"Mark van Rijmenam has written a superb exec̲ ̲ ̲ ̲ ̲ ̲ ̲ ̲ ̲ ̲ ̲
chain, and AI. The book presents hundreds of c̲ ̲ ̲ ̲ ̲ ̲ ̲ ̲ ̲
the actions that business leaders must take to ̲ ̲ ̲ ̲ ̲ ̲ ̲ ̲ ̲ ̲ ̲ ̲ ̲ ̲ ̲ ̲ ̲ ̲ ̲
dynamic environment. Although based on technology, this is a business book.
The author carefully examines the role of collaboration in creating business
change and presents a framework to help any organization become data-
driven and digital. This book is meticulously crafted and researched; It
rewards the reader with insight, practical advice, and greater understanding."
Michael Krigsman – *Industry Analyst and host of CXOTalk*

"In this book, Mark takes us onto an in-depth and exciting journey on how
organisations, our economy and society are transforming today. He navigates
through the maze of new technologies and rewrites the change formulae for
future success based on 4 key ingredients. That future captures our every
digital touch points, predicts and gives it meaning to then distribute it as one
single and decentralised source of the truth. In such a reality, the centrally
organised managerial capitalist structures are making place for ecosystems
that are creating value in a decentralised, self-governed way and where choices are guided by human progress instead of the fear for machine dominance.
A must read for anyone with an ambition to stay relevant and profitable!"
Stephan Janssens – *Organizational Transformation & Blockchain Strategist*

"In *The Organisation of Tomorrow*, Mark van Rijmenam maps the landscape
of today's most disruptive technologies and presents a clear-eyed and actionable roadmap for putting data at the very heart of every strategic decision
your company makes. If you're looking for a compelling, practical guide to
your own organisation's future, there's no better step to take than reading this
book today."
Greg Verdino – *Digital Transformation Advisor & Global Keynote Speaker*

"An intriguing and thoughtful introduction to the current technologies and
their applications which are already having profound impact upon companies,
staff, and consumers alike. The future is set to change in dramatic ways, and
The Organisation of Tomorrow will put you a step ahead."
Josh Ziegler – *CEO, Zumata*

"It is often said that the organisation of tomorrow will be a data-driven
organisation. However, business people in today's world often fail to understand the ins and outs of the digital revolution. The fact that the Internet has
been so pervasive means that such business people really have to get to grips
with digital concepts such as blockchain, AI and the implications of how data
can enhance the power of your business. As well as respect the rights of your
customers. Mark is an expert in this area and has given us a very useful
account of this topic in a little less than 200 pages. His analysis is thorough

and doesn't just rest on the positive sides. It also highlights some of the dangers of not using data-driven technologies properly. Furthermore, it encourages us to rethink the future of the Internet, not just for businesses, but for Society in general. This book is a must-read for all forward-looking business people who care about growing responsibly."

Yann Gourvennec – *Founder of Visionary Marketing and Program Director of the Advanced Master's in Digital Business Strategy at Grenoble Management School*

"Our competitive landscape has changed, for good. This we all (hopefully) know. What is less well known is what the implications of this change entails for how we orchestrate our capabilities and assets to drive impact and value. The 20% of capabilities & assets that made us successful to date will not be the same as the new 20% critical to capture new economic value. Mark's book provides thoughtful and pragmatic insights into the roles and implications of today's emerging (but tomorrow's table-stakes) technologies and how we respond to our changed competitive environment. Making sense of these changes requires navigation as to what to do when – which he provides."

Ralph Welborn – *CEO of CapImpact*

"New technologies and startups are disrupting traditional business models and challenging legacy organizations to think differently. Mark offers his perspectives for organizations on how-to think about leveraging emerging tech such as analytics, blockchain and AI with an eye towards transforming their business into more data-driven organizations. This book is very relevant for business leaders who are interested in preparing their organization for a more digital future."

Mike Quindazzi – *Managing Director, PWC*

"The world is changing at an ever-faster rate as the internet and digital become the drivers of commerce today. With new technology comes new opportunities and Van Rijmenam dives in and explains Blockchain, Artificial Intelligence and Big Data; not in a technical way, but in a way that senior business leaders should easily able to digest."

Timothy (Tim) Hughes – *CEO and Co-Founder of Digital Leadership Associates*

"A compelling read for every data-driven organization who needs to excel and innovate in the rapidly evolving digital world."

Ronald van Loon – *Top 10 Global AI, Machine Learning, Big Data Influencer*

"The book provides a new perspective on how AI, blockchain and analytics can transform a traditional business into a data-driven enterprise. Starting with datafication, the $D^2 + A^2$ model will equip digital economy leaders to engineer a data-driven transformation, powered by some of the most profound technologies of our time. Ultimately to become one of the innovative organisations that will thrive in the new era in business. Avoiding this book would be akin to avoiding the incredible opportunities and challenges that lie ahead for authentic digital economy leaders."

Rob Llewellyn – *Chief Executive and Founder of CXO Transform*

"In his brilliant and extensive work, *The Organisation of Tomorrow*, Mark van Rijmenam dives deeply into the rapidly changing nature of organisations and the radically evolving notions of work in the 21st century. The organisation of tomorrow is no more likely to look and behave like the organisation of yesterday than the world of tomorrow is likely to have much resemblance to the world of yesterday. Mark expertly addresses the drivers and inevitable consequences of the current ubiquitous digital disruption that has become an unstoppable force of nature, human nature, in organisations everywhere. Yes, humans are the creators and beneficiaries of these disruptive forces, due to our curious, creative natures, through our incessant innovation and insertion of new emerging technologies into our life and business processes on timescales that are becoming extremely much shorter than the lifespan of a typical person's career or a typical organisation's existence. Mark takes a deep and wide view of the transformations and disruptions that are taking place. Mark examines these changes from the complementary perspectives of the worker and of the workplace. In particular, Mark illustrates how the notion of work is evolving rapidly at the frontier of the human-machine interface, where the AI that matters will be automated, augmented, assisted, accelerated, and adaptable intelligence. Mark further describes in wonderfully rich detail the emerging digital organization within the context of the three main drivers (data, blockchain, and AI) that define a new $D^2 + A^2$ model for the organisation of tomorrow that he introduces to us in this book. Ultimately, we learn from Mark that the future organisation's success in the global arena will be measured in the three dimensions of trust (enabled by blockchain), efficiency (enabled by AI), and effectiveness (enabled by deep insights that are delivered through data from ubiquitous sensors). The internet of things may just as well be called the internet of insights. The size of an organisation will no longer be a metric of success. As the number of new emerging technologies continues to grow every year, we can be thankful that the most significant ones are converging into a unified business model and that Mark van Rijmenam has illuminated that model for us through an insightful broad vision of the organisation of tomorrow."

Dr. Kirk Borne, *Principal Data Scientist, Booz Allen Hamilton*

The Organisation of Tomorrow

The Organisation of Tomorrow presents a new model of doing business and explains how big data analytics, blockchain, and artificial intelligence force us to rethink existing business models and develop organisations that will be ready for human–machine interactions. It also asks us to consider the impacts of these emerging information technologies on people and society.

Big data analytics empowers consumers and employees. This can result in an open strategy and a better understanding of the changing environment. Blockchain enables peer-to-peer collaboration and trustless interactions governed by cryptography and smart contracts. Meanwhile, artificial intelligence allows for new and different levels of intensity and involvement among human and artificial actors. With that, new modes of organising are emerging: where technology facilitates collaboration between stakeholders; and where human-to-human interactions are increasingly replaced with human-to-machine and even machine-to-machine interactions. This book offers dozens of examples of industry leaders such as Walmart, Telstra, Alibaba, Microsoft, and T-Mobile, before presenting the $D^2 + A^2$ *model* – a new model to help organisations datafy their business, distribute their data, analyse it for insights, and automate processes and customer touchpoints to be ready for the data-driven and exponentially changing society that is upon us

This book offers governments, professional services, manufacturing, finance, retail, and other industries a clear approach for how to develop products and services that are ready for the twenty-first century. It is a must-read for every organisation that wants to remain competitive in our fast-changing world.

Dr Mark van Rijmenam is Founder of Datafloq and Imagjn. He is a highly sought-after international speaker, a big data, blockchain, and AI strategist and author of three management books.

The Organisation of Tomorrow

How AI, Blockchain, and Analytics Turn Your Business into a Data Organisation

Dr Mark van Rijmenam

Routledge
Taylor & Francis Group

LONDON AND NEW YORK

First published 2020
by Routledge
2 Park Square, Milton Park, Abingdon, Oxon OX14 4RN

and by Routledge
52 Vanderbilt Avenue, New York, NY 10017

Routledge is an imprint of the Taylor & Francis Group, an informa business

British Library Cataloguing-in-Publication Data
A catalogue record for this book is available from the British Library

Library of Congress Cataloging-in-Publication Data
A catalog record has been requested for this book

ISBN: 978-0-367-23471-3 (hbk)
ISBN: 978-0-367-23470-6 (pbk)
ISBN: 978-0-429-27997-3 (ebk)

Typeset in Times New Roman
by Taylor & Francis Books

MIX
Paper from
responsible sources
FSC
www.fsc.org FSC™ C013985

Printed in the United Kingdom
by Henry Ling Limited

Contents

Illustrations

Acknowledgements

This book is the result of my PhD, which I undertook at the University of Technology Sydney (UTS) from 2016 to 2019. Undertaking a PhD is a journey and turning my academic thesis into a, hopefully, easily digestible book turned out to be a journey in itself. Doing a PhD and subsequently turning it into this business book would not have been possible without the help of multiple people, whom I would like to thank for their hard work, contributions, discussions, and reviews. Without them, this book would not have become the book it became.

Therefore, first of all, I would like to thank Jochen Schweitzer, my principal supervisor at UTS, for challenging and stretching me intellectually. Thank you for your direct and critical feedback on the work I created, but also supporting me in the intellectual journey that I gave myself. Thanks to your valuable and tireless input, I have been able to write a thesis in the way I did, which subsequently I have been able to transform into this book. Without your input, that would not have been possible. I would also like to thank my other supervisors, Mary-Anne Williams and Danielle Logue, for your input and feedback on the work and papers I wrote. Your feedback helped me improve my work and see things differently when needed.

Once the book was written, I was able to improve the initial version of the manuscript thanks to the great feedback provided by Christian R. Meier, Glen Hendriks, Maksym Koghut, Pieter Bos, Stephan Janssens, and my co-author of my second book, Philippa Ryan. Without your feedback, I would not have been able to improve the book. Thank you so much!

Chapter 1

Welcome to exponential times

We live in exponential times. We are experiencing a paradigm shift, where businesses and technology change and grow at an exponential rate, causing profound social and economic change. The fast-changing, uncertain and ambiguous environments that organisations operate in today require them to rethink their internal business processes and customer touchpoints. The last time such rapid changed happened was the advent of the internet. The internet caused organisations to completely rethink their business and enabled the success of organisations that embraced the new paradigm, including Amazon, Google, Facebook and WeChat, to become monopolists within record time. Now, we are experiencing another change due to emerging information technologies (EIT) such as big data analytics, blockchain, and artificial intelligence (AI) and trends like the Internet of Things (IoT).[i] These technologies make it easier for startups to compete with existing organisations. As a result, and because of the lack of legacy systems, these startups are more flexible and agile than Fortune 1000 companies. Within a short timeframe, startups can become a significant threat if not paid due regard. Therefore, only paying attention to the day-to-day operation is simply no longer enough. Organisations have to become innovative and adaptive to change if they wish to remain relevant and competitive. New technologies can help achieve this shift. When big data analytics, blockchain and AI are combined, it will change collaboration among individuals, organisations and things. When implemented correctly, these technologies can significantly improve consumer engagement, increase transparency, reduce costs and improve production efficiency or service delivery. Thanks to these technologies, we move from "computer-assisted work" to "human-assisted work", particularly as human-to-human interactions are increasingly replaced by human-to-machine interactions and then machine-to-machine interactions. When these technologies converge, it enables organisations to design smarter businesses and incorporating these technologies within your organisation has become easier than ever before.

However, in the words of Commander Chris Hadfield, a retired Canadian astronaut, engineer, and former Royal Canadian Air Force fighter pilot, during a keynote in 2018, "smart only matters when you do something with it". You can have all the technology in the world, but it comes down to what you are going to do with these new tools. How will you put (existing or new) technology to work and how will you take an idea and change yourself and the organisation? In today's world, it is no longer only about collecting as much data as possible, simply because collecting data has become too easy. It is more about doing smart things with that data, while ensuring privacy and security. To achieve that, you need intelligence, human and artificial, to work together seamlessly. Organisations can now leverage data and embed learning in every process. This can empower people with all forms of intelligence and "put smart to work". We now experience the greatest opportunity of all time, forcing organisations to make big bets for the future and to dare to think the impossible.[1] Organisations should go on to the offensive and disrupt their industry if they want to survive in this fast-changing and fiercely competitive world. Emerging information technologies are rapidly changing how we work and live. Organisations have to adapt to these new technologies if they wish to remain relevant in the future.

This book aims to help organisations understand these fast-changing times by providing clear insights into what these technologies are, how they can work together, and how it will change your business. Only if you understand these new disruptive technologies will you be able to incorporate them into your organisation. Therefore, this book will also pay attention to the downside of these emerging information technologies and what organisations should do to prevent consumers from becoming victims of an increasingly data-driven world.

1.1 The importance of data

In constantly changing environments, organisations remain competitive not only by focusing on excellence in the day-to-day business operation but also by being innovative and adaptive to change.[2] Thanks to emerging information technologies, it has become easier to compete as a newcomer in traditionally closed markets.[3] This means that the ability to cope with, react to, and anticipate industry disruption becomes important for organisations if they want to remain competitive. Detecting, anticipating and responding to disruptive changes while displaying industry leadership and managing shifting behaviours of stakeholders is called "organisational ambidexterity".[4, 5] It is considered especially important when facing a fast-changing and uncertain environment.[6, 7] Organisations that wish to achieve this ambidexterity should rely on data as a key resource for their business and develop data-driven business models.[8] This requires organisations to use a variety of internal and external data sources. To apply a variety of activities to that data, including processing, analysing, and visualising, and use the insights of those activities to develop new products and services that target the right customers at the right moment and at the right price.[8] For many, this requires a different mindset, as many organisations still base their decisions on experience and intuition instead of data analytics.[9-11]

Startups that threaten your existing business are already used to this new, data-driven approach. They leverage new technologies and experiment with new approaches. This allows them to benefit from opportunities available in our constantly changing global market. Such startups, which sometimes experience exponential growth, are usually characterised by a so-called "platform approach" to organisational design. A platform organisation is a meta organisation, where members benefit from economies of scale while remaining independent.[12] Well-known examples include Uber, the world's largest taxi company that does not own any taxis; Airbnb, the world's largest accommodation provider that does not own any hotels; or Facebook, the world's largest media company that does not create any content.[13] Another emerging approach to organisation design is that of the Decentralised Autonomous Organisation (DAO). This radical new form of organisation uses blockchain technology and smart contracts to establish governance without management or employees, run entirely by computer code[14] (where *If This Then That* statements are deployed on a blockchain, but more on this in Chapter 4). These approaches fundamentally challenge incumbent industry practices. Almost all new technologies produce large amounts of data, which can be analysed using algorithms to help derive actions and improve decision-making. As a result, these companies are at first data companies that happen to offer a certain service, such as connecting people (WhatsApp), moving people from A to B (Uber), or allowing consumers to experience local accommodation (Airbnb).

Viewing your organisation as a data organisation will completely change all your processes and customer touchpoints. This is a difficult change, but it is required if you want to be able to compete with startups that have been doing this since inception. When you see your organisation as a data organisation, a "gestalt shift" will occur; all of a sudden, you will see your organisation from a different perspective. For example, a car company should no longer see itself as a car manufacturer, but as a software company that is in the business of helping people move from A to B. It should look at how the company can do so in the most reliable, comfortable and safest way. Once the mindset has changed, the organisation can ask whether it wants to produce cars, flying taxis, or develop "Uber-like" apps. The same goes, for example, for a bank. A bank is no longer a financial institution, but a data organisation that enables people to store value and make secure transactions. Whether this is done using a cryptocurrency, as a mobile-only bank or to store digital identity data are then questions that can be asked. Nowadays, any organisation, regardless of industry, should see itself as a data organisation. When doing so, it can remove any barriers that prevent the business from delivering the product or service in the most efficient, effective and customer-friendly way. In the digital world, anything is possible, although it might take some time to figure it out.

1.2 The downside of data

There is also a downside to the abundant presence of data in today's society. Today's tech giants such as Google, Amazon, Facebook, Microsoft, Tencent and Alibaba have long recognised that data is a valuable asset. They have been aggregating vast amounts of data in return for "free" services from the outset. Unfortunately, the problem with "free" services is that you and your data are the actual product. This has resulted in a centralisation of the web and a handful of organisations dominating and controlling it.[15, 16] This has caused problems with truth and trust – such as fake news, clickbait, trolling, spam, lack of privacy and absence of accountability. This book, therefore, will not only help you to change your organisation into a data organisation, but also help you to do it the right way.

This centralisation, where the internet ended up in the hands of a few very powerful companies, is not how the world wide web was originally envisaged. As Sir Tim Berners-Lee said during the Decentralised Web Summit in 2016:[17]

> The web was designed to be decentralised so that everybody could participate by having their own domain and having their own web server and this hasn't worked out. Instead, we've got the situation where individual personal data has been locked up in these silos.

These centralised internet corporations are incredibly powerful. They have access to vast amounts of data of their users, which they use and abuse to follow (potential) customers around the web. They often ignore existing privacy practices.[15, 18] Tech giants use their enormous data silos to make money through advertising (85 per cent of online advertising spend goes to Google and Facebook, according to Morgan Stanley analyst Brian Nowak[19]). They use the data to their liking, often without properly involving or informing the consumer.[20] In addition, while some organisations take data security seriously, many do not. As a result, many consumers have become the victim of one of the hundreds of data breaches happening every year. Their details ending up in the wrong hands, resulting in significant costs for organisations, individuals and society at large.[21]

One of the biggest scandals and privacy breaches happened in 2018, when it became clear how many consumers' Facebook data was stolen and abused by Cambridge Analytica. Cambridge Analytica was a data mining and data analysis company that played a pivotal role in the US presidential election of 2016, the Brexit vote, and a number of other recent political races. Behind the company were key figures backing President Trump, including Steve Bannon, Trump's former strategic advisor, and Robert Mercer, founder of the (ironically labelled) Government Accountability Institute, which uses the dark web and bots to denigrate political opponents. In 2014, the company used personal information obtained without the authorisation of these users to develop a highly effective system to target individual US voters. Under the pretence of academic research, they harvested 87 million profiles without the notice or consent of those whose data was being harvested. Cambridge Analytica then used that data to influence the US election. It was a privacy breach at an unprecedented scale. It showed that Facebook's attempts to protect its users were not working. Already, Facebook faced a huge problem with fake news on its platform. This massive data leak made it clear that it is time for us to rethink how we deal with data. The centralisation of the web has caused consumers to be increasingly dependent on these monopolies and, as a result, we, the internet user, have no control over our data. Instead, companies such as Facebook, Twitter and Google harvest our data and use it for advertising purposes to make billions of dollars. Unfortunately, escaping the power of these companies is rather challenging. Even if you do not have a Facebook profile, the company is capable of tracking you via so-called "shadow profiles".[22] These shadow profiles are possible because Facebook's "Like" button is present on almost every website. This enables the organisation to follow internet users by collecting disparate data such as your location, computer ID, IP address, browsing behaviour and other valuable data sources. Through these live captures, they can discover patterns in that data when they connect them. Mark Zuckerberg claimed to be ignorant about these shadow profiles during the 2018 congressional hearings on the Cambridge Analytica scandal. A surprising and unconvincing remark as it was first brought to light by researchers at Packet Storm Security in 2013.[23]

As if these shadow profiles are not enough, in 2018 it became clear that Google had closed a secret deal with Mastercard that gave it access to the spending patterns of millions of consumers. Google paid millions of US dollars to Mastercard to be able to link clicks on its advertisements to actual online and offline purchases to understand the effectiveness of the ads. Using Mastercard's data, Google can link your ad click to your (offline) transaction, even if the ad click did not convert to an immediate sale. With your Google email address and Mastercard's data, Google can obtain a digital copy of your receipt to know exactly what you are buying, when, and for how much. This information is then shared with a select group of Google advertisers who can use that data to improve their ads and, most likely, increase their spending. Strangely enough, although Mastercard's customers ought to be informed about this – as it directly affects their privacy – many of the two billion Mastercard holders have not been informed about this deal.[24]

These two examples make it clear that there is a significant downside to data. Especially if it is controlled solely by centralised companies that are not held accountable for their data collecting, sharing, and processing practices. Over the years, the objective of a distributed network of nodes, where everyone would be able to participate for the betterment of humanity, has been lost. This is how the web was originally designed by Sir Tim Berners-Lee and colleagues. Today, we have many centralised companies offering centralised services that remove fundamental freedoms such as consumer data ownership rights, privacy, and security. Too often, consumers become the victims of the malpractices of large organisations, that do not take care of their customers' data, leaving their customers vulnerable. In addition, some governments use this centralised web to censor freedom of speech. On a regular basis, countries block important websites such as Wikipedia, Twitter, or Telegram, simply because they host an article or post they do not like. As it may seem, the internet as we know it has a problem. If we want to build the organisation of tomorrow, we need fix the internet as well.

The existing internet has degraded trust among individuals and organisations. The centralised web and the possibility to remain anonymous – but unaccountable – has resulted in a suite of negative behaviours. However, a fully accountable digital society as is currently being created in China, using the social credit scoring system Sesame Credit, is also not the solution. (Sesame Credit is discussed in detail in Chapter 4.) Sesame Credit's proposed solution to problems associated with online anonymity results in the absence of privacy (from the Western perspective of "privacy"), while enabling complete government surveillance and control, due to an even increased centralisation of the web. As a result, we have a trust problem, or as the Lee Rainie, Director of Internet and Technology at Pew Research Center, puts it:[25]

> Trust is a social, economic and political binding agent. A vast research literature on trust and social capital documents the connections between trust and well-being, collective problem solving, economic development and social cohesion. Trust is the lifeblood of friendship and caregiving. When trust is absent, all kinds of societal woes unfold, including violence, chaos and paralysing risk-aversion. There is considerable concern that the way people use the internet is degrading trust. The fate of trust and truth is up for grabs.

The problem lies in how the web and the internet were developed. When the internet was created, the original designers did a lot of things really well. They created standards such as TCP/IP, DNS, HTTP, etc. However, unfortunately, they also forgot two important standards: an identity protocol to use your offline identity online and to have full control over your own data; and a reputation protocol that allows users to be reputable and accountable online, even when they are anonymous. They forgot this, simply because when the web started, only trusted actors had access to the network and these protocols were simply not necessary. Therefore, to build the organisation of tomorrow, we need to restore this (online) trust. We need to restore the original design of the web and replace the web's current anonymity with a reputation system to allow (pseudo)anonymous entities to be reputable and accountable across the internet. In addition, we need a web that limits the influence and power of centralised organisations to use and abuse consumers' data, thereby ignoring their privacy. Instead, we should give consumers full control over their data. In other words, we need a self-sovereign identity (to be explored in detail in Chapter 5).

Apart from centralised control and ownership of data or the lack of an identity and reputation protocol, biased data also causes tremendous problems, as I will discuss in Chapter 6. Due to all these problems, it may seem that emerging information technologies have a lot of negative implications for society. However, there is also hope. Increasingly, organisation, especially startups, and regulators see the importance of data governance, ethics and privacy. Regulations such as the EU General Data Protection Regulation (GDPR) aim to protect consumers and startups such as Berners-Lee's Inrupt aim to give control back to consumers. In 2018, Sir Tim Berners-Lee revealed his new vision, one where the internet becomes decentralised again as he had envisioned it originally. His technology is called Solid POD (personal online data store), which is developed by his company Inrupt. Solid PODs will allow every internet user to store their own data, be it video, articles, wearable tracking data or comments, and share that with anyone or any website that has connected to the Solid ecosystem. Using the Solid POD, the user will remain in full control over their own data and who has access to it and who not. A great new initiative that will hopefully bring us closer to a decentralised society where data is owned by those who created it, privacy is protected, security is a given, and distributed ledger technology will enable trustless transactions among individuals, organisations and things.

In recent years, also media attention to problems of data has grown. Consequently, consumers have become more aware of the consequences of data that is in the hands of technology companies. Increasingly, they demand change or take action themselves. With the discourse growing within the tech community, and among academics, a new type of organisation is required, and fortunately also emerging.[16, 26] This type of organisation applies technologies such as analytics, blockchain, and AI to contribute to creating a better society, which incorporates the initial values of the web: an organisation that respect users' privacy and security; and that will fairly reward users for their work and that gives back control to users over their content and data. In this book, I will discuss how to build this organisation, the organisation of tomorrow. I will do so from a consumer's perspective instead of a shareholder's perspective, as is often the case. After all, if you take care of your customers, your customers will take care of your shareholders.

1.3 The changing face of collaboration

Emerging information technologies change organisations. Exactly how these technologies change an organisation depends not only on the technology, but also on the social actions of the people responding to that technology.[27] As humans interact with technology in different contexts, it changes their behaviour and accordingly the behaviour of organisations.[28] Consequently, organisational change requires breaking down old habits and values, while at the same time altering high impact systems such as decision-making capabilities and governance practices.[29] Technology startups have long understood this and have developed an absorptive capacity and overall innovation capability.[30] They value the opportunity to collect and analyse data and create organisations that are more agile and flexible. Startups are familiar with building digital organisations with data at the heart of their business.[31, 32] With a data-driven business comes new stakeholders, or actors, leading to new ways of collaboration among those actors. Such changes go along with the need to adopt a different mindset to solve the current issues involved with consumer data. For many, this necessitates radical change.[33–35]

To understand how collaboration changes among actors in data-driven organisations, I will take a closer look in the next chapter at how organisations and technologies interact. How does the interaction change when a new, artificial actor joins the scene? Organisations are social entities, and they respond differently to the need for change due to contextual variables such as environment, size, and the technology adopted. Some organisations will show reorientation behaviour, while others will showcase abortive movements, and some will be reluctant to change.[28, 36] For example, online film distribution, digital photography, and online book retailing have seen businesses like Blockbuster, Kodak, and Borders become well-known examples of how once successful companies lacked the innovation mindset or the willingness needed to respond to emerging technological change.[37] Successful organisations continuously adapt to and exploit new, more advanced technologies to survive.[38] Newcomers, such as Facebook, Amazon, Apple, Netflix and Google (responsible for the so-called FAANG stocks) or Alibaba, Baidu and Tencent, have shown such reorientation behaviour to leverage (technological) opportunities that are ignored or overlooked by others.[39] Hence, to avoid what in the mid-2010s came to be known as a "Kodak moment", it is vital to develop the capacity to detect, anticipate, and respond in a timely manner to market changes and competitive pressures.

Resulting from this data-driven approach is a shift in the balance between power and empowerment.[40] This, consequently, creates a shift in collaboration among the involved organisational stakeholders. It does this by (1) including previously excluded actors, such as customers or competitors;[41] and (2) by moving from pure human-to-human interactions to human-to-machine interactions; and, increasingly, even machine-to-machine interactions.[42, 43] This requires an innovative mindset within organisations as a whole. They need to rethink internal processes, customer touchpoints, and structures, and move from traditional product models to collaborative service models and ecosystems. If done successfully, the new ways of cooperation among those stakeholders involved (human and artificial) will ensure continued productivity growth.[44, 45] To successfully incorporate emerging information technologies, organisations need to be thinking like software companies; to see themselves as a data organisation.[11] These organisations must turn existing analogue processes into digital processes that can be analysed and to build a digital platform to grow the organisation. Developing a digital platform not only offers new revenue streams and continuous growth opportunities, but it also allows companies to create new partnerships with previously excluded partners. Such collaborative communities, where organisations share knowledge, engage in collaborative relationships with industry partners and even competitors, and drive innovation have data at their heart.[41, 46] Data and emerging information technologies will allow those organisations to affiliate not only with industry partners but with any previously excluded stakeholder, whether human or machine. The result is new ways to organise activity with the most extreme form of organisation design being that of a DAO. Such an organisation uses blockchain technology and smart contracts combined with AI to establish governance without management or employees, run completely by computer code.[14]

Although the types of actors involved in an organisation have never been limited to human actors, new technologies result in networks that combine social participation and machine-based computation.[47–50] In such organisations, humans and machines interact with each other to produce constantly evolving, synergistic effects. Social interactions become more important, interactions less demanding, and machine–human interactions more prominent.[43] Consequently, big data analytics, blockchain, and AI result in new modes of collaboration among the actors involved, each offering a different take on collaboration. Big data analytics provides insights and information to customers and employees. When more people have access to information and knowledge, empowerment becomes possible.[40, 51] Thus, when organisations provide more people with access to information and knowledge using analytics, power is distributed more equally. This will enable empowerment throughout an organisation and result in decentralised decision-making.[52–55] Conversely, blockchain enables peer-to-peer collaboration by creating distributed value through a network of peer-to-peer actors distributed across the globe, collaborating effortlessly and in real time to create value together for all actors in the network.[56, 57] It is governed by cryptography, consensus mechanisms, and smart contracts, enabling a trustless exchange of transactions.[58] AI is about automating actions, enabling new forms of interaction among humans and machines, resulting in interactions with different levels of intensity and involvement.[43] As such, organisations are engaged with various interactions among humans and machines, resulting in unexpected technical, social, and ethical implications requiring complicated strategies.[59]

1.4 Conclusion

Technology startups in particular seem to value the possibility of collecting and analysing data to create new organisations. These new market entrants often take a different approach to organisation design and, as a result, their business models are more agile and successful than existing organisations.[32] They are better able to leverage new technologies and experiment with new approaches than existing companies. They benefit from opportunities arising from a constantly changing global market. Understanding how these startups do so could help incumbents to remain competitive when challenged by new digital platform organisations and disruptive technologies. Therefore, in the coming chapters, I will discuss how the emerging information technologies of big data analytics, blockchain, and AI can change your organisation. Data is central in all of this as all new technologies now create data. To gain insights from that data, analytics are required. Analytics are used to interpret data regardless of the volume, velocity, or variety. Blockchain is examined because of its potential to fundamentally change how we deal with data and because the cryptography used in distributed ledger technology significantly affects organisation design, decision-making capabilities and existing power structures.[42, 60] Finally, AI is addressed because the mathematical formulae that make up algorithms rely on data to automate and accelerate decision-making and improve business, resulting in an algorithmic business where AI forms an essential part of doing business and where algorithms run multiple aspects of organisations to make sense of data without the intervention of humans.[61, 62] In Chapter 7, I will explain what organisations should do to prepare for the data-driven future, using the $D^2 + A^2$ *model*. I will offer a clear roadmap for organisations to remain relevant and competitive in the fast-changing world they operate in. But before we get to that, let's first examine how technology will change the organisation of tomorrow and how organisations should respond.

Note

i   This book follows industry practices in the writing of Bitcoin vs bitcoin and Blockchain vs blockchain. When written as Bitcoin, it relates to the technology and when written as bitcoin, it relates to the cryptocurrency. The same goes for Blockchain, which refers to the technology/trend as a whole and blockchain, which means one or more blockchain(s); a distributed ledger database.

Chapter 2

How technology changes organisations

To understand how technology will affect the organisation of tomorrow, we first have to go back in time and see how technology affected organisations in the past. The lessons from how organisations responded to new technologies in the past can help in preparing your organisation for tomorrow. The next section might be a bit theoretical but bear with me as it will help you gain a better understanding of the forces that affect your organisation.

How technology influences organisations has been researched for decades. The earliest studies date back to the 1950s when the challenges and implications of manufacturing technology for management and decision-making were examined.[63] In a well-known study, the relationship between organisational structure and organisational performance was considered. The study showed that there are specific organisational designs linked to specific types of technologies. In other words, the type of manufacturing technology in use influenced the design of the organisation, resulting in superior performance if they were in sync.[64] For example, mass production companies such as car manufacturers that produce standardised products based on standard routines reflect mechanistic structures, while organisations that use technology to produce one or several products simultaneously reflected organic structures. The emphasis of these early studies in the 1950s and 1960s was on how technology influenced organisational structures and production processes, especially in relation to manufacturing technology.[64-67] Central to this earlier research was that the social – management, employees, and customers – and the technological – the machines and equipment – were equal parts in the organisational structures and both deemed as important to the success of an organisation.[68, 69] In those days, technology was perceived as having a predictable impact on organisations, where the design of the technology determined the impact.[38, 70, 71] As technology evolved from traditional 'offline' technologies, such as manufacturing equipment, to information technologies (IT), such as computers and spreadsheets, researchers started to view technologies as material elements of organisations to understand the impact of IT on organisations.[12, 38, 72, 73] This resulted in the perspective that human stakeholders are the focus of attention to understand how individuals create social worlds and that, at the same time, institutional properties influence human actions and social relationships. Meaning that humans shape the world, and the technologies around them, and the world shapes them.[74] Human interactions consist of structures of meaning, power, and moral frameworks. If you wish to analyse human interactions, you should analyse these structures. This theory, which was developed in the 1980s, combined how humans interpret behaviour, how they realise intentions, and what is appropriate conduct.[75] It resulted in the idea that technology is both a physical object and a social product. Technology is the enabler between action and structure, and how humans use technologies could change organisational structure.[76] Thus, technology can change action that can result in a changed organisational structure (such as centralisation or decision-making).

With the appearance of advanced IT in the 1990s, the nature of organisation design, intelligence, management, and decision-making changed.[38] The idea was that these technologies increased communication among stakeholders, thereby reducing the breadth, depth, and width of an organisation, enabling empowerment among employees, reducing the number of face-to-face meetings, and making an organisation's decision-making processes more efficient and effective. Of course, what was deemed advanced IT in the 1990s we no longer see as advanced IT but rather early stage information technologies. Nevertheless, the lessons from how organisations adopted IT in the 1990s can be applied to the organisations of today. Technology and social interaction were seen as related, whereby social structures are the norms and behaviours that govern decision-making capabilities.[77] Technology was deemed capable of offering new affordances or reconfiguring organisational structure. However, the effect of technology varied depending on the affordances that the technologies could provide. Thus, sometimes enabling activities and sometimes limiting them.[78] Technology was seen as both facilitating and constraining social action. Human actors could continuously shape IT so it remained flexible and would not become a fixed constraint. For a long time, the development and deployment of IT have been considered a social phenomenon, where social and material dimensions influence organisations. This perspective can help to understand how IT is used and institutionalised within organisations. Importantly, IT is considered a product of human actions and a medium for human actions that could "only condition and never determine social practices".[75] Although, with the increased capabilities of EITs, this argument becomes increasingly blurred as we will see the following chapters.

Increasingly, IT was seen as a product of time and context. How people use technology determines the organisational structures, instead of the technology itself changing the organisational structure. Thus, how people use IT was important, and often the management of an organisation determined how technology was to be used within the organisation. However, technologies have different degrees of interpretive flexibility, meaning there is flexibility in how people design, use, and interpret technology. As such, employees can ignore the instructions of management, which would result in changes in the organisational structure.[79] This flexibility is determined by the material affordances of the technology, the institutional context, such as power or knowledge, the interest of human stakeholders and time. Because technology tends to become routinised within an organisation. With 'the generative and unbounded materiality' of today's emerging information technologies, this notion becomes increasingly significant as increasingly technologies have the power to change the institutional context.[80]

As technology became more advanced over the years, these views changed. How technology is used and combined creates certain (organisational) structures, thereby giving technology a more socialised view.[28] However, this approach has also been criticised for being too social a view where technology "is subject to the whims of their users", suggesting users can apply the technology as they deem suitable.[81] Therefore, technology was increasingly treated as a structural property. The focus moved to seeing technology as material, where technologies exist in the "realm of structure" and technology-in-use in the "realm of action".[81] This means that technology itself was seen as part of the organisation. How the technology was applied and used depended on the actions taken by the people within an organisation. The consequence of this view is that technology does not have agency, rather people attribute agency to technology when they use it.[82] In other words, technology does not have its own intent or its own free will. Rather, how humans use technology determines the outcome. A central component of this position was the concept of performativity. Performativity shows how relations and boundaries between technologies and humans are enacted in practice and, therefore, are not fixed or pre-given. Something is performative when it contributes to the creation of the reality it describes. For example, performativity can be applied to understand algorithmic trading: models that describe the world of option pricing are later used in algorithms, and thereby enact that world. In other words, the theory is used to build the market it described. As such, the models contribute to the development of the reality they first described. It can be seen as a catalyst that helps start a process, or mediate user participation, to achieve a certain objective or to make sense of and engage with a changing environment.[83]

This approach helped researchers discuss the materiality of objects (as in the physical or digital characteristics of an object). It led to the introduction of the concept of *sociomateriality*, thereby shifting away from technological artefacts and technologies-in-use to *the social* and *the material* and emphasising more the role of technology.[84] Sociomateriality is a theoretical concept that helps researchers understand how technologies and organisations interact. However, it can also help managers to gain a better understanding of how future technologies will affect their organisation and what sort of response is required to successfully incorporate those new technologies and with that to remain competitive. Therefore, bear with me a little bit longer as I explain the concept of sociomateriality and the different arguments that scholars have as it will all become clear at the end of this chapter.

2.1 The concept of sociomateriality

Organisations are created by "material forms and spaces through which humans act and interact".[84] As people interact with each other, it influences technologies. Consequently, technologies influence how people interact with each other. They are *constitutively entangled*.[84] This means that the social (management or employees, i.e. the organisation) and the material (technologies such as chairs or computers) are entangled and inextricably related. The social shapes the materiality of technology and materiality is present in every phenomenon considered social.[27, 84] Basically, this means that technology influences people and organisations. How people use those technologies then influences the outcome of that technology, thereby influencing the organisation again, and so on. So, within the entanglement, the material influences the social and vice versa. All organisational aspects are bound by the material. This becomes visible when dealing with online (social) media where technology both facilitates and constrains the behaviour of media users.[85] For example, initially, influencers on Instagram used the social media network to connect with their followers using photos only. The number of likes they received influenced their popularity and their popularity likely influenced how they would use Instagram. When Instagram introduced the possibility of uploading videos in 2013, thereby changing the technological affordances of the network, influencers immediately adjusted their behaviour and started to produce videos specifically for Instagram. However, these videos are only limited to 60 seconds, thereby constraining again the behaviour of the media users, etc.

The concept of sociomateriality moves the analysis from the development of technology to the use of the material. The technology is not sociomaterial but the practice in which it is embedded is.[86] Social and material agencies become interlocked and produce technologies and organisations. Some researchers even expand this notion with the concept of the inseparability of the social and the material. They stated that matter has no properties and only exists when it actively participates in a network.[87] Sociomateriality sees the material and the social as intrinsic to organising activities, which is why some argue for the entanglement of the social and the material when dealing with information technologies.[86] With organisations increasingly subject to multiple, emerging, changing, and interdependent (information) technologies, materiality becomes integral to everyday life.[84] Just as how the internet has become so pervasive in today's world that often we no longer notice that we use it and completely rely on it in our daily lives. When that happens, it alters existing relationships and power balances within organisations.[88, 89] To understand how exactly, let's first discuss the concept of social and material agency as it will help you grasp the importance of looking at your organisation from this perspective.

Social agency, in this context, refers to how humans define and use technology. How people apply (new) technologies to achieve their goals. While material agency is the capacity of non-human actors to act without human intervention.[90] As such, social and material agencies both relate to actions, but they differ in intent. Social agency is a coordinated exercise to achieve certain goals. Material agents exercise agency using performativity; that is, non-human actors do not have inherent intention and do not act to realise their own goals, as non-human actors do not have goals of their own making.[82, 91, 92] Instead, people attribute agency to objects and technology when they use them and interact with it. People are free to enact technology in ways they deem necessary, so technology is at the discretion of human agents.[82, 93] As we will see, this no longer applies when dealing with emerging information technologies. From this stance, neither human nor material agency should be given priority when dealing with how people reach their objectives as "each contributes equally to shaping the other".[59, 90, 94] As such, humans and technologies acquire form, capabilities, and attributes through their interpenetration. The social and the material are inseparable.[59, 94] What material artefacts are is important, as artefacts are more than an organisations' representations. Technologies also help create the organisation when users interact with it and develop a new understanding of that organisation.[95] Subsequently, material artefacts mediate and shape interactions and affect internal power relations. Since the social and the material are directly linked to power when strategising, incorporating the notion of power in sociomateriality is important.[96, 97]

Power dimensions play a role in changing or maintaining a specific organisational model. Some actors have more influence than others in how technology is used, thereby reinforcing existing power structures. For example, managers often determine how a new piece of technology should be used within the organisation.[36, 98] However, the adoption of new technologies can also lead to conflict and change existing power distributions, social orders, and established patterns of interactions among groups since new technologies often result in actors having access to new information or previously excluded information, as we will see in Chapter 3.[30, 75, 96, 99] Having access to new and more information changes how people behave, the tasks they conduct, and changes communication among people, as we have seen when email was first introduced in organisations; it completely changed how people worked and communicated. This can trigger changes in interaction patterns and work roles.[27, 100] As such, technological change can result in political change, changes in the social order and/or shifting existing power balances within the organisations.[76] Different emerging information technologies will have different implications and trigger different changes in existing interactions. Therefore, to understand how new technologies affect an existing organisational model, it is important to understand the intricacies of the technology being implemented. Big data analytics, for example, can lead to empowerment, because "the more blurred the distinction between what workers know and what managers know, the more fragile and pointless any traditional relationships of domination and subordination between them will become".[101] Therefore, in the coming chapters, I will discuss the intricacies of big data analytics, blockchain, and AI to provide insights into how they will affect your business. People are flexible to change their routines if required when dealing with technologies and, therefore, technology can cause relations among people to become less hierarchical and more collaborative.[90, 102] As such, sociomaterial arrangements related to EIT result in certain changing power relations; those that previously were excluded from information, can, thanks to digitalisation, obtain access to valuable insights and information. As such, digitalisation fundamentally shifts the power balance between the social and the material, thereby altering existing relationships and decision-making processes.[38, 76, 88, 103]

In other words, agency is a capacity realised by human and non-human actors. It is an effect of the relations and interactions between those human and non-human agencies in a network.[104] Hence, as social and material agents interact, their agency shifts and they develop a complex web of sociomateriality.[86] Understanding the difference between social and material agency helps to understand how emerging information technologies will interact with your organisation. Crucial to understanding why is a clear understanding and definition of what technology is in the first place. Therefore, in the next section, I will explore what technology is in the context of EIT.

2.2 The concept of technology in organisations

In the 1990s, IT was defined as "rationality-enhancing technology that transmits, manipulates, analyses or exploits digital information and thereby facilitates easier, cheaper and more controlled communication and information transfer, which will enhance organisational intelligence and reduce management levels in decision-making".[38] Despite the advances made in technology, this definition still stands firm. Information technology consists of three aspects: mechanical systems (hardware), human systems (skills and human energy), and knowledge systems (abstract meanings and concepts). Technology is descriptive (the type and role of technology within organisations) and relational (the relation between technology and structure).[105] Hence, as people use technology, it influences their behaviour, which influences how they use the technology. It is often observed as an external force that drives change within an organisation.[28, 73] As such, technology is not neutral but an integral and material part of constituting a certain phenomenon.[73] It is the result of continuous interactions of humans, actions, choices, social histories,

and institutional contexts. Its material artefacts are socially defined, produced, and only relevant to people engaging with it.[73] Technology used to
produce certain identifiable impacts on organisations. However, with technology rapidly becoming more complex, it becomes increasingly difficult to
understand or predict the impact of technology on organisations.[73] Therefore,
we need a new way of thinking of how technologies and organisations influence each other.[91, 103] The original idea that IT only has social and material
practices that are constructed by human actions may no longer apply due to
the exponential changes in technology we are currently experiencing. Thus,
looking at technology from a purely social and material perspective might no
longer be sufficient. As a result, what defines matter when we talk about
digital technologies and whether IT can be perceived as materiality have
become unclear.[106, 107]

Aristotle, already, referred to materiality as being perceptible (that which
can be perceived) and intelligible (that which cannot be perceived).[108] Materiality such as chairs, tables, books, buildings, pens, data, or computers can be
perceived as technology but so are columns, records, numbers, or algorithms.
So, on the one hand, digital technologies can be defined as material as people
can directly interact with binary signals and, hence, it can be perceived.[27]
Digital technologies are developing at such breakneck speed that increasingly
form and function are becoming detached from matter, such as the example
with quantum computing. They are developed from materials of such a
granular level previously unthinkable. However, that does not mean they are
no longer material as binary signals, and even atoms, are available to all users
in the same form. Although they might not be directly observable (have you
ever actually observed ones and zeros?) they still have material consequences
and can, therefore, be perceived as material.[91] Thus, as long as the material
conditions and characteristics of digital technologies endure across differences
in place and time, it can be perceived as matter. However, on the other hand,
digital artefacts change and evolve continuously as they cannot be contained.[103] Digital elements have no weight and lack any spatial mode of
being, so they should be considered immaterial (in 2011 it was estimated that
all the data that exists today on the internet weighs approximately 50 grams
or the equivalent of a medium-sized egg).[84, 88, 89, 109, 110] This would mean
that digital technologies cannot have any material agency that is associated
with it. Despite that they play an active role in the material world, with significant consequences, there is no "thing" and, thus, digital technologies are
not material.[111] Whether information technologies are material or not might
seem like an unimportant semantic discussion, but it becomes important
when we start talking about how this reflects with emerging information
technologies.

IT can redistribute knowledge, resources, and conventions in organisations,
but today, IT can also (re)create new knowledge and information technologies.
I am talking of course about artificial intelligence. Increasingly, AI uses neural

networks and deep learning algorithms that are not trained by humans. Rather, they are exposed to massive data sets, millions of videos/images/articles, etc. and the algorithm must figure out for itself how to recognise different objects, sentences, images, etc. As a result, it can come up with solutions no humans could have thought of. For example, in 2016 researchers from Google created a set of algorithms that had to communicate with each other and had to prevent a third algorithm from eavesdropping on their conversation. Consequently, the algorithms developed an encryption method that managed to do so. However, the encryption method created, used patterns that humans would never use and as a result, humans could no longer decipher it.[112] This works well in a closed environment but can become quite scary if released into the wild. Moreover, the general view is that technology becomes stabilised over time. Human actions do not refine and modify technology, which in a world of self-learning algorithms using reinforced feedback loops, is no longer the case.[28] In addition, the concept of technology-in-practice, explaining how people deal and interact with technology, does not help either, since it assumes that only humans deal with technology. Technology can be constructed with certain materials and assumptions, but only when it is used by human actions does it structure those actions. When an actor decides to use a technology, the actor also decides how to interact with it and these interactions can be different over time (i.e. like driving a car in different countries with different rules). However, physical properties result in boundary conditions on how to use an artefact and the more it is integrated into a system, such as an organisation, the narrower its alternative uses. Unfortunately, none of these concepts offers any guidance when dealing with emerging information technologies; for example, with AI and blockchain, non-human actions structure technology actions and technology even creates new technology but also adopts and uses that technology. For example, organisations such as the Associated Press use algorithms to write financial reports at a rate of 2,000 stories per minute. Of course, these are not in-depth award-winning articles, but business-related stories, such as quarterly earnings, involving stock market performance and corporate profits. Stories, however, that used to be written by humans. Another example in the financial world is the venture capital (VC) firm Deep Knowledge Ventures. In 2014, this Hong Kong VC fund appointed an algorithm to its board of directors. The algorithm gets to vote on whether an investment in a certain company is made or not. The VC fund focuses on life sciences and age-related disease projects and the algorithm, called VITAL, analyses data from multiple sources including clinical trials, financial details, previous funding rounds, intellectual property, and others. Although the algorithm is not yet running the VC fund by itself, it is a giant leap forward in how VC firms approach investments. Or what about Lapetus? A startup that uses artificial intelligence to analyse your selfies to determine whether or not you will be accepted for life insurance, within two minutes. Increasingly, such technology is embedded in organisations and thereby changes the interactions between the social and the material.

The use of technology is also influenced by the understanding of the user.[28] When using technology, humans are influenced by the materiality and characteristics of technology, those inscribed by the designer and previous users. In this case, previous use affects how technology is used. Even if that might be in ways not intended by designers, human actors might continue to use it in that way (e.g. due to corporate pressure, unavailability of staff, users' expectations or because they become more knowledgeable about the technology). However, when dealing with advanced technologies, in particular when dealing with AI, this is no longer the case. Artificial actors are not bound by corporate pressure or unavailability of staff, just like robots do not require a lunch break or cannot go on strike. AI removes unsuccessful behaviour if it does not contribute to achieving its ultimate goal.[113]

Technology is not sociomaterial, but the practice in which it is embedded and practised is "the space in which the social and the material become entangled".[73] However, within this practice when no social is involved, as in the case of AI, does this entanglement still take place? How can we conceptualise this interaction when no social is involved, but an intelligent actor that has been created by technology itself is? In the following section, I explore our understandings of AI as it relates to the emerging concept of sociomateriality to start to grasp how emerging information technologies affect organisations.

2.3 The introduction of the artificial

With rapid advancements in AI, organisations are increasingly dealing with (intelligent) artificial actors. This requires a different approach, since AI is fundamentally different from human intelligence.[114] Intelligence is "the complex expression of a complex set of principles", consisting of various interdependent subsystems all linked together.[115] Intelligence exists because of evolution, and it enables humans to model, predict, and manipulate reality. This unique ability allows us to reason backwards and forwards from a mental image and reason on possible (un)desired future outcomes. Evolution created our intelligence, but evolution is an inherently dumb process. It achieves its goal by trial and error and does not possess the foresight capabilities that we humans have. In fact, the unintelligent process of evolution has resulted in flaws in human intelligence.[116] Due to various constraints, such as food availability, trade-offs with other organs and biological materials, it is possible that our brains have not evolved in the most optimised way.[117] Artificial intelligence, on the other hand, will be developed by (artificially) intelligent beings/things which do possess the foresight capabilities that evolution misses. As such, it is better capable of understanding which materials and what processes work best for intelligence. It can apply the knowledge of others to improve (initial) designs and as such improve its intelligence.[117] Consequently, artificial intelligence will look and act in ways unfamiliar to mankind today and, hence, requires a different approach.

Evolving technologies such as artificial intelligence result in constantly evolving organisational processes. Especially, because the basic elements of computational systems, data and algorithms, have become central to everyday life. Understanding these fundamentals (a research stream that has become known as *computational thinking*) and how they affect organisations is as important as understanding mathematics or logic.[88] The more intelligent artificial intelligence becomes, the more it will affect and change organisations and the evolution of AI will not stop. In fact, Demis Hassabis, CEO of Google DeepMind, the division within Google responsible for ground-breaking research on artificial intelligence, said "the goal is to harness artificial intelligence for grand challenges. If we can solve intelligence in a general enough way, then we can apply it to all sorts of things to make the world a better place".[118] As technology continues to be improved, it is time for organisations to start incorporating the artificial perspective in their strategy, as it behaves so differently from human intelligence. In addition, how organisations use technology depends on the context, which changes all the time. Especially when dealing with AI. Simply because AI incorporates a great deal more context than humans ever could. However, only limited research has been conducted, and many questions arise when talking about the artificial as an independent actor within organisations. I do not intend to answer all these questions but simply pose them to show the need for additional research. For example, what structures emerge when people interact with the artificial remains unclear for now. How do existing structures, common practices, and culture determine the artificial and vice versa? How does the incorporation of the artificial within organisations change how organisations deal with new IT? What is artificial agency and how does it affect technology adoption, change collaboration, and influence traditional organisational tasks such as decision-making, strategising, or organisational design, normally performed by humans? In addition, how do artificial actors affect technology, what are the motivations of artificial actors, and do artificial actors' motivations change over time when they learn more? To understand these questions and how the artificial effects sociomateriality, we need to more closely examine the artificial agent and artificial agency.

As we discussed, traditional IT used to be at the whims of its users. Artificial intelligent agents, however, have the power to change its behaviour and make decisions independently and autonomously. With that, they can affect the context without being subject to the whims of human action. The increased availability of advanced AI within organisations, resulting in increased automation of tasks and jobs, leads to an algorithmic organisation built around smart algorithms. Algorithms that can define company processes, that can deliver customer services, that can take action when necessary, and, as such, can define the way the organisation works. With AI increasingly becoming pervasive in organisations, the balance that exists between the social and the material seems to be shifting, in favour of the artificial. Advanced computer-assisted information processing technologies will result in a reduction of human nodes in an information network. By doing so, it would lead to flatter organisations.[38] When dealing with AI, it is no longer always the case that humans can use the technology as they deem suitable, as AI can make decisions based on its internal logic and the outcome is often a given.[62, 119] In addition, it is no longer true that social actions "always involve interactions between humans",[75] as today's artificial actors also interact with artificial social agents such as chatbots. Even more, when AI is combined with smart contracts and distributed ledger technology, the possibility appears of developing organisations that are completely built up with code, without management or employees involved – so-called Decentralised Autonomous Organisations or DAOs – where artificial agents act completely autonomously with intentionality.

Organisations and technologies are both social and material, and the same goes for the artificial; it has both human agency (as it has intentionality) and material agency, but at the same time it is difficult to label it as social or material. Artificially intelligent agents have the capacity to act autonomously in response to human and material agency. It is social as it is developed by humans and it is not social as increasingly artificial intelligent artefacts are created by artificial intelligent artefacts, without any human involvement (to complicate matters, this does not mean that at some point in the future artificial intelligence cannot become a social "being").[120] In addition, it behaves differently when interacting with humans or without humans and rapidly it is becoming more intelligent than humans, albeit currently only in narrow domains. Artificial general intelligence (AGI) – AI as intelligent as human beings – is still decades away.[113] Next to that, it is material as it consists of binaries that are perceptible by humans,[108] but these material characteristics can change, unexpectedly, over time, "driven by large, varied and uncoordinated audiences".[121] The artificial continues to develop and evolve once designed, while what it does can remain the same, albeit becoming better over time. In addition, artificial agency can act on its own; it showcases intelligent behaviour, it has goals, can reason and monitor its behaviour.[113] It can even reproduce and evolve without the need for human action. The best illustration of how this works is AlphaGo Zero, the improved version of the AlphaGo algorithm developed by Google's DeepMind in 2017. While previous versions of AlphaGo had been trained using human data, this version of the algorithm was completely self-trained, without human intervention or historical data. A mind-blowing feature, especially because within three days of teaching itself how to play the game, it beat the version that beat Lee Sedol in 2016. It did so by applying a new form of reinforcement learning where the algorithm became its own teacher. It played against itself, hence it always had a component of equal strength, and learned from every move it made. While the previous version that beat Lee Sedol already surprised the world champion with moves he had never seen or thought about, the new version applied completely unknown strategies that it had taught itself. As a result, after 40 days it surpassed all previous versions of AlphaGo and, arguably, became the best Go player in the world. Such unexpected moves and strategies as developed by AlphaGo Zero increasingly start to appear in AI development. In 2017, AI developers from Google built algorithms that had to compete for scarce resources, resulting in increasingly advanced strategies to beat the component.[122] In 2016, another project from Google Brain developed algorithms that created new encryption methods, unlike any seen before developed by humans, to protect information from other neural networks. Finally, in 2017, Facebook developed two algorithms that created their own secret language, unsolicited, and used advanced strategies to get what they wanted. Consequently, Facebook had to shut down its algorithms.[112, 123] As these examples show, artificial agency is fundamentally different from material agency and, hence, a new science of the artificial is indeed required.[103, 124]

Developing a new way of dealing with the artificial in organisation studies is critical as increasingly the artificial is affecting organisations in multiple, unexpected ways. Until now, the artificial has been viewed as part of technologies (such as chairs, buildings, books, pens, data computers) that affect organisations. However, since AI is fundamentally different from human intelligence, with artificial agents operating independently of humans, the artificial is deeply changing organisations. Hence, it requires a new approach to deal with it in organisations, and a definition of an artificial agent as well as artificial agency is required. In the past, social agency has been defined as "coordinated human intentionality formed in partial response to perceptions of a technology's material agency" and material agency as "ways in which a technology's materiality acts. Material agency is activated as humans approach technology with particular intentions and decide which elements of its materiality to use at a given time".[91] Neither of these definitions is sufficient for the artificial. As such, I define artificial agents as "artificially intelligent actors that have the ability to act upon their own, apart from human intervention". As artificial entities, they can exercise agency through their performativity; that is, by doing things that are out of the control of users or other artificial or human agents. As such, artificial agency is "coordinated artificially intelligent intentionality formed in partial response to perceptions of human agency and material agency". Understanding what artificial agents are and how they perform agency helps to incorporate emerging information technologies in general and artificial intelligence in particular within the organisation of tomorrow.

2.4 Towards a tripartite analysis of sociomateriality

The concept of sociomateriality as discussed so far fails to explore the generative and constitutive rules of digital (made by humans) and artificial (made by AI) artefacts.[103] The entanglement of the social and the material raises ethical questions of consequences, responsibility, and accountability.[106] This requires further discussion, especially when incorporating artificial intelligent agents. Artificial agency becomes increasingly important now that there is a continuous stream of AI breakthroughs, made possible through increased "computational capabilities, algorithm design and communication technology".[125] Since technological artefacts can now be created by artificial intelligent actors, the important characteristic of sociomateriality, that technological artefacts are created by social action which in turn shapes human action, no longer applies. Thus, no longer are "all information technologies created by people and the result of social processes".[81] Therefore, we need to add an additional, artificial, agent to the concept of sociomateriality. One that can become entangled with the social and material in action. Within this extended concept of sociomateriality, time becomes important in relation to the artificial. AI continuously changes over time and improves based on new input it continuously receives, thereby changing its materiality but not its social usages (its objective or goal). This brings us to a new approach to sociomateriality, whereby not only the social and the material become entangled by means of action but in which it seems the artificial also becomes entangled with the social and the material by means of action, as shown in Figure 2.1.

Within this tripartite, the social, the material, and the artificial seem to imbricate over time and through an exercise of their agency. The social, the material, and the artificial are independent entities, becoming entangled when they are put into a relationship with one another through human, material, or artificial agency. Separating the artificial from the material is required because it combines characteristics of the material and the social but is none of those.

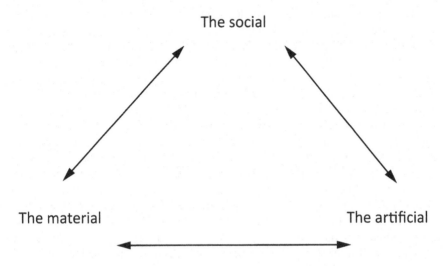

The social

The material   The artificial

Figure 2.1 Tripartite of sociomateriality

As such, seeing the artificial as an independent actor allows for a better understanding of how emerging information technologies will affect your organisation and what you should do to ensure a sustained competitive advantage in these ambiguous and uncertain times.

Within this tripartite analysis of sociomateriality, the social creates the material and the artificial, while the material and the artificial influence the social. The material creates the artificial, while the artificial influences, creates, or changes the material. The focus is on how the social, material, and artificial agency influence each other and how they acquire form, capabilities, and attributes through their interpenetration and how they interact with each other. Relations and boundaries between the social, the material, and the artificial are enacted in practice and are not fixed or pre-given; that is, the context matters. Since the impact of the artificial on organisations is growing, managers need to understand the sociomaterial (re)configurations as they organise activities. Within the tripartite analysis of sociomateriality, the notion of performativity remains relevant for understanding organisation design in times of artificial actors. These artificial actors are often developed within a certain framework and based on certain models that, when set free in an organisation, will then influence that organisation and how actors interact. As such, a tripartite analysis of sociomateriality will help you understand how humans, technology, and AI are interrelated with each other and how they affect each other in action as we will see in the coming chapters.

2.5 Conclusion

So, you might wonder now, what does this all mean? Why is it important to separate the concepts of the social (humans), the material (technologies), and the artificial (AI)? In this, rather theoretical, chapter my objective was to help you understand how the appearance of the artificial intelligent agent within organisations will change how organisations work. Looking at your organisation from a social, material, and artificial perspective might be a new way of defining the organisation. Doing so will help you better align your strategic goals as the organisation of tomorrow will face new challenges due to the appearance and continuous evolving of emerging information technologies. Especially the introduction of the intelligent artificial agent, which will take over many of the jobs currently done by humans, will significantly affect your organisation. Organisations that are capable of incorporating the artificial agent and combining it with other advanced information technologies stand the best chance to remain competitive in a truly data-driven future. Even more, when big data analytics, blockchain, and artificial intelligence are combined and integrated, organisations can move to become a Decentralised Autonomous Organisation. These organisations datafy their processes, distribute their data via the cloud or using distributed ledger technologies, analyse their data using descriptive or predictive analytics to sense and seize opportunities, and automate their decision-making using AI.

In today's world, data-driven organisations cannot function without humans as organisations remain social entities, but the more organisations turn into DAOs, the more jobs will be taken over by AI and robots.[126, 127] However, almost certainly, most of the existing organisations will never transform into complete DAOs, which are absent of management and employees and run completely by autonomous code. Consequently, there remains a human element to organisations and, as a result, *the social, the material*, and *the artificial* should exist in coherence and interact with each other without negatively affecting one another. This means the artificial adheres to the ethics valued by the social (which is a challenge in itself, as we will see in Chapter 6), the material is bound by the norms and principles of our society and the culture within an organisation, and the social is not subordinate to the material and the artificial. All three should exist in balance with each other, and organisations that ignore the human side of doing business are likely to face difficulties.

In the coming chapters, I will discuss how big data analytics, blockchain, and artificial intelligence will challenge existing organisational practices and will require you to rethink your strategic priorities. Especially when these emerging information technologies converge, the impact on your organisation will be significant and affect how your stakeholders, whether human or artificial, collaborate with each other.

In Chapter 3, I will discuss that adapting to changes in the environment is a complex, social, process that involves a wide variety of stakeholders on different organisational levels.[128] Organisations are integrated and dynamic entities where strategic management choices related to technologies, structures, and processes determine how a company can cope with these changes in the environment. Hence, not only changes in the environment, but also strategic management choices determine the behaviour and culture of an organisation. Next to organisational flexibility to respond to changes in the environment using the right technology, processes, and structures, an organisation needs to develop capabilities to understand the environment.[128] These, so-called dynamic capabilities consist of using analytics to understand the environment and customer needs, to develop products or services that match those needs and to adapt the organisation accordingly. These components can be integrated, developed, or reconfigured, depending on changing internal or external circumstances, and I will discuss how the material (big data analytics) can influence the social (organisations, management, and employees).[129]

In Chapter 4, I will discuss what blockchain is, its potential influence on organisation design, and how it is likely to result in new ways of collaboration among humans and artificial actors. This will contribute to an understanding of how the material (distributed ledger technology) affects the social (trust and decision-making within organisations) and how the artificial (automated decision-making through smart contracts) affects the material and the social. The emergence of blockchain technology in general and smart contracts, in particular, seem to re-define two forms of organisation design; the *decentralised* organisation and the *autonomous* organisation. These organisations use distributed ledger technologies and cryptography to remove the need for intermediaries and enable peer-to-peer transactions. Within these distributed organisational forms, technology is playing an increasingly important role resulting in new forms of organisation design and behaviours.[42, 130–132] Blockchain and smart contracts enable an organisation to control and reduce opportunism while automating decision-making, which has a direct impact on organisation design and inter-organisational relationships.[133, 134]

In Chapter 5, I will dive into the convergence of big data analytics and blockchain. When an organisation is capable of integrating both emerging information technologies within its business, significant change will occur, resulting in sustained competitive advantage. Some have argued that blockchain would do for value what the internet did for information: facilitate trustless peer-to-peer transactions without intermediaries.[135] Blockchain is a distributed ledger, and the data recorded on it is immutable, verifiable, and traceable. These new characteristics of data will help organisations solve issues related to data-sharing, data governance, data provenance, security, data ownership, and privacy. As a result, the convergence of big data analytics and blockchain will greatly affect how organisations should approach data and how they can derive insights from it. This chapter explores these applications and looks at startups developing solutions to ensure data provenance, privacy, security, and data ownership.

Chapter 6 will then take a deep dive into artificial intelligence and how it can be used to automate your business. This chapter will help you to understand the impact of AI, its corresponding risks, and what can be done to control it. Human-machine-networks, which are intensely connected, should be seen as nodes that have multiple dimensions with each other.[43] Since we are dealing with human, non-human, and artificial actors that interact and collaborate, I will not only discuss what AI is, how it will automate certain departments within your organisation such as your customer service department, but I will also discuss how we can ensure that AI does what we want it to do. How we can minimise harm to those actors involved, i.e. how the social can control the artificial. AI is not without risk, and as we will see, it is vital for organisations to develop AI correctly and responsibly.

In Chapter 7, I will bring everything together and explain how organisations can apply the lessons from this book using the $D^2 + A^2$ *model*. This model will provide you with the tools and a roadmap to make sure that your organisation sustains a competitive advantage in the increasingly data-driven and fast-changing future. I will discuss how actors interact with each other in an ever-changing network when faced with big data analytics, blockchain, or AI. I will then conclude the book with a note on the importance of globalisation in a digital world.

Chapter 3

Big data analytics to understand the context

Organisations face a constantly changing environment and those organisations wishing to remain competitive in such an ambiguous and uncertain environment should focus on detecting, anticipating, and responding to disruptive changes.[136, 137] Adopting to these changes is a complex process including both technological and social dimensions. It involves a wide variety of stakeholders on different organisational levels.[128] Organisations are integrated and dynamic entities where strategic choices related to technologies, structures, and processes determine how a company can respond to changes in the environment. Not only changes in the environment, but also these strategic choices determine the behaviour of an organisation.[128] Therefore, an organisation needs to develop the right capabilities to understand the fast-changing environment and remain competitive. A deep understanding of the context, which can be achieved using the right analytics, is required for leaders that face increasing uncertainty. In this chapter, we will see how the material (data and analytics) can influence the social (organisations, management, and employees) and how the social can change because of that.

Contemporary (business) environments are inherently ambiguous and uncertain. Ambiguity refers to unknown situations, where organisations face unidentified risks, which may be interpreted differently. Uncertainty refers to a changing environment in which the organisation lacks information to determine the reasons for change.[7] Organisations that have access to sufficient data and analytical tools can better understand the causes and effects of change and can anticipate environmental risks. Such organisations are better capable of dealing with an ambiguous and uncertain environment.[138, 139] Often, these environments are characterised by startups that are able to create better products and services using fewer resources as they leverage emerging (information) technologies. They often originate in low-end markets that are ignored by the incumbents who focus on the most profitable customers.[140] Those startups that are able to get a foothold in the lower end of the market and can become profitable due to the application of more advanced technology often disrupt the incumbents. Since these startups are more agile and can respond faster to the ongoing change in the environment than incumbents, they stand a better chance to remain relevant and competitive.[3] For example, companies such as Borders, Blockbuster, and Kodak are well-known examples of once-successful organisations that lacked the agility to respond to technological changes in their environment, such as online book retailing, online film distribution, and digital photography.[37] On the other hand, startups such as Amazon, Netflix, and Instagram have been able to leverage and benefit from the emerging information technologies that were overlooked or ignored by the incumbents.[39] Therefore, to avoid a "Kodak moment" it is crucial for organisations to not only develop the capacity to quickly detect and anticipate changes in the environment, but more importantly also respond to market disruptions and competitive threats.[141]

Detecting technological market disruption in a complex and fast-changing environment is difficult.[142] Often, disruptive startups go undetected until it is too late.[143] Nicholas Taleb, the well-known scholar and essayist, labelled such disruptions "Black Swans" – or unknown unknowns.[144] Black Swans are events that deviate from the expected, have an extreme impact, and, although they are difficult to predict, they have retrospective predictability. Moreover, they are unappreciated when they are first discovered and, therefore, often ignored and labelled as a fad or irrelevant. Unintended outcomes and unexpected events not only happen from environmental forces, but also from the unintended consequences of deliberate choices made by management. Choice, chance, and environmental circumstances interact, resulting in both positive and negative consequences that impact the organisation in the most unexpected ways. These events are what is meant with Black Swans; outliers that are unlikely to happen but have a major, long-lasting impact if they do. A well-known Black Swan was the Financial Crisis in 2007 and 2008. Those that discovered the biggest credit bubble of all time before it was about to burst made a killing, while millions of others lost tremendous amounts of money. This story has been turned into an award-winning movie – *The Big Short* – and clearly shows the impact a Black Swan can have on consumers, organisations, and societies.

Black Swans that surprise an organisation are the result of many (unintended) consequences of a long string of decisions made, based on a constantly changing environment, but with a lack of information at hand to truly understand what the implications of those decisions will be.[145] For example, the astronomer Clifford Stoll famously predicted that the internet was a "fad";[146] yet, in hindsight, we all know how disruptive the internet has been and how much it has changed our world. A Black Swan that is currently unfolding is the move to a decentralised society; its effect on global economies and organisations remains unknown, many have called it a fad and would not think it could ever happen. Yet, it has been predicted to greatly disturb economies and organisations.

Organisations that wish to remain relevant face the challenge to correctly and timely detect the changes in their environment and to correctly respond to those changes. Research indicates that data and analytics can assist in identifying and responding to Black Swans.[138, 139] Already, for many organisations, the role of data has become increasingly important in detecting and understanding environmental ambiguity and uncertainty (hedge fund manager Michael Burry was able to see the housing crisis coming and benefit from its collapse only by thoroughly analysing the housing market and the corresponding subprime loans in the United States).[147, 148] Data-driven organisations are in a strong position to deal with environmental ambiguity and uncertainty when they have a flexible, empowered, connected, and decentralised organisation and the technological capabilities to innovate across time and space.[52, 149, 150] Firms that embrace a data-driven approach often find that they have to change the design of the organisation.[52] The analysis of data and sharing that information internally shifts internal power structures. Moving power away from leaders with years of experience to those employees who have access to data and the means to analyse it to make strategic decisions.[40, 55] Although access to data may prevent organisations to be surprised by disruptive changes in the market, access to information alone is not enough. Instead, the organisation should have implemented the right decision-making processes within the organisation not only to anticipate but also respond to industry disruption when detected.[144, 145] Therefore, those organisations that anticipate the changing environment are not fooled by randomness.[151] Instead, they have developed the right capabilities and structures to be able to deal with ambiguity and uncertainty.[6, 7] These capabilities enable them to leverage opportunities and remain relevant and competitive.[152] In this chapter, I will discuss what those capabilities are.

Black Swans are not impossible to identify. We simply have to know where to look, be willing to expect more the unexpected, and act swiftly and decisively once a Black Swan happens. This requires faster decision-making processes (whereby multiple interdependent parties need to obtain a common understanding), better antennas to scan the horizon, and a better ability to interpret weak signals.[153] The strategic challenge that organisations face is to continuously adapt their strategy to the constantly, rapidly, and unpredictably changing environment. This requires strategic sensitivity, a long-term approach, an open mind, and flexible decision-making processes.[137] Above all, it requires a data-driven approach.

3.1 Datafying your business

Imagine it is Friday afternoon, and after a long week at work, you and your colleagues decide to go to the bar to unwind and refresh with a nice cool glass of beer. You go to your favourite pub and upon reaching the bar order a few pints. However, instead of the bartender giving you your beloved beer, he hands you a plastic card and tells you that from now on, you can pour your own beer as much as you want and as often as you want. Of course, if you wish, the bartender can still serve you, but with the new system you can try any beer that you wish and have as little or as much as you want. You want to try out the new American Pale Ale but only want a small glass because you are not sure if you will like it? Go ahead. If you feel more like a pint of a Summer Ale, it's all up to you. The new system automatically calculates the amount of beer you consume. You pay your tab at the end of the evening, just like always. As the evening progresses, you and your colleagues try out various new types of beers, which you would normally never order as you were limited to buying a half-pint glass or larger. In the end, your bill is higher than normal, but you had a great evening.[154]

This might sound like a far-off scenario, but in reality, it is already possible. It shows exactly the enormous possibility of analytics. The Israeli company WeissBeerger has developed a system that enables bar owners to equip their kegs of beer with sensors to datafy their beer-pouring activities. This system enables customers to tap their own beers and pay for exactly what they consume. It also enables the bar owner to know exactly which beers are selling when, at what time of the day, and to whom.[154] This is valuable information for the bar owner, as it enables the bar owner to order new kegs at the right time, since they know exactly how much of which beer is consumed when. However, it also shows which bartenders are giving beers away for free, pouring for their own consumption, or how much of the draught beer pour is inaccurate. For many breweries and bar owners, this information would be the holy grail of beer pouring. Especially, because breweries often spend vast amounts of money on marketing activities and market research but remain in the dark in terms of the "last mile" of information. Research by the company WeissBeerger showed that bars that installed their system not only had more information about who consumed what and when, it also helped them to take simple corrective actions for the "generous bartender". Those bars that installed the self-serve system saw their consumption rise by a whopping 30 per cent.[155]

WeissBeerger's sensor technology and consumption analytics show the power of big data analytics. Providing relevant insights can contribute to improving your organisation and increasing your revenue. It shows that access to the data alone is not sufficient. Only if you are capable of doing something with the insights derived from the data, can you actually make a difference for your customers and shareholders. Nevertheless, it starts of course with data and only if you have access to data, you can analyse that for insights. Therefore, the organisation of tomorrow can only succeed if it has digitised and datafied every, or at least most of the, ideas, processes, and customer touchpoints.

It is important to note the difference between digitalisation and datafication. Digitalisation refers to the conversion of information into digital format. For example, converting music into MP3 files, photos into JPEG, text to HTML, and analogue video to YouTube videos. Doing so will increase your available data exponentially. Digitalisation, therefore, means capturing human ideas in digital form for transmission, manipulation, re-use, and analysing.[156] Datafication, on the other hand, refers to turning analogue processes and customer touchpoints into digital processes and digital customer touchpoints. This means collecting data within every part of your organisation: HR data, financial data, social media data, sales data, customer data, and even data from devices that you connect to the internet. The Internet of Things (IoT), which is a network of connected products and devices linked to the internet, is an enabler for this process. Connected devices enable you to analyse all kinds of processes within your organisation. You can think of how people move through your office (workforce analytics). How drivers behave on the road (transportation analytics). Or how different products are being used (product behaviour analytics). The possibilities to datafy your business are endless. Basically, any process, device, infrastructure, or customer touchpoint can be made smart by including sensors that are connected to the internet. Moreover, with the number of connected devices available growing exponentially, this is easier than ever before. In the near future, sensors and connected devices will result in smart homes, smart offices, and smart cities. Currently, there are approximately 10 billion connected devices, with the number reaching 29–42 billion in 2022, and 75 billion in 2025. By 2030, we will have over 100 trillion connected sensors. In 2035, the prediction is that we will interact with a connected device every 18 seconds, or 4,800 times a day.[157–161] Whether these numbers are correct or not, the fact is that the number of connected devices will increase exponentially in the coming years. With that, the amount of data that we will create annually will explode, easily driving us into the era of the brontobytes (10^{27} bytes), and that will enable you to truly datafy your business. Once you are growing the amount of data within your organisation, your analytics will become more meaningful and provide you with more and better insights.

The first step in building the organisation of tomorrow is to datafy your organisation. While doing so, you will notice that it is far from only a technical challenge. The datafication process touches upon every aspect within your organisation including business workflows, strategy processes, data governance, privacy aspects, security, and company culture. All these aspects should be considered when you want to datafy your businesses and that is not an easy task.

3.2 From data to information to wisdom

Raw data is plentiful in today's digital age. Approximately 90 per cent of today's online data represents a compilation of data that was generated in only the last few years.[162] Consumers create billions of messages via instant messaging apps and social networking sites, such as Facebook, Twitter, or WeChat. We generate upwards of six billion queries on Google every day on our mobile devices and desktops. In addition, all the data coming from the

Internet of Things will only further grow the available data. However, this raw data does not create value on its own. It must be processed in a way that delivers valuable insights to your organisation for it to be resourceful. Raw data that is analysed, allows you to identify patterns, build models based on these patterns, and make data-driven projections to solve business problems. In recent years, it has become increasingly important for organisations and many of the Fortune 500 companies have developed and implemented big data strategies.[147, 148]

Once you have created, stored, and started to use the data within your organisation – a process collectively referred to as Big Data and which has been around since 2001[163] – you have made the first step in preparing your organisation for the data-driven world of tomorrow.[164] Once you start to incorporate big data within your organisation, it will change how your organisation is managed, how your organisation is designed, your culture and identity, and how decisions are made.[138, 139] Already, for many businesses, the most likely path to creating competitive advantage is by using big data and subjecting it to (advanced) analytics.[165] Hence, it is not only newcomers such as Airbnb, Netflix, and Amazon that can benefit from a data-driven approach.[13] Any company, small or large, can benefit, as we have seen with the bar example. Big data analytics offer insights by extracting structured information from unstructured data using tools such as descriptive, predictive, or prescriptive analytics.[166] In fact, some suggest that analytics have become a prerequisite to understanding the business environment and to remain competitive.[167, 168] There are several levels of practices of analytics, each increasing in complexity and the value they create: descriptive analytics, diagnostic analytics, predictive analytics, and prescriptive analytics. Let's discuss each of them briefly.

Descriptive and diagnostic analytics are all about the past and the present. Descriptive analytics is about what happened and diagnostic analytics about why something happened. They enable organisations to sense, filter, shape, learn, and calibrate opportunities by providing insights into what has happened in their internal and external environment, from one second ago to decades ago.[169, 170] Descriptive and diagnostic analytics are like looking into the rear-view mirror of your car. Using multiple structured data sources and statistical methods you can obtain insights about what has happened.[171] Descriptive analytics is also known as business intelligence and it only offers insights into the past. It does not offer recommendations on how to move forward. A well-known example is Google Analytics that many organisations use to analyse their web traffic. It provides clear graphs to help you understand what happened to your website but does not provide recommendations on how to change your website to generate more traffic. Diagnostic analytics is about why did something happen, and it goes one step further than standard business intelligence. It is about asking the right questions to understand why something happened in the past, what the patterns and trends in the data are, and what the insights are that you can derive from it.

Predictive analytics, on the other hand, is all about the future and predicting what will happen.[171] It uses machine learning and algorithms to find patterns and capture relationships in multiple unstructured and structured data sources to create foresight.[172] Predictive analytics allows you to make future projections based on historical and present data. There are many different providers who offer predictive analytics solutions, including KNIME, Sisense, GoodData, Dataiku, or TIBCO Spotfire. Predictive analytics enables you to use the known raw data and process it so that you can make predictions on the information you do not know.[172] As such, predictive analytics contributes to improving decision-making processes across the organisation.[173] It is about the future and predicting what will happen.[171] It is like your car's navigation system, directing you to the fastest route around a traffic jam. The assumption is that organisations that use predictive analytics will gain a competitive advantage since they can anticipate the future.[174] However, insufficient data and flaws or biases in algorithms and data could significantly harm organisations and their customers, which is why data governance is so important.[175] I will discuss data governance in detail in Chapter 5.

The final stage in understanding your business is prescriptive analytics. It is about what to do (now) and why to do it, given a complex set of requirements, objectives, and constraints. It not only offers recommendations on how to act upon predictions to take advantage of those predictions and transform an organisation accordingly, but it can also make decisions autonomously based on those recommendations. It leverages predictive analytics and descriptive analytics to derive ideal outcomes or solutions. Prescriptive analytics helps you solve business problems based on foresight achieved from continuously analysing a wide variety of (un)structured data sources.[176] Prescriptive analytics not only allows you to make sense of raw data but also allows you to determine the actions to take now. It leverages machine learning, simulations, mathematical formulae, as well as optimisation and data modelling techniques to help enterprise leaders make better-informed, data-driven decisions.[177] It is the final stage in understanding your business and offers you a thorough understanding of the environment to improve business performance.[177] When given several options to choose from, prescriptive analytics is helpful in identifying the best outcome or solution based on known limitations and scenarios.[176] It is about scenario planning to determine the best option for (autonomous) decision-makers, which can reduce the amount of uncertainty.[6] It takes predictive analytics a step further by not only helping you to decide what business decision to make, but even to make that decision on behalf of you, often autonomously. In continuation of the car metaphor, it is a self-driving, autonomous vehicle that can pick you up and take you to your destination.

When facing big data, prescriptive analytics comes with multiple benefits, such as improved utilisation of resources and increased insight into patterns and habits of consumers. It also offers organisations better insights on the impact of new technologies or techniques.[178] For example, you can use prescriptive analytics to determine the best social media engagement opportunities to take. The company Lithium Reach helps organisations accomplish this by recommending the best time of day to post content via social media channels.[179] Prescriptive analytics is also useful for front-line workers. For example, it can be used to determine the best-personalised option and with that enhance the customer experience. For instance, Wine.com uses prescriptive technology to encourage customer chat sessions with wine experts to increase customer loyalty.[180] Moreover, prescriptive analytics enables industrial-scale data analysis so that enterprises can scale internal decision processes.[181] Prescriptive analytics is being used successfully in a variety of businesses. General Electric (GE) and Pitney Bowes forged an alliance to leverage prescriptive analytics using data produced from Pitney Bowes' shipping machines and production mailing.[182] GE developed customised applications for asset performance management (APM) for Pitney Bowes with its Pedix software platform. This allows Pitney Bowes to offer accurate job scheduling capabilities and productivity and client services to its enterprise clients. PopSugar, a lifestyle media company, also uses prescriptive analytics to produce engaging content that its readers will find relevant and valuable. The company uses prescriptive analytics to better understand its audience and business value drivers. For instance, PopSugar was able to determine from 231,000 social shares and seven million views that childhood nostalgia and recognisable product names helped increased social shares and readership.[183]

In the near future, prescriptive analytics will further facilitate analytical development for automated analytics where it replaces the need for human decision-making with automated decision-making.[184] Automated analytics will enable organisations to choose the best marketing email to send to customers instead of needing a marketing director to make this decision. The prescriptive analytics market is also growing exponentially and is expected to reach US$1.1billion in 2019.[185] Moreover, it is projected to be built into business analytics software by 2020.[186] This means that increasingly analytics is becoming part of the capabilities of an organisation. However, for big data analytics to have the most effect, it needs to become a dynamic capability.

3.3 Analytics use cases

Descriptive, diagnostic, predictive, and prescriptive analytics can each provide insights into the business and as such improve and optimise your performance and increase your competitive advantage. Descriptive and diagnostic analytics enable organisations to learn, sense, filter, shape, and calibrate opportunities by providing insights as to what has happened in their environment.[187] This will allow your organisation to better sense opportunities than the competition. Predictive analytics can improve your decision-making across your organisation to help you understand which opportunities are best to be seized depending on their future outcome.[187] As an example, predictive analytics can predict future customer demand based on detailed customer profiles, which will build loyalty and commitment if carried out correctly. When predictive analytics is successfully incorporated in your organisation, you can start to predict a lot more, including:

1   Customer churn: when is your customer about to leave you and for what reason? Knowing this information will enable you to take proactive action to prevent your customer from eventually leaving you.
2   Sentiment: what do your customers think of your new product, service, campaign, or commercial? Knowing this information enables you to change it before or shortly after launch to ensure that it matches your customers' needs.
3   Customer support: when can you expect an increase in customer support and what will the customers be looking for? Knowing how your customers use your product would enable you to predict customer service requests if you notice a fault in your product. This information will certainly improve your customer service.
4   Customer Lifetime Value (CLV): when you have a detailed understanding of your customers, you are able to better predict their CLV. Having a better understanding of the CLV will allow you to invest more, or less, in the right customers.

Finally, prescriptive analytics transforms an organisation and can be seen as the final stage in understanding your business. It enables a continuous and in real time alignment and realignment of tangible and intangible assets based on foresight achieved from continuously analysing a wide variety of structured and unstructured data sources, exactly what is necessary to detect Black Swans.[136, 137, 153, 187]

There are many different use cases with analytics to improve your organisation. This may seem daunting, but in general the opportunities can be divided in nine use cases across three different pillars (see Table 3.1): your customers, your product, and your organisation.

Table 3.1 Analytics use case framework

Your customers	Your product	Your organisation
Develop a 360-degree customer view	Personalise website/ offering	Reduce risk/fraud
Understand the market	Improve your service	Better organise activities
Find new markets	Co-create and innovate	Understand the competition

- *Develop a 360-degree customer view*: developing a complete view of your customer is important for every organisation, as it helps to understand what your customer wants, what the needs and preferences are and how the customer has to be approached. When you combine and analyse internal data sources, such as your CRM data, sales data, or call centre data, with external sources, such as social media data or news data, you are capable of creating segments of 1, meaning that you know each customer as well as you know your friends, even if you have millions of customers.
- *Understand the market*: when you mix different data sets such as sales data, market news data, and social media data, you can get real-time insights what the market thinks of your product and when you launch for example a new commercial, you can get insights in real-time how it is perceived.
- *Find new markets*: analysing various data sources such as web statistics and social media can help you find new markets or customers with latent needs that you were not aware of. Using techniques such as Natural Language Processing (NLP) or machine learning you will be able to anticipate better what (potential) customers are looking for, which could result in finding completely new markets.
- *Personalise website/offering*: today it is all about relevancy and offering the right product/service to the right person for the right price via the right channel at the right moment in time. Google personalises its search results based on your profile and Amazon offers different homepages, with different products on offer, to almost every visitor. It comes back to completely knowing your customer by combining different data sources to really know what they are looking for.
- *Improve your service*: using analytics, you can optimise your customer service, resulting in happier customers. A great example of this practice is Southwest Airlines; it uses speech analytics to extract in real-time deep and meaningful information out of live-recorded interactions between staff and customers. This data, combined with other sources such as customer profiles, flight information, and social media data enables it to offer a consistently high-quality service.
- *Co-create and innovate*: analytics not only provides you with insights about your customers but can also give you information regarding the products and how these are being used. When you are capable of monitoring how the product is being used via sensors and telematics, you gain a deep understanding of how you can improve the product. This allows you to co-create and innovate together with your customers. In addition, simulation analysis using massive amounts of data and supercomputers will enable you to drastically speed up the innovation of your products.
- *Reduce risk/fraud*: analytics can help you with detecting anomalies and outliers. These anomalies and outliers could indicate fraudulent actions. It can also reduce the risk you are facing. When you have a better

understanding of your customer, you can better determine their risk profile (whether it is a customer or a business looking for credit, a mortgage, or insurance).

- *Better organise activities*: employees can generate massive amounts of data at the office. Sensors installed on office furniture and throughout the office can provide insights into how employees behave at work. These insights can be used to organise the workplace better. You can also monitor all unstructured data such as emails, documents, and meetings to know which employee is knowledgeable about which topic and which employees interact with each other (of course taking privacy into account). This should not be seen as spying on your employees but will help employees to find the information they need faster and more efficiently.
- *Understand the competition*: what you can do for your own organisation can also be done, more or less, for your competitors. When you monitor the pricing strategy of your competitor, analytics can inform you in real time when they adjust pricing, allowing you to respond faster. Of course, this strategy is not completely without risks as when two algorithms start interacting, strange things can happen; such as a book about flies for sale for over $23 million, as we will see in Chapter 6.

3.4 Sensing, seizing, and transforming

Developing the right capabilities for your organisation is vital in today's competitive world. Instead of just focusing on ordinary capabilities, organisations should focus on dynamic capabilities. Ordinary capabilities are like best practices that are common across all organisations within one or multiple industries. They started in one or two companies and over time, are copied by other organisations. An example is Toyota's efficient production system, which over time has been implemented by all car manufacturers. Ordinary capabilities can be taught by taking an engineering or management class. They are a minimum requirement to run a business nowadays. However, if your organisation wants to develop sustained competitive advantage, then you should not only focus on ordinary capabilities, but you should pay special attention to develop so-called dynamic capabilities. These are the capabilities that are idiosyncratic. They are unique to the organisation and often take years to develop but are rooted in the organisation. Dynamic capabilities are what differentiates a successful organisation from an unsuccessful organisation.

Dynamic capabilities were first described as those capabilities that enable an organisation to develop new products and services depending on changing market circumstances.[188] An organisation should integrate, develop, or reconfigure different components depending on changing internal or external circumstances.[129] Dynamic capabilities are especially important in high-velocity, fast-changing markets.[189] The context, experience, and timing of dynamic capabilities determine the level of sustainable competitive advantage that can be achieved in rapidly changing environments.[190] Dynamic capabilities, when developed successfully, offer organisations the capacity to sense and shape opportunities and threats. To seize those opportunities sensed. To maintain competitiveness through enhancing, combining, protecting, and reconfiguring tangible and intangible company assets. Dynamic capabilities enable highly adaptive behaviour and organisational agility to manage deep uncertainty and there is a direct link between dynamic capabilities and superior performance in changing environments.[6, 191, 192]

Organisations that have successfully turned analytics into a dynamic capability are, for example, the city of Barcelona. It analyses user-generated content to understand tourist profiles.[193] By analysing 100,000 travel blogs and reviews written by tourists who have visited Barcelona, the city obtains valuable insights into its "customer", resulting in detailed profiles of those who visit Barcelona.[193] As such, Barcelona employs descriptive analytics to obtain insights on changing tourism behaviour to identify new markets and customer trends.[187] On the other hand, the Indian industrial company Ramco Cements Limited (RCL) analyses operational data and enterprise resource planning (ERP) data to enable "more intelligent business decisions".[194] The company employs various data visualisation techniques and predictive capabilities to analyse distinct data sources, such as geographical data of trucks, plant data, or customer data, to optimise processes and improve decision-making.[194] As such, the predictive analytics that RCL implemented are a dynamic capability as it offers the company a competitive advantage since it can improve its processes, make better decisions, and respond faster to changes in its environment.[141, 195, 196]

Although companies need to focus on developing dynamic capabilities, executives often rely on experience and routines to develop ordinary capabilities, such as functional and operational processes in areas like manufacturing and marketing, to create competitive advantage.[197] However, access and ownership to such difficult-to-replicate assets are no longer enough for organisations. Only those dynamic capabilities that offer an understanding of how the market and environment change can result in competitive advantage.[187] They are created by learning from mistakes, repeated practice, and experience.[189] Dynamic capabilities are particularly relevant for network organisations that operate in an international, global, and open environment that are well-developed for exchanging goods and services, face rapid technological change where organisations need to combine multiple innovations to address customer needs but where it is difficult to exchange technological and managerial know-how.[187] Especially those organisations that operate in multiple countries and span multiple jurisdictions and territories, so-called Multinational Enterprises (MNEs), where variables such as technologies, infrastructure, markets, and customer demands are different, dynamic capabilities must be amplified.[198] Therefore, big data analytics can be seen as a dynamic capability. It helps to understand the environment and enables managers to act and as such provides organisations with sustained superior performance and competitive advantage.

To be more specific, dynamic capabilities are those capabilities that sense and seize opportunities and, subsequently, transform and realign the assets of an organisation. Sensing is the ability to scan, search, and explore across markets, technologies, and customers to understand customer needs, the latest technological possibilities, the evolution of markets and industries, or the potential responses to that from suppliers and competitors. Sensing relates to understanding the constraints that affect changes (including laws and ethics) and includes elements such as R&D activities to find new technologies, processes to understand supplier innovation, and processes to identify new markets and customer needs. These are the activities that help an organisation to understand the stakeholders and the context of an organisation.[190] Sensing can be done through traditional market research, but it is better to start combining and analysing disparate data sources such as social media data, (latent) customer demands, geopolitical trends, market prices, and many more. Using business intelligence tools such as Tableau, ClearStory Data, Qlik, or Sisense you can prepare those data sources and combine them to find patterns that could indicate important market dynamics. It can help to understand the environment and to discover patterns in customer behaviour or market trends. As such, analytics can enable organisations to detect opportunities in times of ambiguity and uncertainty. It offers the antennae required to detect the weak signals that indicate a changing environment and changing customer behaviour.[153, 190, 199]

Once you understand your customers and market trends, and hence you are able to better detect Black Swans, you should prepare the business to be able to seize those opportunities sensed.[187] This requires investments in the development and commercialisation of activities to ensure the right structures, procedures, designs, and incentives are in place to seize opportunities.[187] Seizing activities include selecting decision-making protocols, designing product and revenue architectures, improving processes and managerial activities such as leadership, communication, and organisational culture.[196] In short, it means improving and preparing the organisation for seizing the sensed opportunities. These activities help an organisation to anticipate detected Black Swans and prepare for a potential response. The company Netflix is particularly good at using predictive analytics and using detailed customer information to "improve members' retention, reduce cancellations, achieve long-term loyalty, and obtain positive satisfaction ratings for their product".[200] Netflix applies predictive analytics to offer product recommendations and facilitating customers' decision-making, on, in Netflix's case, what to watch.[200] By analysing vast troves of data, Netflix is able to seize opportunities based on its deep understanding of its customers' preferences.

Sensing and seizing opportunities, or detecting and anticipating changes in the environment, prepare an organisation for profitable growth and competitive advantage.[187, 191] However, key to sustained competitive advantage is the capability to develop new products and services depending on changing market circumstances, i.e. respond to the Black Swans.[152, 188] This requires a continuous (re)alignment of (in)tangible assets and includes elements that are involved in embracing innovation.[187, 201] It ensures that your organisation can build value-enhancing product development or knowledge management skills to be able to respond to disruptive innovation.[202] The objective is to (co)create and innovate new products and services that match the sensed and seized opportunities. However, currently, not many organisations apply prescriptive analytics to transform their business or (re)align their assets. This may be because prescriptive analytics is a nascent technology that is applied only by few organisations (e.g. Facebook and Google). In addition, although prescriptive analytics is likely to offer the greatest benefits for organisations, a lack of available software, high-quality and bias-free data, and computational requirements may prevent organisations from applying prescriptive analytics.[176]

When faced with industry disruption, a company that developed dynamic capabilities is on the lookout for unknown unknowns, while an organisation that applies big data analytics to enhance its dynamic capabilities can create additional value.[203–207] The routines, skills, and capabilities underpinning sensing, seizing, and transforming combine to give organisations a competitive edge in uncertain and changing environments.[187] As we will see in Chapter 7, when I will explain the $D^2 + A^2$ model, an analytics strategy underpins and facilitates dynamic capabilities to respond to changes in a dynamic environment.[206, 208, 209] But first, let's discuss how big data analytics will change the power balance within your organisation and enable a new way to develop your strategy.

3.5 Empowerment and open strategising

Although big data refers to the creation, storage, and usage of large volumes of data, analytics offers insights from any type of data, regardless of the volume, velocity, variety, variability, or veracity (as long as the data is unbiased and of high quality of course).[163, 164] The various types of analytics enable organisations to detect, anticipate, and respond strategically in an ambiguous and uncertain business environment.[166, 173, 177, 210–212] By doing so, analytics changes how organisations are managed, how organisations are designed, their culture and identity, and how decisions are made.[138, 139] Access to such knowledge and information not only results in a better understanding of the context and improved decision-making capabilities but also results in a shift in power within organisations.[35, 52, 55] Shifting the power balance within an organisation, however, requires a different way of working and a change in company culture. Traditionally, the power to make (strategic) decisions within organisations resided with those leaders who had the most experience and were on top of the hierarchy. Leaders have the power to make decisions because they have access to limited, tangible resources and knowledge not available anywhere else in the organisation. After all, knowledge is a form of power and knowledge can be gained from power.[51] However, through observation, new knowledge can be created and, thus, when data and insights from data are widely accessible in real time, the locus of power changes. Within organisations that face disruption and where data becomes more and more important, data shifts the power structure within the business. Moving it away from leaders with years of experience to whoever has access to data and who has the power to analyse that data for understandable insights to make (strategic) decisions and create new opportunities.[35, 52, 55] When more people have access to knowledge, empowerment is a possibility.[51] Organisations that empower their employees and customers, and partner with previously excluded actors, whether human or machine, are less likely to be surprised by changes in the environment.[129, 187] Therefore, increasingly organisations should adopt an open strategy approach, which is the decentralisation of strategy formulation across previously excluded, internal and external actors.[213] An open strategy is possible thanks to big data analytics, and it significantly changes how *the social* interact with each other.

Traditionally, organisations focused on ownership and control of (in)tangible assets to achieve competitive advantage. However, ownership of resources is no longer vital for success.[213] Data is so widespread due to the rise of new technologies and it can be used to fuel innovation. Embracing external ideas and knowledge and combining it with internal research and development will enable organisations to create new business models and opportunities and remain competitive in the digital age.[214] Collaborating with new actors increasingly gains acceptance, thanks to the plummeting costs of communication, the availability of digital artefacts, and the possibility to safely share proprietary data, as we will see in Chapter 5. [213, 215] This enables organisations to use the intelligence of the crowd to create better solutions, improve innovation, and make better decisions.[216, 217]

It is called *open strategy* and has been around for over 20 years. It is an extension of open innovation, which focuses on discovering, exploring, and exploiting innovation opportunities.[218–220] Open strategy embraces the advantages of an open approach to create value instead of raising barriers.[213] As such, it goes one step further than open innovation. It allows previously excluded stakeholders, such as employees, customers, suppliers, connected devices, or even competitors, to join in the strategy-making process and create increased value for the organisation. Open strategy allows organisations to better understand the fast-changing environment by offering new, internal and external, data sources, which, when analysed correctly, can result in new strategic opportunities.

Open strategising consists of two important principles: inclusiveness and transparency.[221] Inclusiveness is about involving previously excluded actors in the strategy-making process while transparency is about being transparent when communicating with those actors.[215, 219, 221-224] Both principles are only possible because of the availability of data and analytics. It enables organisations to actively incorporate input from previously excluded actors during strategy making who must actively engage and interact with each other, since sensemaking "takes place in interactive talk".[223, 225] Within collaborative decision-making, transparency and inclusiveness are, therefore, important. Inclusiveness ensures actors can actively participate in decision-making processes, while transparency ensures all actors remain aligned.[223] Although open strategising changes collaboration within human-to-human networks by empowering employees and customers, it can also result in an extra burden of work due to the need to digest large amounts of information. This is where big data analytics comes in.[226-230] Big data enables inclusiveness by collecting and aggregating ideas (of course, only with full consent of the stakeholder), while analytics enables transparency by summarising the conversations and detecting actionable ideas among the data, using Natural Language Processing and text analytics. This can result in new business lines or strategic directions for the organisation.[220, 231-234]

One of the first examples of a successful open strategy project was IBM's Annual Innovation Jam, a concept developed in 2001 to unite the organisation and to understand what ideas reside in the organisation. Everyone in the organisation can contribute and, through game theory, the ten best ideas are selected that will receive funding to be developed further. After some time, those ten ideas are evaluated. Some will be developed further, while others will be stopped. The IBM Jamming Sessions show that many people within an organisation have important strategic ideas. Often, in a closed-strategy process these are not used as strategy-making is done near the top of the organisation. The Jam Sessions, however, bring many ideas together. It has resulted in many new big product lines or smaller ideas that contributed to bigger ideas. The IBM Jam Sessions also show that people want to be engaged. That they want to share their ideas with a wider audience, even if those ideas do not generate as much attention. Since 2001, IBM's Innovation Jam has been developed into an IBM product, which is successfully applied by dozens of organisations to include their employees, customers, and even competitors in the strategy-making process.

Therefore, not only does big data analytics offer the insights to better interpret a fast-changing environment and improve the decision-making capabilities, but it also changes how *the social* collaborates when organising activities, enabled by *the material* and *the artificial*. Though open strategising is one form of collaboration made possible due to data and data-related technologies, there are more forms of collaboration that organisations should be aware of in these changing times, especially when *the social* and *the material* become involved with blockchain and AI, as we will see in Chapters 4 and 6. First, let's pay some attention to the risks associated with data and analytics, because if these are not managed correctly, all your work could be in vain.

3.6 Security and privacy

In a world that increasingly revolves around data, security is key. Unfortunately, too often organisations do not take security seriously. As recently as December 2018, the global hotel chain Marriott confirmed the Starwood data hack, where 500 million customer profiles and credit card details were stolen. A few days later, Quora acknowledged that 100 million user profiles were hacked. In addition, even big tech giants like Facebook allow firms such as Cambridge Analytica to syphon away 87 million user profiles. Moreover, the average Internet of Things device is so easy to hack that a kid can do it, even if it is meant to be a highly secure crypto wallet.[235] In the years to come, data will only increase in importance and as such in value. With that will come increased attention by hackers to steal data or hack your products, services, or servers. More than ever, data security is vital if we wish to benefit from data. It is a key requirement for the organisation of tomorrow, because one hack can ruin your organisation (in 2011, the Dutch company DigiNotar, a commercial certificate authority, was declared bankrupt after it was hacked). Data security comes in many flavours, which, roughly speaking, can be divided into three different streams:

- processes and organisational solutions;
- technical and hardware solutions;
- data and software solutions.

Let's briefly discuss the first, which should be obvious for all of us by now, and take a deep dive in the second and third stream.

Processes and organisational solutions

Security processes and organisational solutions are very straightforward, or at least should be. By now, every organisation should enforce a hard-to-guess password, preventing users and employees from using passwords such as *123456* or *qwertyui*, which, unfortunately, still happens. The best way to ensure difficult and different passwords for different services is to use a password manager such as 1Password or LastPass. These services can generate and store difficult passwords (which go beyond the outdated "at least 8 characters and a capital letter and a number") to make your life easier and more secure. Other practical solutions include educating staff not to use a random USB stick that they found somewhere, enforce clean desk

policies as well as having and enforcing a security policy within your organisation. Processes and organisational solutions are so straightforward that
every organisation should adhere to them. Unfortunately, that is still not
the case.

Technical and hardware solutions

To improve your security, you should have not only organisational solutions
but also secure hardware solutions as well as secure connected devices. Connected devices are vulnerable, as seen in the DDoS attack on October 21,
2016, which took down the DNS provider Dyn. Large websites such as Etsy,
Twitter, PayPal, Verizon, Comcast, and Reddit were among the many that were
virtually unusable during this attack. The hackers turned to unsecured IoT
devices to create an extensive botnet, so they could push enough traffic to take
down Dyn. While this was the largest attack caused by IoT security issues, it
certainly isn't the first. The IoT market needs to find a way to properly secure
these devices before more high-profile attacks completely negate the benefits of
having this connected technology in your organisation. Especially, because IoT
devices add countless potential attack surfaces to an organisation, whether you
have an official policy or people are bringing in their own technology. Each
connected device that is connected to your network has the potential of giving
attackers a direct entry point to your infrastructure.

Hardware-based security helps to prevent hackers from accessing your servers. Using, for example, dongles in combination with security tokens can be
a requirement to access a certain service or server. The dongle can include
biometric technology to prevent anyone being able to use it, except the owner.
Without the required dongle and having the right biometrics, it is impossible
for hackers to gain access to secure data. Of course, this does not count if the
hardware itself contains a backdoor or has been tampered with before being
installed. This is especially relevant for Internet of Things devices, which are
often developed using many different products from many different suppliers.
While there are several unified platforms emerging that cover IoT security
standards, such as MIDAS, Unify IoT, and Universal Internet of Things
Platform, you could be dealing with dozens of devices whose suppliers don't
have the same protection in place. Outdated firmware and software could also
make it easy to exploit your IoT technology and use it as a point of attack.
The sheer variety of form factors, operating systems, feature sets, and vendors
introduce complications that your current IT security resources may be unable
to cover. Therefore, when you are datafying your organisation and introdu-
cing connected devices in your organisation or you are developing connected
devices for you customers, a complete re-evaluation of your IT security strategy and the personnel's mindset is important. You do not want that your
connected device is "responsible" for the next DDoS attack that will bring
down the internet again. Thus, your staff needs to understand that every

connected device being developed or integrated into your organisation could represent a vulnerability point.

Vulnerable IoT devices can have significant consequences and do much harm to your organisation and your customers, which could even lead to potentially life-threatening situations. Consider smart devices used in manufacturing applications. If an IoT safety sensor gets compromised, it could result in your employees or your customers ending up in unsafe situations that could cause injuries or death. This is especially the case in the medical field, which is adopting a wide range of speciality IoT devices to improve patient care. If a monitoring device reports the wrong sugar levels on a diabetic patient, they could end up in a coma. Alternatively, even something as simple as a thermostat could have long-term consequences for a company if compromised. If the heating or cooling is run at inefficient levels, the overhead costs could slowly start to eat into your budget. Data centres with cooling systems that are being maliciously controlled could lose their ability to regulate heat and even lead to hardware failure. This problem is only going to get worse as IoT continues its rapid expansion over the next few years. Unfortunately, many organisations are not prepared to deal with the security issues that they bring to the table. However, like any other technology, the Internet of Things is not going to stop because of this, therefore, organisations have to act to ensure safe connected devices.

Data and software solutions

Even if you have the best security policies that everyone adheres to and you have implemented all the possible hardware security solutions, it is still possible that your organisation will be hacked. Every organisation can be hacked, and if you are not hacked, you are simply not, yet, important enough. Therefore, the starting point of your organisation should be that hackers will obtain access to your data. Even if you have implemented the right organisational procedures and hardware preventions.

So, what measure should you take if you know that hackers will obtain your data? Of course: encryption! If hackers have access to your data but cannot read your data because they do not have the right encryption key, the stolen data remains useless to the hackers. However, unfortunately, many organisations don't have encryption, and if they do, they don't have end-to-end encryption. A 2015 survey showed that of those organisations researched, only 44 per cent made use of extensive data encryption technologies.[236] The main barriers for organisations not to implement encryption is, according to the survey, a lack of budget (37 per cent), performance concerns (31 per cent), and lack of knowledge (28 per cent). One per cent of the respondents believe that encryption is not effective in protecting their data, which to me points to a lack of understanding encryption in the first place. Those companies that do not ensure encryption leave their data vulnerable in case of a data breach.

With that, you breach your customers' privacy, and that could make you liable, especially under the GDPR.

However, even if you have implemented encryption, you could still face problems with the advent of quantum computing. Most of the existing encryption will end up useless when we have working quantum computers. The problem with existing cryptography is that a sufficiently powerful quantum computer could easily solve the mathematical problems that are currently used by most encryption algorithms. If that happens, any data that is currently encrypted using those algorithms will become accessible to those with access to such quantum computing. As such, intelligence agencies are, most likely, already storing currently unbreakable intercepted data in the hopes that quantum computing will give them access. Once hackers gain access to quantum computing, your encrypted data is anything but safe. As such, despite offering enormous opportunities to solve some of the world's biggest problems, quantum computing is also one of the biggest security risks.

Therefore, organisations should adopt quantum-computing proof encryption, also known as post-quantum cryptography or quantum-resistant cryptography. Fortunately, it is gaining more attention from researchers as well as organisations. However, developing new quantum-resistant cryptography takes time while the developments around quantum computing are accelerating. In 2018, Google revealed a 72-qubit gate-based superconducting system, bringing us rapidly closer to quantum supremacy (meaning a quantum computer that outperforms the world's fastest supercomputer). By the time you are reading this book, it might be that quantum supremacy has already been achieved.

End-to-end encryption that is resistant to quantum computing will become very important in the near future. Therefore, the organisation of tomorrow that wants to protect its data, that wants to protect its customers' data and as such comply with regulations such as GDPR, should ensure that its data remains secure, now and in the upcoming era of the quantum computer. Fortunately, quantum-resistant encryption is not the only measure organisations can take to secure themselves. The other option is to start using security analytics.

3.6.1 Security analytics

Security analytics can help you understand what is happening within your company and can help you act when it is needed most. Protecting your organisations from (would-be) hackers is difficult. Many organisations believe that security management has become more difficult over the past years. There are several reasons why security management has become more difficult including more complex IT systems that are required and limited talent that is available to develop the security measures. In addition, the threat landscape has become a lot worse with more sophisticated and successful hacks carried out in the past years. One of the reasons for this is that organisations have not yet adopted security analytics in their organisation but are still relying on near obsolete processes and technologies. Often, monitoring still depends on too many manual processes and tools that are not integrated with each other, resulting in an incomplete overall picture. As a result, organisations face a lot of false positives, due to the lack of intelligent analytics resulting in too much noise. Very few organisations correctly protect their business, let alone store their sensitive documents or passwords correctly. In the 2014 Sony hack, hackers found a folder on a server containing unencrypted passwords. To make matters worse, that folder was called *passwords*.[237]

It is time that organisations face the facts and start protecting themselves, and their customers. Security analytics can help you handle the complex data landscape, especially for organisations that have large data centres, thousands of employees that use their own devices, and employees and customers that use vulnerable connected devices. With security analytics, you can gain the data and insights required to protect your IT resources. A few vendors operating in this area include NetSentries and Argyle Data. Security analytics can identify the red flags that often precede a breach or attack. You can find devices or hardware that are communicating with unauthorised systems or networks and lock them down before someone can use that device to get into your infrastructure. IT security specialists can use security analytics solutions to look beyond perimeter-based protection and determine whether they need to act based on the network traffic they are seeing. With security analytics in place, you will have the possibility of derailing zero-day attacks (software bugs discovered by hackers that are unknown to the developer) before they cripple your organisation or cause a costly data breach. Machine learning plays an important role in automating at least parts of this process. It will prevent your IT security staff from becoming overwhelmed by the sheer volume of information that they need to look at. As your organisation fends off attacks related to your hardware and connected devices and discover more markers for potential vulnerabilities, the security analytics solution can use this data to handle lower priority issues. Your IT security analysts can then focus their attention on complex exploits and other concerns that require a hands-on approach. Security analytics is becoming a prerequisite for the organisation of tomorrow, but security analytics alone is not enough. Especially in larger organisations, it is time to introduce the Chief Information Security Officer (CISO).

3.6.2 The Chief Information Security Officer

The Chief Information Security Officer is not only responsible for your security analytics but has the responsibility over anything data related. The CISO should be an important role within the board and should look at combatting persistent threats and mitigating exposure of the company's IT systems to (large) cyber-attacks. The CISO should focus on reducing the possibility of fraud on business processes, preventing hacktivism on company networks as well as identifying insider threats. The CISO should create a secure environment that is capable of dealing with large quantities of data. Security analytics involve terabytes or petabytes of data due to log information from monitoring your network, database information, identify information, and all kinds of other system data that needs to be analysed in real time to know what is going on. Within a true security analytics environment, an organisation should be able to combine security intelligence with business transactional data as well as unstructured company data such as emails to obtain a complete picture of what is going on. This will allow you to find all kinds of unique patterns and anomalies that actually might be, for example, a very slow-moving attack that in the end could do much harm.

The introduction of the Chief Information Security Officer is just the beginning. The world of digital security is changing rapidly, and organisations should evolve as well. Cybercriminals are constantly changing their tactics, finding new ways to attack companies. If a company refuses to stay up-to-date, it is almost begging to be hacked. This new reality requires a new approach to security. Protecting your company should be focused on prevention, detection, and response. On the one hand, you should make it as difficult as possible for criminals to hack your systems and exploit your data. Encrypt your data, and especially your passwords, and use firewalls to protect your systems from outside intruders. On the other hand, focus on monitoring and detection to know what is going on within your network and company. Combine different, real-time, automatic tools to discover patterns and anomalies that could expose an intruder, identify offences as well as find security incidents that require your attention. Remove any manual activities and make use of automated intelligent processes that analyse deep internal and external security intelligence. Once a security threat is detected, you should focus on the response to minimise the possible damage.

Security analytics is a difficult field, which involves large volumes of data, smart algorithms, and extensive encryptions. The brightest minds and/or smart software tools should be used. It should be on top of the agenda for every company. For many organisations, it will be an expensive investment to make, but not doing it could turn out to be a lot more expensive.

3.7 Conclusion

Big data has often been coined the next "management revolution", the Fourth Industrial Revolution, or "the next frontier for innovation, competition, and productivity".[34, 170, 238] While only a few years ago, organisations were still struggling to understand the impact of these trends on their business, big data has now emerged as the corporate standard.[167] Big data analytics affects all organisations, big or small, has an impact on every industry around the globe, and is a key characteristic of the organisation of tomorrow.[164] Especially in these ambiguous and uncertain times, analytics enables organisations to sense opportunities. Using large amounts of structured and unstructured data and applying it to advanced analytics enables organisations to understand their environment and seize opportunities, which enables them to remain competitive. Data analytics, when conceptualised as dynamic capabilities, can help to interpret the business environment, enable managers to act, and result in sustained superior performance and competitive advantage. Therefore, the introduction of descriptive, predictive, and prescriptive analytics means that the traditional way of decision-making, based on experience and expertise, is exchanged for data-driven decision-making. When organisations provide more people with access to knowledge, power is distributed more equally, enabling employee empowerment within an organisation. This power shift is necessary to fully benefit from big data analytics.

A great example of a company that became a data organisation is the company Kaeser Compressors. The company used to be a very traditional company that sold air compressors. A lot of them, in an industrial context. As David Judge, Vice President SAP Leonardo, explained to me, Kaiser Compressors managed to transform from a traditional product company, which has been around since 1919, to a service company providing Air-as-a-Service to its customers. In 2015, using sensors and smart IoT technology, it was able to change its product into a service, which ultimately became a platform. After all, when you can sell a product as a service, it means you can create data with it. When you have datafied a product, new possibilities arise such as selling a subscription to fresh air and offering a predictive maintenance programme and other analytics. In addition, you can then start to apply machine learning and AI to offer additional intelligence to your customers.

In the past, Kaeser sold the air compressors to companies and servicing them was a revenue producer. Now, Kaeser sells air by the cubic meter. It remains the owner of the air compressors and maintenance is included in the price. It uses predictive analytics capabilities to reduce maintenance costs, while customers have a guaranteed supply of fresh air for their machines. Since then, Kaeser has extended its cloud-based solution with artificial intelligence and machine learning capabilities. This allows it to deal with real-time data and display the air compressors as a digital twin to ensure it is online and operational. The digital twin, including documentation and all historically important events, are visible to Kaeser, the customer, and relevant industry partners. A great example of how a traditional product company transformed into a data company that takes care of its customers.

The development and application of big data analytics as a dynamic capability within your organisation takes time to mature. Especially, because a change in culture takes time. Organisations that want to achieve that, should first develop a shared *understanding* of what analytics means for their organisation to make initial *investments* in isolated environments, a.k.a. Proof of

Concepts. Once the business recognises the importance of developing analytics capabilities, the organisation can *adopt* these capabilities, including data governance practices and security analytics, more broadly across geographies and business unites. The next step of analytics maturity is to monitor and *control* multiple types of analytics across the business and implement the right data governance until descriptive, diagnostic, predictive, and prescriptive analytics are completely *integrated* across the organisation and used in parallel to make decisions, develop strategy, and create sustained competitive advantage. It is likely that organisations will go through each of these five analytics maturity phases (understand, invest, adopt, control, and integrate) before moving on to the next level of analytics. The more mature an organisation becomes, the more it will employ employees in various roles such as the Data Scientist, Data Engineer, Chief Data Officer, and Chief Information Security Officer that deal with data-driven, real-time decision-making. As a result, analytics can become a dynamic capability, leading to a competitive advantage for the organisation of tomorrow.

Chapter 4

Blockchain to distribute the organisation

When the web was developed over 25 years ago, the technologies in place significantly lowered the cost of building a global company. Thanks to the internet, it has become possible to reach a large part of the global population simply from behind your computer. Those companies who first understood the power of the web, and managed to execute their vision correctly, are now the leading global monopolies we are so familiar with: we use Google or Baidu for finding information, Facebook or WeChat for social activities, Amazon or Alibaba to shop, and Apple or Huawei for our hardware, etc. For years, these companies have understood that data is a goldmine. Since their beginning, these companies have rigorously been collecting and storing data. This has resulted not only in them becoming powerful monopolies but it also contributed to a centralisation of the world wide web. This centralisation is in stark contrast to Sir Tim Berners-Lee's vision of a decentralised web in which everybody participates and has full control over their data and the content that he or she creates. For the past years, it seemed that centralisation of the web was a new reality and that there was not much we could do about it. But then things changed when in 2008 a paper was distributed among a small group of cryptography enthusiasts.[239] The author, Satoshi Nakamoto – a pseudonym for an unknown person or group of persons – described the concept of a cryptocurrency called bitcoin that solved the long-standing problem of double spending of digital funds.[240, 241] At first, the impact of the paper did not become immediately clear, although those involved in the early years of bitcoin immediately saw the potential it could have. While the world was in the midst of the biggest financial crisis in decades, created by centralised organisations and a lack of regulation, the first truly decentralised cryptocurrency was born. The story of bitcoin, its underlying technology blockchain, and how it has progressed in the past decade reads like a thriller. Where centralised organisations such as banks and governments are opposed to libertarians who see in bitcoin the resolution to many, if not all, their problems. However, bitcoin is only one application of blockchain, and as we will see later on, I do not believe that bitcoin has a bright future.

Blockchain, however, does have a bright future and some say that it is a bigger invention than the internet or the steam machine, with which I concur.

A blockchain is a shared and decentralised public or private ledger that describes a single version of the truth of ownership. It is a distributed ledger that uses database technology to record and indefinitely maintain an ever-growing list of data records, which are immutable, verifiable, and traceable. At first, these data records were bitcoin transactions. Today, applications have moved to any type of online transaction across any industry. Blockchain not only offers us a chance to fix many of the problems that exist due to the centralisation of the web but also enables us to take over where the internet has fallen short. But first, to understand the impact of blockchain on your organisation, let's first discuss how organisations have changed so you will appreciate the impact blockchain can have. Then, I will discuss what blockchain actually is, because an understanding is important to see the enormous potential of it. For that, I will paraphrase parts of chapter 2 of my latest book, co-authored with Dr Philippa Ryan, *Blockchain: Transforming Your Business and Our World*.[242] If you have read that book, you can skip sections 4.2.1–4.2.6. If you believe you want to learn more about blockchain after finishing this chapter, I would highly recommend reading that book as it will inform you how blockchain can be used for social good. How blockchain can contribute to solving some of the United Nations Sustainable Development Goals and solve wicked problems such as identity theft, poverty, climate change, fraud, censorship, democracy, and fair trade. After discussing what blockchain is, I will discuss the intricacies of crypto-currencies and tokenomics, the impact of blockchain on privacy and reputation. I will conclude with discussing how blockchain will affect several industries.

4.1 Introduction

The earliest organisations of the twentieth century where seen as rational entities. They were evaluated based on their economic output and they had a strict hierarchy of authority. Power was distributed unevenly. Only a few people at the top of the organisation made all the decisions. These were so-called bureaucratic systems, where bureaucracy was deemed the most efficient way to create an organisation.[243] Closed bureaucratic systems result in authoritative organisations, where authority and responsibility are owned by management.[244] In the 1930s, this evolved to organisations that were seen as natural systems. Bureaucracy was no longer the leading paradigm, but humans were seen as the core of the organisation and deemed the most important resource. Within such organisations, the focus was on teamwork, cooperation, and motivation, and employees of such an organisation are pursuing multiple interests. The informal structure that develops among employees is more important than the official structure of the organisation.[245]

In the 1960s, organisations as open systems emerged where the focus is on the interaction of an organisation with its environment.[245, 246] Open system organisations have to be flexible and adaptive to changes in the environment. Management facilitates interactions among stakeholders rather than imposing rules on how to behave.[245, 246] Within such organisations, employees are empowered to adapt their behaviour in real time, depending on the needs of the environment. For example, a salesperson can adjust his/her presentation style and duration depending on the client, instead of having to stick to a format defined by management. In recent decades, this has again evolved into open network organisations. These organisations focus on collaboration with industry partners and customers. They use technology to innovate, connect with, and adapt to internal and external stakeholders.[41, 247] Especially the network organisation, the Multinational Enterprise (MNE), has become vital in today's data-driven world that requires organisations to be flexible and adaptable and technology allows the organisation to do so. The most common administrative structure for MNEs is a decentralised network organisation.[248] They operate through a network of market-sensitive, self-organising business units which are vertically or horizontally integrated.[249–251] Especially within today's fast-moving business environments, involving global markets and competition, network organisations are more receptive for market and technological developments and as a result can better anticipate and respond to disruption.[129] Open system organisations are often built around democratic designs, where employees at all levels participate in accomplishing the organisation's strategy. Network system organisations result in delegative organisations, as self-governed teams that do not report to leadership to accomplish a company's strategy.[247, 252] Recently, we have seen organisations built around collaborative communities where organisations that want to succeed share their knowledge and engage in collaborative relationships with industry partners to drive innovation.[41] A great example of such an organisation is Nike. In the past, Nike sourced its materials from vendors that were often 2–3 steps removed from Nike. As a consequence, Nike did not have an overview of who was involved in which materials and its supply chain was not optimised. Therefore, it started to collect data on all the materials it sourced, perform a lifecycle analysis on the materials and brought it all together into a central database. But then, Nike decided to share that data with the rest of the industry and the supply chain. This enabled the entire supply chain to populate the materials database, which enabled everyone in the supply chain to make better decisions.[253] Lately, the holacracy has also been added to the domain of possible organisation designs, which is especially relevant for organisations facing rapid changes and using technology to enable dispersed actors to collaborate.[254] A holacracy is an organisation where power is distributed across the organisation, enabling self-management and empowerment. It applies decentralised management and organisational governance, whereby authority and decision-making are distributed and delegated using self-organising teams.

Within each of these organisational designs, technology is playing an increasingly important role. Thanks to emerging information technologies, future forms of organisation design will increasingly move to a delegative style of organisational design and decision-making. The availability of distributed ledger technology within the organisation enables self-governed actors to create value. As we will see in this chapter, blockchain technology (which is one type of distributed ledger technology) can create value by enabling a network of peer-to-peer actors distributed across the globe, collaborating effortlessly and in real time, to create value for all actors in the network.[56, 57] Within this 'Internet of Value', miners create value by validating transactions, smart contracts create value by executing certain tasks automatically, and organisations create value through increased efficiencies within supply chains resulting in increased value creation for society as a whole.[132] When implemented to the extreme, the technological features of distributed ledger technology can result in completely new forms of organisation design, unlike any seen before, thereby affecting organisations and inter-organisational relations.[42, 130–132] Such organisations use distributed ledger technologies and cryptography to remove the need for intermediaries and enable peer-to-peer transactions. Blockchain and smart contracts enable an organisation to control and reduce opportunism while automating decision-making. To understand the impact blockchain will have on organisations, let's first explain what it is.

4.2 What is blockchain?

Since Nakamoto's paper, distributed ledger technology, also known as blockchain technology, has rapidly gained popularity. Although ledgers have been around for millennia, for the first time in history they can be updated across multiple organisations and computer networks simultaneously. This functionality significantly reduces the possibility of "gaming" the system. That is, the distributed and decentralised nature of distributed ledger technology prevents any single party from controlling and manipulating the ledgers. The underlying cryptography ensures a "trustless" system. This removes the need for intermediaries to manage risk. This is a true paradigm shift. It is why so many organisations are exploring blockchain's potential to improve their tracking and audit systems. Although blockchain technology has only been around for a decade, businesses, government organisations, and consortia alike have significantly invested in this modern phenomenon.[241]

Blockchains can serve as a record-keeper for societies, including registration of any type of document or property.[42] Data records are stored chronologically in *blocks* that are *chained* together cryptographically. Every node in the network has a copy of the block, and in order for a transaction to be added to a chain, there has to be a consensus among the nodes in the network. Already, there are a wide variety of distributed ledger technologies, ranging from the "traditional" bitcoin blockchain (often referred to as blockchain 1.0) to blockchains that focus on smart contracts (Ethereum, often described as blockchain 2.0), blockchains that are not a blockchain at all but instead use a Directed Acyclic Graph (IOTA, seen as blockchain 3.0), or blockchains that use a delegated consensus mechanism (EOS, also known as blockchain 4.0). For the sake of the argument, I include other variations of distributed ledger technologies under blockchain (although technically these variations, of course, differ, sometimes even significantly). Otherwise, you could be lost by the enormous possibilities at the end of the chapter. The result of this new technology is that peer-to-peer transactions become possible. No longer is a certifying authority required, such as a bank that usually takes a small commission to carry out the work. The removal of third parties and the ability of organisations and consumers to execute peer-to-peer transactions almost instantaneously is a true paradigm shift. This is what makes blockchain technology so important.

There are different types of blockchains. The type of blockchain selected determines how participants in the network interact with each other. There are public and private blockchains as well as permissioned and permissionless blockchains, each with different characteristics, rules, and actors. The most well-known public and permissionless blockchain is the bitcoin blockchain. Anyone can join a public permissionless blockchain by connecting a computer to the network, downloading the blockchain, and starting to process transactions. Anyone who wants to join the network can do so. There is no approval required nor a previous relationship with the ledger. No one controls or owns the blockchain and anyone can contribute at any time. Trust within the system is created through game-theoretical incentives and cryptography. On the other hand, private blockchains do not require these artificial incentives since all participants in the network are known to each other. A private blockchain is by definition a permissioned blockchain. If you want to join, you have to be approved by the existing participants in the network. This enables more flexibility and efficiency in validating transactions.[58] Private blockchains are generally used by organisations that like to keep a shared ledger for settlement of transactions, such as, for example, within the financial services industry or as part of a supply chain. They are owned and operated by a group of organisations and transactions are visible only to members of the network. An example of a private blockchain is the Utility Settlement Coin (USC) developed by 11 of the biggest global banks, led by Swiss bank UBS.[255] The USC is the digital counterpart of each of the major currencies backed by central banks. The objective is to develop a settlement system that processes transactions in (near) real time, rather than days. The aim of the project is to enable global banks to conduct various transactions with each other using collateralised assets on a custom-built blockchain and to make financial markets more efficient.[256] In May 2019, it became known that the companies involved with the USC invested another US$50 million in the project. With the technology advancing and more organisations seeing the benefits of a shared ledger among industry partners, more enterprise block-chain solutions are being developed, including Maersk, British Airways, and UPS.

Maersk: streamlining and securing international shipments

Already in March 2017, the world's largest shipping company developed its first blockchain Proof of Concept. Together with the Dutch Customs and the US Homeland Security, it explored how blockchain can be used to access cargo data remotely to speed up customs processes. The first test was built using IBM's Hyperledger Fabric framework. The objective was to streamline the settlement of global trade transactions. On average, 30 people and organisa-tions are involved in a shipment using a shipping container, resulting in over 200 interactions, each requiring separate documents.[257] There is plenty of room for improvement. In 2018, Maersk launched an IBM-Maersk blockchain plat-form for the global supply chain. The initiative, called TradeLens, quickly grew to 92 participants, including 20 ports and various customs authorities.[258] In 2018, the platform streamlined over 154 million shipping events and continues to grow at one million shipping events per day.[259] Each participant within TradeLens has its own node that participates in the blockchain, enabling participants to cut out as many as five middlemen per transaction.

British Airways: solving the flight information problem

In 2017, British Airways, together with three airports (London, Geneva, and Miami) and SITA (an IT company focused on the airline industry), created a small Proof of Concept to test synchronising operational flight data across multiple stakeholders.[260] The FlightChain project ensured that all stake-holders involved in the operation of a flight could use a single version of the truth of important flight data. Within the test, each stakeholder in the net-work published its own data to the blockchain. For example, the departure airport published the departure gate, while the arriving airport published the arrival gate. In total, more than two million flight changes were processed and stored on a permissioned blockchain.[261] Since everyone in the network has access to the same data, it allows for more streamlined processes. Smart contracts will play an important role within a decentralised flight information ecosystem, and the performance, resilience, and scalability of a private blockchain can be a useful tool to improve the air transport industry.

UPS: tracking global shipping data

Maersk is not the only logistics company that is looking at blockchain tech-nology to improve its business processes. Another company is UPS, which has been streamlining its business processes with data and analytics for years. Already in 2017, UPS joined a transportation-focused blockchain consortium to develop blockchain standards for the freight industry. In 2018, it filed a patent for the use of blockchain to track and trace sending packages across the globe.[262, 263] It is clear that UPS wants to play a key role in developing the global smart logistics network. As with Maersk, UPS also understands that shipping logistics involve dozens of different stakeholders and numerous transactions. Making the data of these interactions immutable, verifiable, and traceable will significantly increase efficiency in the global logistics industry. UPS aims to contribute by developing a system that routes packages autonomously through different logistic service providers and settles transactions among those stakeholders (nearly) instantly.[264] Although it is still early days, such a decentralised system would contribute significantly to improving the global logistics industry.

Kellogg's: food quality and safety first

Food supply chains are complex, which makes it difficult to quickly respond to product recalls. However, one in ten people fall sick every year as a result of poor food quality, and 420,000 people die each year from a foodborne disease, according to Paige Cox. In addition, 30 per cent of the food produced is lost or wasted, while a lot of people are still malnourished. The food industry needs to be improved, which is why SAP launched a Farm-to-Consumer blockchain initiative together with ten customers to improve material provenance and traceability. Kellogg's, the American multinational food-manufacturing company, is one of those companies. It aims to achieve full transparency within the food industry. By creating an undeniable and immutable history of food (and the individual ingredients), Kellogg's wants to improve food safety and security. According to Ramesh Kollepara, Senior IT Director at Kellogg's, blockchain has the potential to improve how products move from farm to plate, offering upstream and downstream provenance and genealogy. This provenance will enable peer-to-peer collaboration without intermediaries among industry partners and improve food safety thanks to automated supply chain traceability. By integrating blockchain in the food supply chain, Kellogg's shows it can solve real-world problems related to food.

As these examples show, blockchain has a lot of potential to optimise supply chains. Especially, because global supply chains are complex processes. Different companies, with distinctive objectives, are working together to achieve a common goal; to bring something from A to B. For a supply chain to work, partners have to trust each other. To do so, there are multiple checks-and-balances, extensive documents and different checkpoints all interacting in a web of bureaucratic processes. The processes in place are time-consuming, expensive, and they don't always prevent growing problems such as counterfeit products, fragmentation and falsification of data, lack of transparency, extensive settlement times, and incorrect storage conditions. Knowing the amount of paperwork and the number of processes and stakeholders required to send a product from farm to plate, it is remarkable that we have managed to develop global supply chains.

Thanks to the availability of new technologies, however, supply chains are already transforming. Wholesale companies are more and more selling directly to consumers. e-Commerce companies are moving from same-day delivery to same-hour delivery (Amazon), physical inventory is increasingly being replaced by digital inventory (thanks to 3D printing). And, organisations are moving from products to solutions (the example of Kaeser Compressors, who moved from selling air compressors to now selling Air-as-a-Service). As it seems, the balances and roles are shifting in global supply chains, making them more complex than ever before. This requires new technologies to ensure the provenance of data and products across different geographies. Fortunately, blockchain technology enables organisations to develop new applications that can significantly improve the supply chain. All of a sudden, transparency, the provenance of data and products, and seamless trust are achievable, resulting in reduced costs, more effective supply chains, and happier customers. Sharing data in a more trusted way leads to improved collaboration. This will enable organisations to develop efficient, network-based business models. Blockchain has been touted as the next big thing, but for the supply chain industry, it will be truly transformative. After all, decentralisation is about a resilient architecture so that a network cannot be taken down and problems can be easily traced, whether this is a computer network or a global supply chain. Once there is product and data provenance, using immutable data records, it becomes possible to create effective and efficient trustless transactions among industry partners. Therefore, one of the main applications of enterprise blockchain solutions is located in global supply chains. Blockchain can help reduce paper handling during shipments, increase food safety, security, and traceability while reducing food waste from farm to plate and enable quick and efficient recalls if something goes wrong. With more enterprises experimenting with blockchain solutions, blockchain is quickly becoming the gold standard for any supply chain.

The type of blockchain that an organisation could opt for depends on the objective of the organisation and on the type of transactions that need to be stored on a blockchain. Some transactions, such as financial transactions, should not be visible for the general public, while other transactions, such as ownership of (digital) goods and land titles, benefit more from a public blockchain.[265] Regardless of the type of blockchain, the data stored becomes immutable, verifiable, and traceable, due to four key components of a blockchain. Every distributed ledger technology makes use of cryptographic primitives, such as public key infrastructure (PKI) and hash algorithms, time stamps, and consensus mechanisms. These characteristics have the potential to significantly change decision-making within and across organisations.

4.2.1 Cryptographic primitives

Cryptography is a key component of any blockchain system. Among other things, it consists of two important features: the digital signature and the hash algorithm.

Digital signatures

Digital signatures are based on public key cryptography, also known as asymmetric cryptography. Asymmetric cryptography means that two keys, a public and a private key, are mathematically related to each other. This relationship means that any data encrypted by one key (public key), can only be decrypted by the other (private key), and vice versa. It is impossible to encrypt data with a public key and use another public key to decrypt that data.[266] As a result, you can use a key pair to identify the owner of a certain digital asset. Since the public key is publicly available, any data encrypted with a related private key can only be decrypted by the corresponding public key. It works like a mailbox, where everyone has a key to deposit a letter to that mailbox, but only one person has the right key to open the mailbox and take the mail out of the mailbox. Public key infrastructure has since been widely deployed. Almost anything online uses the PKI, from sending emails to visiting websites (a website is encrypted using PKI if it has an SSL certificate and the website shows https). It means that we can be certain that the data that is sent between you and the server is not interrupted. PKI is also used to ensure the authenticity of a certain document, which is done using the hash algorithm.

Hash algorithms

Each block of data on a blockchain receives a *hash id, as a database key*, calculated by a Secure Hash Algorithm. The block hash is fixed. In other words, the hash id allocated to the block never changes. Hash algorithms are used in a variety of components of blockchain technology. One of them being the hash id, which is a unique string of 64 numbers and letters that is linked to data in each block. The United States' National Security Agency (NSA) has designed a second generation of cryptographic hash functions called Secure Hash Algorithms 2. It includes SHA-256, a highly efficient secure hash algorithm that creates a unique hash id for every piece of data. Hash algorithms create the same hash if the data is the same.[267] Altering only one bit in the data will result in a completely new hash id. The hash id of a block that is added to a blockchain is the starting data for the next block and as such the blocks are chained together. This means that if data in a block is changed, it will change the hash of that block, which in turn will change the hash in the subsequent block, etc. To tamper with the data, the blocks would have to be revalidated by consensus. This will not happen because the other nodes in the network do not have an incentive to work on "old" blocks in the chain. Besides that, a blockchain keeps on growing, so it requires considerable computing power to revalidate old blocks, which simply makes it not worthwhile.[268]

A hash algorithm is also used to check whether or not a certain document has been altered. If the hash of a document detailing the ownership of, for example, a piece of art is on the blockchain, you can always check if that document has been altered by simply running the hash algorithm on the document. If the hash matched the one on the blockchain, the document has not been altered. The hash makes data on a blockchain immutable and verifiable that it has not been changed over time.

4.2.2 The consensus mechanism

Consensus decision-making has been used by humans for many years.[269] Although it began as a concept applied to politics and societies, it has become an important part of computer science.[270] Consensus algorithms ensure that connected machines can collaborate independently without the need to trust each other and can continue working even if some members of the network fail.[270, 271] There are many different consensus algorithms that take different approaches to authenticating and validating values and transactions on a blockchain. Consensus mechanisms are key to any blockchain. Thanks to the consensus algorithm, there is no longer the need to trust the other party. As a result, decisions can be created, implemented, and evaluated without the need for a central authority.[42, 134, 271] The result is intermediary-free transactions, whether it is human-to-human, human-to-machine, or machine-to-machine.[42]

With the lack of a trusted intermediary, participants in the network have to agree upon the rules that govern the blockchain and how these rules must be applied, before a blockchain is deployed. The nodes in the network execute the agreed-upon algorithm, and a pre-defined majority must agree on the outcome. Consensus algorithms use cryptography to validate transactions (and thus decisions) and it solves the long-standing problem of double spending. Double spending refers to actors who want to cheat the system by spending the same digital token more than once. With fiat money, this problem is solved through the usage of a central authority (a bank). In a decentralised system, without a central authority, it can be solved by consensus. To understand the issue, a thought experiment was proposed: *The Byzantine Generals' Problem*.[272] This thought experiment is about a group of generals who are each commanding a different part of the Byzantine army and need to agree upon a plan to attack and conquer an enemy city. The generals can communicate only via messenger, but the problem is that at least one general is a traitor. The question is how many traitors can the army have and still function as one force? Every consensus algorithm is a Byzantine Generals' Problem solution. The first algorithm that solved the Byzantines Generals'

Problem was the PBFT algorithm.[273] Since then, many PBFT algorithms have been developed before bitcoin was introduced. PBFT algorithms can be applied in a decentralised, permissioned network. A central aspect to PBFT algorithms is that a membership is required, which has to be approved by a centralised authority. The Proof of Work (PoW) algorithm solved this problem.[241, 271] This consensus algorithm operates in a decentralised network, without a central authority. It assumes that a majority of the actors are "honest" actors and reduces the risk of dishonest actors.

Proof of Work

The PoW algorithm solved the requirement for a centralised authority. Normally, the centralised authority is the one that controls the state of a network. For example, a bank keeps track of who owns how much money. As a society, we have agreed to trust banks and usually this works fine. As a reward for this, banks receive a fee. The technical innovation of a PoW consensus algorithm is that a central authority is no longer required to control the state of a network. The PoW algorithm is used in public or permissionless blockchains, where actors do not have to know or trust each other. When there is no central authority, all the participants in the network have to come to a consensus about the state of the network. However, with millions of participants this is not viable. That is where consensus algorithms come into play. The PoW consensus algorithm requires participating actors to solve a difficult computational problem. The validation is done using cryptography, which means that the actor has to find the solution of an inequality, which requires considerable computing power (and energy). When a solution is presented, it is immediately clear that it is correct. This can be compared with a crossword puzzle, which can be difficult to solve, but once completed you immediately know that it is done correctly. The first node that solves the equation can determine the state of the network. The rest of the network agrees to the new state. The node who solved the equation first receives acknowledgement for the effort. In the case of the bitcoin blockchain for example, the actor receives a certain amount of bitcoin (which is also required to cover the costs for the energy required to run the computations).

Proof of Stake

Proof of Stake (PoS) is another common consensus algorithm that takes a different approach. Within PoS, as within PoW, validators are selected randomly. However, where validators within PoW have a larger chance of being selected if they have more computing power, within PoS the amount of money (that is, the number of tokens or the amount of cryptocurrency) that a member holds determines the likelihood of being selected.[274] Once a block is produced, a transaction fee is paid to that validator and signers commit the block to the blockchain (i.e. the state of the network). These signers can all be nodes in the network or a randomly selected group of nodes that do the signing for the complete network. To "incentivise" nodes to hold a larger stake, the more stake a node has in the network, the less complex the puzzles the node has to solve. As a result, nodes that already have a large stake can easily become larger. PoS still requires a consensus agreement on the current state of the network, but the more tokens an actor owns, the higher the stake in the success of a blockchain. As a result, PoS requires far fewer computer processing unit computations and therefore is more energy efficient.[275] The assumption underlying PoS is simple: if an actor has a higher stake in the system, they have a higher incentive to ensure that the network is secure and correct. After all, the pain felt when the price and reputation of the crypto-currency are damaged (due to attempts to game the system) increases with the number of tokens an actor has. It is expected that the Ethereum network will implement a PoS consensus mechanism in 2019.

Other consensus mechanisms

Proof of Work and Proof of Stake are not the only consensus mechanisms. In recent years, the number of available consensus algorithms has exploded. It seems that every blockchain is developing its own consensus mechanism. Here is an overview of what is out there:[276]

- *Delegated Proof-of-Stake*: same as Proof of Stake, but the number of tokens you own determines who gets to vote and elect witnesses.
- *Leased Proof-of-Stake*: users can develop their own tokens, which they can use to improve their security on their server farms.
- *Proof of Elapsed Time*: similar to a Proof of Work algorithm, but the difference is that this algorithm focuses more on the duration of the computation.
- *Simplified Byzantine Fault Tolerance*: there is one validator that can bundle multiple transactions to create a new block.
- *Delegated Byzantine Fault Tolerance*: this consensus mechanism uses game theory to verify blocks among professional miners.
- *Directed Acyclic Graphs*: they do not have a blockchain structure, but often require users to validate two transactions if they wish to add one transaction. This verification can use a simplified Proof of Work algorithm.
- *Proof-of-Activity*: a combination of Proof of Work and Proof of Stake to make sure that tokens offered as a reward are on time.
- *Proof-of-Importance*: the more you send and receive transactions on the blockchain, the more tokens you will receive.
- *Proof-of-Capacity*: used especially for decentralised storage as it utilises the availability and capacity of storage space on a user's drive.

- *Proof-of-Burn*: miners have to show proof that they burned tokens, which means sending them to verifiable unspendable addresses.
- *Proof-of-Weight*: similar to Proof of Stake, but it depends on various other variables, called "weights", which basically means combining various features of various consensus algorithms.

By the time you read this book, the above list might have been updated, simply because some algorithms are no longer used and new consensus mechanisms have been developed. Consensus mechanisms are constantly evolving and which consensus mechanism would work best for your application depends on many different variables.

Timestamp

A consensus mechanism implements a timestamp service, which ensures that every block that is added to a blockchain is timestamped to prove temporal relations between different events.[241, 277] The timestamp confirms that a certain transaction occurred on the blockchain at a certain time. If an actor tries to cheat the system and offer the same transaction again, nodes will check the transaction against the timestamp. If the transaction is found in a previous block, the nodes in the network will come to a consensus that the transaction is invalid. In addition, the timestamp feature, in combination with the hash, enables users to prove at any given moment that a certain document was owned by a particular user at a certain moment in time and that since then the document has not been altered. It makes data fully traceable.

4.2.3 Transactions

Blockchain enables intermediary-free transactions as it removes the need for trusted centralised third parties (who generally take a commission for verifying transactions). Taking out the middlemen completely changes how actors can interact with each other and how decisions are developed, implemented, and evaluated.[275] Bitcoin transactions may have been the first transactions recorded on a blockchain, but since then many other transactions have become possible. Any financial transactions related to any digital currency, financial contracts, or hard and soft assets can be recorded on a blockchain.[42] In fact, any type of transaction, whether related to digital or physical goods, can be recorded on a blockchain. This includes land registrations, tracking of goods throughout a supply chain, Internet of Things devices exchanging transactions, identity, reputation, natural resources, as well as peer-to-peer exchanges such as taxi rides or home sharing.[14, 132, 265, 278, 279] The list is endless, and a complete overview can be viewed at the website of Ledra Capital, which is collecting the wide range of potential uses of blockchain on an ongoing basis.[280]

In 2016, for the first time, a transaction took place between two organisations across the globe that was paid for using the blockchain and smart contracts.[281] The Commonwealth Bank of Australia and Wells Fargo from the United States used blockchain in, according to them, the world's first global trade transaction between independent banks for a shipment of cotton from Texas to Qingdao in China. Further, in December 2017, Dutch agriculture trading house Louis Dreyfus Co. collaborated with Dutch banks ING and ABN AMRO, and French bank Société Générale SA, to sell a cargo of US soybeans to China using a blockchain platform. The digitised documents were able to match data in real time. This prevented duplication and handled the entire transaction in half the time it normally took.[282] In 2018, the World Bank announced that it launched the bond-i: a blockchain operated new debt instrument. Together with the Commonwealth Bank of Australia, it developed the world's first bond to be created, allocated, transferred, and managed through its lifecycle using blockchain.[283] It used the Ethereum blockchain to sell a two-year bond worth $110 million Australian dollars to seven investors. In the coming years, we will likely see more of such financial products.

Ownership of physical products can also be transferred and stored on a blockchain when owners sell their assets (such as art) by transferring a private key attached to that asset.[42] When this is done automatically using smart contracts, it is called smart property. Smart contracts are a special branch of transactions that can be stored on a blockchain, using, for example, the Ethereum or NEO blockchain.[130] Smart contracts can have a major effect on organisational design and decision-making.[42, 130, 132]

4.2.4 Smart contracts and Ricardian contracts

The term smart contract was first coined as "a computerised protocol that executes the terms of a contract".[284] It can be seen as a traditional agreement which is automatically defined and executed by code, leaving no room for discretion.[42] Smart contracts are analogous to scripts for processing transactions and/or decisions. They run on a blockchain and are considered "the killer application for the cryptocurrency world".[285] With the arrival of smart contracts deployed on a blockchain, the concept of what defines an organisation and how organisations can achieve competitive advantage changed drastically.

Smart contracts can be seen as *If This Then That* statements, compiled into code (although a lot more complicated). They are software programs that will execute certain transactions or decisions, which were agreed upon by two or more actors.[133] They are created by choosing events or preconditions and providing what needs to happen when those preconditions are met. The protocol is then recorded on a blockchain. Once deployed on the blockchain, these scripts can no longer be altered and will always execute once the preconditions are met.[286]

Smart contracts have three distinctive characteristics: they are *autonomous* (after deployment on a blockchain they can no longer be altered), they are *self-sufficient* (they can accumulate and spend value over time), and they are *decentralised* (they are distributed across multiple nodes within a network).[42, 131] Once a smart contract is on a blockchain, it is final and cannot be changed (technically this is not true; smart contracts can be altered if the majority of the network agrees to do so. Within public permissionless blockchains this is very difficult to achieve, within private blockchains this is easier since there are fewer participants). However, certain parameters can be altered only if the original code allows for this. Therefore, it is vital for organisations to ensure that the code is 100 per cent correct and that no bugs or errors remain in the smart contract when it is recorded on the blockchain. Mistakes can be extremely costly, as we have seen with *The DAO Hack* which lost US$50 million due to a mistake in the smart contract.[287] The only way to fix a bug in a deployed smart contract is through a *hard fork* on the blockchain. A *hard fork* is a radical change to the protocol and makes any previous transaction invalid. It basically creates a fork in the chain and it requires all nodes to start working on the new path. It is exactly what happened with *The DAO*. Nevertheless, do not expect blockchains to create a hard fork every time an organisation deploys a faulty smart contract.

Smart contracts not only have an impact on contract law but, more broadly, also on social contracts within societies and organisations. This is because smart contracts are automatically and autonomously executed, thereby taking out the need for human judgement and minimising the need for trust.[42] In addition, smart contracts remove the need for developing, implementing or evaluating decisions by management or employees. When multiple smart contracts are combined, together with artificial intelligence and analytics, it becomes possible to automate decision-making capabilities.[42, 130] This will result in a completely new paradigm of organising activity, which can result in new organisational designs that are completely run by computer code, so-called Decentralised Autonomous Organisations (DAOs).[42, 58, 130] However, there is one problem with existing smart contracts, which is that they are not legally binding. As a result, in 2018, there has been a renewed interest in Ricardian Contracts. These types of contracts differ from smart contracts that they are legally binding, and it records the agreement between multiple parties in human-readable and machine-readable text (contrary to smart contracts, which only executes what is defined in an agreement).[288] This means that it is a legal contract that is easy to read and understand by everyone, so not only your lawyer or developer.

Ricardian contracts were first introduced by Ian Grigg, one of the earliest pioneers in financial cryptography, in 1995. Ricardian contracts use cryptographic signatures to bind different parties into a legal agreement. They will automatically execute when certain pre-conditions have been met. Ricardian contracts not only define intentions but also execute instructions automatically.

The main advantage of a Ricardian contract is that if there is a dispute among parties involved, the case can be decided in court. This is not possible with smart contracts, which are only the instructions based on what is defined in an agreement. If something goes wrong, proving a scam or fraud in court is difficult since a smart contract is not a legally binding agreement. Another benefit of a Ricardian contract is that once a human-readable agreement is turned into a machine-readable agreement, it can be hashed. The hash can then be stored on a blockchain. This would ensure that each part of the document can be uniquely identified by its hash and it becomes impossible to change the original agreement without the other parties knowing. As a result, Ricardian contracts are extremely secure.

It is important to note that there is no legal framework with smart contracts. As a result, if an unexpected event occurs, smart contracts lack the ability to evolve as there are no guidelines on how to proceed. Ricardian contracts, on the other hand, do come with a legal framework and this adds clarity for all stakeholders. This means that, contrary to smart contracts, you require lawyers to create and deploy a Ricardian contract.

Smart contracts may seem revolutionary, but they are nothing new and have been around for a long time. Smart contracts are already in place in most modern office buildings. For example, access cards that determine whether you are allowed entry to a certain area are pre-defined by a piece of code and linked to a database.[289] As such, smart contracts have been around for a long time already. The only difference now is that when they are deployed on a blockchain, they remain accessible indefinitely and will carry out their pre-defined tasks whenever certain conditions are met. Smart contracts offer tremendous opportunities for organisations. Organisations that deploy smart contracts to facilitate inter-organisational transactions become more intensely connected with each other, since they share the same database across time and space. In the coming years, we will likely see a wide variety of applications using smart contracts that will change how we work, how we do business, and how we run our daily lives. This will increasingly take away the middleman, managers, and employees.

Organisations adopting blockchain technologies can be viewed as Human-Machine Networks (HMNs), where combinations of humans and machines interact with each other. Here the *social* and the *material* work together to produce synergistic effects.[43] The more an organisation moves towards a DAO design, the more efficient and autonomous it will become. Ultimately, organisations can operate completely independently using a blockchain, a combination of smart contracts, connected devices, and analytics.[130] The interactions between actors will be guided purely by autonomous software algorithms increasing the need for careful deployment of smart contracts on a blockchain by shareholders of a DAO.[14, 42, 131] A DAO is run by immutable code under the sole control of a set of irreversible business rules.[131] A DAO will have different actors from today's organisations. It requires extensive data governance processes that ensure data reliability and accuracy. It will result in a fundamentally new organisational structure.[42, 290–292] A DAO is a self-organising framework that uses automated decision-making based on consensus in which actors interact with each other without the need to trust each other. Within a DAO there is no traditional organisational hierarchy since hierarchy is determined by ownership (i.e. how trusted an actor is as well as the merits earned by that actor as a result of behaviour). This change in organisational structure affects the balance of power. In traditional organisations, power is distributed either by hierarchy or by knowledge. Often these are related; the higher up the hierarchy, the more information you have and the more power you have within the organisation.[51] Within a DAO, this works differently. Power is determined by the number of tokens an actor owns, an actor's trust level, and their achieved merits. This will shift the power balance within an organisation from a hierarchical structure to a distributed structure, thereby affecting the governance structure.[293]

The process of completely automating a company using smart contracts, big data analytics, artificial intelligence, machine learning, and the Internet of Things can be achieved in any sector.[294] Within a DAO, multiple actors, human and non-human, have to cooperate independently. Within such systems, mathematical models of conflict and collaboration can incentivise actors to act in the best interest of the system as a whole. DAOs are an exciting opportunity to redesign our society and how we do business, and to create more efficient organisations that offer better products and services for lower pricing.

4.2.5 The decentralised ecosystem

Although we have seen many variations of distributed ledger technology, there is still a lot of work to be done. Blockchain is still a nascent technology, and for blockchains to achieve wide-scale adoption, a decentralised ecosystem has to be developed. To achieve a decentralised society, many more components need to be built, requiring global standards and large investments. My estimate is that it will take another 3–5 years before the ecosystem is ready for full-scale, enterprise adoption. Apart from the different industry layers that need to be developed, we will also continue to see new blockchains being created. For a blockchain to be useful for the organisation of tomorrow, several criteria are required. Therefore, if you aim to develop your own blockchain technology or if you plan to implement an existing blockchain technology, look for the following four criteria.

Zero or very low transaction fees

It may be obvious that for a blockchain to become a success it should enable fee-free transactions or at least very low transaction costs. The beauty of tokens is that you can divide it into extremely small portions, such as the

Satoshi, or a hundredth of a millionth of a bitcoin. However, if transferring such a small amount comes with any transaction fee, no matter how small, it becomes unfeasible. Especially with a future where connected devices will be able to trade bits of data, transaction fees are impractical. Although for larger transactions, minor fees are less of a problem.

Infinite scalability

Visa is capable of handling 2,000 transactions per second, with a peak of 56,000 transactions. Any blockchain that can handle fewer transactions than this is not suitable to replace traditional payment methods. In a future where everything is connected and makes transactions with everything, infinite scalability is a requirement because in the future we can expect millions of transactions per second.

Complete decentralisation

The main advantage of distributed ledger technology is that it is decentralised, meaning no government or central bank controls the product, service, or token. It is governed completely by market economics of supply and demand. Obviously, governments do not like this, which is why we will see governments developing their own cryptocurrency, such as the crypto euro or dollar, which will compete with other cryptocurrencies. In 2018, Sweden announced the introduction of the e-krona, a crypto version of the krona to enable a cashless society. However, for a blockchain to function without the government being able to interrupt or block it, it should be completely decentralised. This means that bitcoin is not a suitable solution as bitcoin is not truly decentralised. When bitcoin was started, the power of it was the fact that it was decentralised. Not one centralised stakeholder could control the network. Unfortunately, that is no longer the case. Today, 70 per cent of the bitcoin's collective hash rate, i.e. the mining power, is controlled by Mining Pools (which are groups of cooperating miners who agree to share block rewards in proportion to their contributed mining hash power). The four biggest mining pools control over 50 per cent of the network's collective hash rate. This centralisation of mining is a logical consequence of how the protocol was developed. It rewards economies of scale. As a result, bitcoin is no longer the decentralised network that it was supposed to be when it was developed. This does not have to be a problem, as long as the mining pools can be trusted and have an incentive to do the right thing. However, if things change, such centralisation can pose a real threat to the future of a blockchain.

No or very low ecological footprint

Bitcoin's ecological footprint is completely unsustainable, even if it will use only renewable energy sources. The Proof of Work consensus mechanism requires tremendous amounts of computing power. A single bitcoin transaction uses roughly enough electricity to power 1.57 American households for a day, which is approximately 2.55 gigawatts of energy required to run Bitcoin's software.[295, 296] This results in an estimated annual energy consumption of approximately 22 terawatt hours. In comparison, Google's annual energy consumption was approximately 5.7 terawatt-hours in 2015, and CERN uses approximately 1.3 terawatt-hours per year to power the Large Hadron Collider.[297, 298] It is almost 30,000 times the energy consumption of Visa (which happened to process 82.3 billion transactions in 2016, compared to the approximately 100 million Bitcoin transactions in 2016[299, 300]). Any cryptocurrency or blockchain that will be used by millions if not billions of people and things should have a minimal ecological footprint. As such, any blockchain using the Proof of Work consensus mechanism, which requires substantial computing power, will not work. Fortunately, there are plenty of new consensus mechanisms, many of which that do not require extensive computing power.

Developing a blockchain that is infinitely scalable, has very low or zero transaction fees, can handle millions of transactions per second and is environmentally friendly is difficult to develop. However, if we want to make blockchain mainstream, there is no other option. That is why, I do not believe bitcoin has a future in the long run. Unless the above challenges are resolved and the Bitcoin community is able to completely change the existing protocols, Bitcoin does not have a future and will ultimately fail. It will become the Myspace of cryptocurrencies; paving the way for a new future, but eventually not being the solution we are looking for.

4.2.6 Changing organisation design

Blockchain-enabled products and services are commonly referred to as Decentralised Applications, or DApps. A DApp has at least two distinctive features: (1) any changes to the protocol of the DApp have to be approved by consensus; and (2) the application has to use a cryptographic token, or cryptocurrency, which is generated according to a set algorithm.[42] The development of decentralised products and services changes organisation design. Blockchain does not require a centralised authority for maintenance, as the database is stored on millions of decentralised computers. Its decentralised infrastructure ensures that a single case of mismanagement resulting in a point of failure, does not affect the entire network.[60] Blockchain removes the need for trust in the absence of a centralised governing body. It, therefore, follows that any organisation developing DApps should still have a strong focus on data governance. After all, only data authenticity can be ensured; reliability and accuracy cannot. With Blockchain, it becomes possible to embed data governance directly within the network, bringing the code to the data.[60] Laws and regulations can be programmed into a blockchain itself, so

Table 4.1 Traditional and new decentralised organisations

	Traditional decentralised organisations	*New decentralised autonomous organisations*
Trust	Experience and relationships	Cryptography
Decision-making	Expertise and seniority	Automatically using smart contracts
Governance	Established by board of directors	Embedded in the code

that they are enforced automatically, which makes governance easier.[301] Hence, the ledger can act as legal evidence for data and increase the importance of data ownership, data transparency, and auditability. Thanks to all these characteristics, we will see that blockchain technology and smart contracts will drastically affect organisation design, creating *decentralised* and/or *autonomous* organisations. These forms differ from past discussions on decentralised and autonomous organisations (see Table 4.1), in which decentralisation and autonomy were achieved by re-organising human interactions and decision-making.[302–304] Within traditional decentralised and autonomous organisations, trust is created by experience and forging relationships, decision-making is based on expertise and seniority, and governance is established by a board of directors.[302–306] Thanks to blockchain and smart contracts, a *decentralised organisation* can be defined as an organisation that uses consensus mechanisms and cryptographic primitives to ensure trust among actors, who are decentralised across time and space.[134] An *autonomous organisation* is an organisation that is run completely by immutable code, in which decision-making is automated using smart contracts and governance is embedded in the code.[42, 60, 134] A decentralised organisation does not have to be autonomous, but an autonomous organisation has to be decentralised.

Now that you have a better understanding of what blockchain is and how it works, let's discuss blockchain's most well-known application: cryptocurrencies.

4.3 Cryptocurrencies and tokenomics

When most people think of a cryptocurrency, the first thing to come to mind is probably bitcoin. However, bitcoin is just one of many. At the time of writing (June 2019), there are over 2200 cryptocurrencies, with a total market cap of over US$250 billion. Each of the available tokens offer different values and benefits. Traditional currencies like the dollar and the euro have a fixed value regardless of how and where you use them. Different types of cryptocurrencies and tokens, however, perform differently across platforms. Each is designed to solve different issues and problems in the digital world. The current cryptocurrency marketplace has been likened to a "Wild West", with massive daily and monthly fluctuations. In April 2017, the total market cap of the cryptocurrency market was US$25 billion. Nine months later, on January 8, 2018, the market cap reached its highest point of US$813 billion. A staggering increase of 3,252 per cent in just nine months. However, one month later, as of February 6, 2018, the market cap dropped to US$308 billion. A drop of 62 per cent in just one month. End of November 2018, the market dropped to US$122 billion, another drop of 60 per cent since February 2018. It is clear that the cryptocurrency market is, at the time of writing, still in its infancy. As such, unfortunately, there is a lot of market manipulation going on, which is, at least partially, responsible for the fluctuations. Of course, with any new technology there is a lot of opportunism. That also happened within the crypto market. This is nothing new. When gold was discovered at a new location in the mid-nineteenth century, there was also a rush and opportunism to make a quick buck. In the coming years, the market will stabilise due to regulations, a better understanding of the technology, and an appreciation of the actual value that some cryptocurrencies have. As such, in the coming years, flawed products and ICO-scams will become less frequent. Just as we saw happening with the internet bubble in the 1990s. Just like then, it will take some time before we get rid of the bad apples and we may never get rid of them completely. This is nothing new either. As long as the internet exists, we have hackers and criminals trying to steal money and data from innocent citizens and organisations.

Well-thought-through global regulation and education is what the market needs. Regulators should focus on the Initial Coin Offering (ICO), as a more streamlined process around ICOs could prevent scams and Ponzi schemes. Similar to the Initial Public Offering (IPO) regulations we have, ICOs should comply with certain regulations to protect investors and keep founders accountable. With nearly 50 per cent of the companies that did an ICO in 2017 having already failed within a few months, despite having raised over US $104 million, it is quite clear that this is necessary.[307] These regulations could include requirements such as to:

1   disclose financial, accounting, tax, and other business information before performing an ICO and making this information easily available and understandable;
2   implement escrow functionalities with smart contracts to ensure funds only get released upon reaching certain milestones. When those milestones are not met, funds will be returned automatically;
3   have a board of advisors that is actively involved with the company, understands the market, and can control founders who all of a sudden have access to millions of dollars;
4   require organisations that want to do an ICO to have a prospectus that informs potential investors of the risks involved with the ICO.

These regulations, of course, require additional work for organisations that want to do an ICO. In the end, it will protect not only the investors but also the founders and employees of the company. However, since we are dealing with a product that does not know traditional borders, such regulations can only be effective if they are adopted globally.

Whether the organisation of tomorrow will do a public ICO, a private ICO, or no ICO at all, it is very likely that cryptocurrencies, or tokens, will become commonplace in future for every type of organisation. The organisation of tomorrow, despite differences in industry, location, products and services on offer, will all have one thing in common: they use some sort of token as the key enabler to the platform. Organisations have multiple options when selecting the type of crypto token. The token economics they opt for influences the likelihood of success for the organisation. Tokens are the fuel of the decentralised economy and William Mougayar, author of *The Business Blockchain* and Managing Partner and Chief Investment Officer at JM3 Capital, describes a token as:[308]

> A unit of value that an organisation creates to self-govern its business model, and empower its users to interact with its products while facilitating the distribution and sharing of rewards and benefits to all of its stakeholders.

Although there are over 2,100 different tokens, there are three types of tokens: currency tokens, utility tokens, and security tokens. Especially security tokens offer a completely new approach to funding and investing.

4.3.1 Currency tokens

Currency tokens are the most well-known tokens, simply because the first crypto token ever, bitcoin, is a currency token. A currency token is a medium of value exchange. The value of the token is determined by supply and demand. Contrary to fiat money, which is backed by gold, currency tokens are only backed by the demand and trust in the market. Therefore, a new currency token faces the chicken and egg problem; for a currency token to be used by a lot of people, the currency token needs to have value and high liquidity. However, to have high liquidity and value, there needs to be a lot of users. Therefore, it took bitcoin and ether a lot of time to increase in value. The more currency tokens there will be, the more difficult it will be to overcome this problem. As a result, in the future, there will only be a few dominant currency tokens.

Perhaps one of those cryptocurrencies will be the Libra Coin. In June 2019, Facebook launched their Libra coin. They call it a "new global currency powered by blockchain technology." It will be mobile-first and accessible with an entry-level smartphone and data connectivity. Contrary to existing cryptocurrencies, the objective is to have minimal price volatility. To achieve that, the Libra is backed by a reserve of low-risk assets such as bank deposits and short-term government securities. Libra aims to become a global cryptocurrency, resulting in open ecosystem products and services made available to internet users. However, don't expect Libra to be a "pure cryptocurrency" that is available all over the world. Sanctions will probably prevent it from operating in Iran, and the Libra Association Council can, most likely, block transactions if necessary. Nevertheless, with founding members including companies such as Spotify, Booking.com, Vodafone, Uber, Lyft, Visa, Mastercard and eBay there will be instant demand. After all, it seems likely that upon launch, internet users can pay for services offered by these companies with Libra. It is an interesting initiative, backed by reputable companies although initially immediately opposed by European and US governments. Will Libra succeed in developing a truly permissionless, trustable blockchain and global cryptocurrency? A lot remains to be seen, but it is great to see that large multinationals are adopting blockchain and cryptocurrencies. One thing is for sure; Libra will receive close scrutiny by governments, organisations and internet users. Only by operating in full transparency they can gain the trust they so much need to make this a success.

The chicken and egg problem will not apply to government-backed currency tokens, such as a hypothetical crypto euro, crypto dollar, or the e-krona, since the government can simply enforce the usage of the currency token, thereby automatically creating demand.

4.3.2 Utility tokens

The second type of token is the utility token. This is a token that is backed by some sort of asset. It is a token that has a use case and has not been developed as an investment. Most of today's blockchain startups aim to develop their token as a utility token. Although these tokens are not designed as an investment, they can still increase in value if the demand for the linked platform or service increases. A utility token, therefore, offers future access to a product or service and can best be compared to a gift card or loyalty points.[313] An example of a utility token is ether (ETH), which is used on the Ethereum blockchain and allows you to run smart contracts and transactions. A utility token allows you *to do things.*[314]

4.3.3 Security tokens

A security token is a token that allows the owner of that token a (future) stake in a company or another asset such as a painting, a car or a building, whether it be in the form of dividends, revenue share, or a price appreciation.[309] It constitutes an investment contract and, hence, attracts the attention of the Security and Exchange Commission (SEC). In November 2018, the SEC sent shockwaves through the crypto community by announcing it had charged two blockchain startups with conducting illegal digital token sales. The two companies, Airfox and Paragon, did not commit fraud, they simply did not register their tokens with the SEC (as is the case for the vast majority of token sales in the years 2015–2018).[310] According to the SEC, most tokens can be considered securities and are, therefore, subject to regulation.[311] Security tokens offer the buyer certain rights and obligations. To determine whether a token is a security token, the SEC uses the Howey Test (developed in 1946).[312] The Howey Test boils down to four questions, which when all answered as "yes" means that the token is a security token:[313]

1 Is the token being sold as an investment with an expectation of profits? In other words, are tokens purchased because an increase in value is expected or because the purchaser receives some sort of product or service in return?
2 Is there a person upon whom investors rely? In other words, any profit comes from the efforts of a promoter or third party and is outside the investor's control.
3 Is it an investment of money or other assets?
4 Is it an investment in a common enterprise?

Most crypto startups aim to avoid being a security token as it means additional scrutiny by the SEC. However, most crypto startups sell their tokens before they have a product and, therefore, the value of the transaction depends on another's, future, work.[312] As such, these tokens can be considered an investment contract during the ICO, which further down the track can be changed to a utility token.

The security token offering

The ICO appeared in 2013 when the Mastercoin project raised US$5 million in the first ever ICO. One year later, Ethereum raised US$15 million for the further development of Ethereum. Unfortunately, with the rise in value of cryptocurrencies, we have also seen a significant increase in scammers who tried to get rich quickly. These scammers negatively affected many honest startups who saw the Initial Coin Offering as a relatively simple way to raise funds for their project. However, due to the nature of ICOs, investors have no protection, resulting in many governments creating ICO regulations to protect them better. Unfortunately, these regulations differ across the globe and with ICOs being a global product, startups have to comply with a wide variety of regulations. In addition, ICOs require roadshows to promote the ICO, which add up to the costs. As a result, doing an Initial Coin Offering is now very expensive, and it is better to use that money for the development of the actual product or platform. Therefore, I believe that the era of the ICO, or the Token Generation Event (TGE) as it is sometimes called now, is over. The idea of using a token to raise funds, however, offers a lot of benefits. With an ICO, these benefits are predominantly for the startup: large sums of money without losing any equity or voting rights. The investor, on the other hand, can only hope that the startup founders stick to their promises, as there is zero investor protection. This explains why investors have lost interest in this now, which is a sign of market maturity. It is, therefore, not a surprise that a new funding model appears. One that benefits not only companies but also investors. If executed correctly, the organisation of tomorrow can attract a lot of value when launching a security token.

Distributing security tokens is done during a Security Token Offering (STO). Depending on how the STO is structured, it can give the investors a lot of benefits, such as the ability to voice their opinions through voting, gain access to dividends and other rights based on the proportionate ownership in the underlying asset or company. However, an STO not only benefits the investors, but it also has significant benefits for the issuer as well as other stakeholders such as regulators.

There are multiple stakeholders involved with a security token, including the issuer, buyer, regulator and exchanges. Traditionally, accessing public markets as a funding source was only possible for the biggest companies, but with an STO also smaller companies can now target the public market for funding. It offers investors a tool beyond speculation, provides transparency to regulators and offers a new business model for (crypto) exchanges. In general, there are five major benefits of an STO compared to traditional securities:

1. *Security Tokens are Programmable:* the main benefit of security tokens over traditional financial securities is that they are programmable. This means you can incorporate certain rules within the security token that automatically apply. These rules could be related to dividend release (the longer you hold a token, the more dividend you will get), voting rights (the longer and the more tokens you have, the more voting rights you will get) or other privileges. These rules can then become an effective way to incentivise ownership and ensure price stability.

2. *247 Full Liquidity:* current securities can only be traded from 9am to 5pm on weekdays. In addition, often securities require a few days before they are settled. Using blockchain technology tokens can be settled instantly or within a few minutes. As such, a utility token can be settled a lot faster than traditional securities and this will change the concept of liquidity as we know it. Until today, real estate, collectables and art have been perceived as illiquid, but with the advent of security tokens, this might drastically change. When these assets are tokenised and sold across the globe, they have the potential to become highly liquid. That would result in an influx of liquid assets that could significantly change global markets. However, a security token by itself is not a liquid asset. First, we need the right infrastructure because even a token remains illiquid if you cannot sell it to someone else. Only when a security token can be easily exchanged on a secondary market, it becomes liquid. And only if there is sufficient demand for the security token. After all, a token that nobody wants to buy is still illiquid. In short, for security tokens to become liquid assets, there needs to be an infrastructure, and there needs to be demand.

The infrastructure goes beyond just having (de)centralised exchanges for security tokens such as tZero (which was launched end of January, 2019), OpenFinance or the upcoming Malta Security Token Exchange. It also requires clear disclosures about the projects at hand as well as approved liquidity protocols to enable the programmability of security tokens (arguably the biggest advantage of security tokens). According to Jesus Rodriguez, managing director at Invector Labs, the security ecosystem should also include P2P-Swap trading protocols, debt tokens, custody, future and other derivatives as building blocks to unlock the liquidity in security tokens. Once the security token ecosystem is in place, it becomes possible to make illiquid assets liquid. Thanks to distributed ledger technology and smart contracts, asset ownership transfer can be automated while adhering to global/local private security laws. If you are 25 per cent owner of a tokenised building, you could decide to sell in the morning and have your cash before you finish your cup of coffee. That would revolutionise financial markets and the world economy. All the administration generally involved in trading (il)liquid assets can be done using blockchain technology, thereby significantly reducing costs while improving efficiency. After all, required steps such as KYC/AML checks, investor accreditation checks as well as compliance checks in both the buyer and seller's jurisdictions can be done "on chain".

3. *Global Market Accessibility:* whenever an organisation decides to create an Initial Public Offering, it has to decide where they want to do their IPO. This can be in the country where the company's headquarter is, or in another country depending on regulations, market demand or other reasons. However, with an IPO, an organisation can never offer their shares across the globe. This is different for security tokens.

As we have seen with ICOs, blockchain technology does not care about borders and startups have raised funds from everywhere in the world. As an example, the company Origin Protocol raised US$6,6 million from 1800+ investors across 50 countries. The same applies to STOs. All of a sudden, an organisation can offer their security to the global market, giving it a much higher chance of success. In addition, launching an IPO in multiple markets would generally involve a lot of fees to banks and advisors in the different markets. This is not the case during an STO, thereby lowering the fees to raise funds.

4. *Fully Traceable and Embedded Compliance:* regulatory compliance is key for security tokens. However, regulations vary depending on investor type, asset type or jurisdictions. Incorporating them all would normally be a hassle. However, since security tokens are programmable, the regulations can be embedded in the code. It means that regulations become exponentially easier and automatic once the system is set up. In addition, security tokens are fully traceable, similar to utility tokens. With any cryptocurrency, it will always be possible to trace a coin throughout the years, to see who owned it and for how long. This will bring transparency to the markets and those stakeholders involved.

5. Fractional Ownership: last but not least is the possibility of fractional ownership. Investors like to divest to hedge their risks. However, in the current situation, fractional ownership is very complicated when dealing with high-priced assets such as real estate or art. With a security token, it becomes possible to own a small part of a building in one side of town and another part of a building in a different area. Instead of spending all funds on one building, thereby increasing your risk, you can now divest your money across multiple properties. This would greatly reduce your risk. Since these assets are now also highly liquid, it gives an investor a lot more options.

Security tokens promise to fundamentally change trading currently illiquid assets. That would require investors to completely rethink their portfolio as they obtain a lot more possibilities to reduce risks while benefiting from opportunities. If 'all of a sudden', trillions of dollars become liquid, it will have a major effect on the world economy.

4.3.4 Tokenomics

Despite there being three different types of tokens, they all adhere to token economics or tokenomics. Token economics is an emerging field that studies tokenised ecosystems. With the rapid adoption of tokens, it is a field that becomes increasingly important. In the years to come, it is likely that many universities will start to offer specialised degrees to help future leaders understand the economics of tokens. Tokenomics is all about how your token will work when the token has been launched. Every organisation that wants to launch a new token has to determine the economic models of their token. The economics of a new token should adhere to several laws. These laws were first written down by Fred Krueger, CEO of WorkCoin, and in summary, these laws consist of:[315]

1   Your token should have a high "Token Hold Time" to ensure long-term demand for the token. Having a token that is only briefly used, for example, to purchase a ticket, does not make sense; there is no need for that token.
2   Your Hold Time should be higher than the Transaction Time. The transaction time to purchase your token should be lower than the amount of time people hold on to your token. If it is the other way around, there is no incentive to purchase the token as it takes too long to join the game.
3   The rate of the transaction volume should be low; meaning that the Transaction Volume should be, significantly, lower than the Token Market Cap to ensure upward pressure on the token price.
4   People need to have a reason to purchase tokens and not only be given to them, although this is not always the case. The token should offer a certain value, and it should increase the network effect, i.e. it should provide a utility in the ecosystem it is part of. Token velocity is one of the key

characteristics that will impact long-term, non-speculative value. It relates to whether people will hold on to the cryptocurrency as it can increase in value or they will sell it immediately. Any cryptocurrency that offers no value has no future.[316]

5   The higher the percentage of tokens being held in the ecosystem the better as any new growth will translate into a surge in prices.

6   Growth matters. A lot. Ceteris paribus, growth in transactions result in growth in prices. The more tokens that are held inside transactions or by participants, prices will go up.

7   You need an ecosystem of sellers and buyers; all parties need to be buyers and sellers at the same time to ensure a long Hold Time and use for your tokens.

As Fred Krueger mentions, modelling your token and developing your token economics is hard. There are a lot of different stakes at play and many considerations to consider. William Mougayar goes as far as to offer 20 questions that any crypto startup should ask itself when developing their token.[308] Questions include:

1   Is the token tied to product usage, i.e. does it give the user exclusive access to it, or provide interaction rights to the product?

2   Does the token result in a monetizable reward based on an action by the user (active work)?

3   Is the token required to run a smart contract or to fund an oracle?

Tokens are the fuel for the decentralised economy. Without tokens, blockchain startups cannot run their platforms and offer their services and products. Tokens will become an important characteristic of the organisation of tomorrow. However, it is vital that the token has a *raison d'être* as otherwise it can be perceived as a scam or a fraud. Only when there is a real use case for the token, and it adheres to the existing regulation and the laws of token economics, will it have a viable chance to become a success.

By now, it should become clear that incorporating blockchain in your organisation is not as straightforward as building a website. There are a lot of different components to think of. One being especially important, particularly when data becomes immutable, verifiable, and traceable until eternity: GDPR.

4.4 Blockchain and privacy regulation

In an era where data privacy is an increasing concern, blockchain technology is moving towards a more transparent and more verifiable security model. Blockchain is a decentralised database where any data stored is read and write and not editable. That puts blockchain in direct opposition to the General Data Protection Regulation (GDPR) that went into effect on May 25, 2018. With regulations pushing for more consumer control of personal data, can block-chain technology work within this new framework? Absolutely, but not as it currently processes data. Of course, there are many different privacy regulations across the globe, but the next section is based on the, at the time of writing, globally thriving GDPR. The GDPR is designed to allow individuals greater control over their personally identifiable information. Specific to the EU, new rules require data storage to enforce consumer rights such as:

- Erasing personal data when the need for its storage expires, e.g. when you withdraw consent for the storage or when it is no longer legal to continue processing that data.
- Corrections for incorrect data.
- Restricted processing when data is under contention, awaiting an amendment, or you withdraw permission.

Erase is the word that goes directly up against the blockchain. Under these new rules, all companies storing personally identifiable data must offer the required levels of control. They must have an EU representative on staff to handle data deletion and control requests. Even if the company has no phy-sical location within the EU, a local representative is required. Failure to follow these rules can lead to stiff fines on data controllers and processors. These fines are administered by individual countries. The amount of the fine depends on ten criteria, including the nature of the infringement, actions taken to mitigate any damage, or history of previous infringements. Whenever a firm infringes on multiple criteria, the fine will be according to the gravest infringement. As such, the organisation of tomorrow has to think carefully how to deal with all its data.

While privacy protection is a laudable goal, regulatory changes continue to lag behind the realities of technology, the same applies to GDPR. The ability to trust blockchain systems comes from the knowledge that the information, once entered, is permanent. Deletion on demand is not compatible with the blockchain as it exists today. On a blockchain, all transactions are clearly visible and highly transparent for those with access to the blockchain. There-fore, following the GDPR rules becomes tricky when also using blockchain technology. While GDPR was designed to be platform agnostic, the require-ments for data deletion and data editing seem to be a direct contradiction of the way the technology functions. In addition, GDPR is simply not applicable to a decentralised system. The regulation assumes that a single controlling entity can delete the stored data. The whole idea of a decentralised ecosystem is that there is no central entity to take control. No company or single indi-vidual can affect the entire ledger, making it impossible to delete data on these types of networks. Even the individual, organisation, or thing that added the data to the blockchain cannot delete or edit the data. Therefore, it becomes difficult, if not impossible, to hold the entity that added the data to a public blockchain accountable. Private blockchains offer more control and a place to point the finger, but erasing information is still tricky.

Given the nature of blockchain, it seems clear that the GDPR as written will be incompatible with existing blockchain uses. That doesn't mean that compromises aren't available. While you can't delete data from the blockchain and maintain the current level of security, you can segregate the types of data stored on the chain. For example, the blockchain could retain records of contracts and changes with hashes that reference information that contains personal identification. If you buy a song using, for example, Voise, a P2P platform for musicians that enables direct-to-consumer sales, the details of the transaction would be stored on the blockchain. Your personal information (payment details, name, address, etc.) would go through a third party. That third party would control your music access and library of songs. By separating the types of data and putting personal information on centralised systems, blockchain becomes compliant. That's not how things work now, but segregating data is possible. Of course, with segregation, your data is suddenly much more accessible and secure, right? Well, not completely. The GDPR gives you more control over your data, but it doesn't increase security. As discussed in Chapter 3, data security is vital in data-driven organisations, and blockchain does contribute to that because on the blockchain, information is highly encrypted, decentralised, and secure. Centralising personal data to enable erasure, and with that to comply with GDPR, removes that added security. So, how to make this work?

One thing the GDPR does not do is define "erase". While it might seem clear what it means to erase data, there is definitely some grey area. Even "erased" data is often recoverable. If data is inaccessible, even to the entity providing storage, does that count as erased? If yes, blockchain technology can rapidly rise to the challenge by simply destroying the cryptographic key associated with certain information. The data will still be there, but it will be unreadable. This solution preserves the integrity of the ledger and offers a greater level of personal control over what information you share publicly. However, it should be ensured that the cryptographic keys are quantum-proof. Data that is encrypted and where the cryptographic key has been deleted may be deemed "erased" now but might become visible again in the future. Therefore, erasing data on a blockchain by deleting the cryptographic key would only work if the encryption used is quantum-computing resistant.

Although blockchain technology seems to be incompatible with GDPR in terms of erasing data when using non-quantum-resistant encryption, it is a worthy trade-off; blockchain offers increased provenance, transparency, privacy, and security of data, offering better protection of consumers than existing centralised technologies. Therefore, hopefully regulators and developers will come to an understanding about how to blend privacy controls with transparent transactions and bring the spirit of GDPR to the blockchain and vice versa. GDPR is also very much linked to another important concept in doing business: trust.

4.5 Trustless transactions

Blockchain has the potential to revolutionise the way we leverage trust and even the way we think about trust. Trust is a fundamental good that, while largely intangible, is key to the functioning of practically every meaningful interaction in society. We tend to think of trust concerning business, banking, relationships, and finance since the necessity of trust in these areas is clear and undeniable. In fact, without trust, no transaction can go forward. The very idea of even the simplest negotiations becomes implausible without it. Without trust, the law becomes tyranny and business become piracy. At present, trust has been made to diffuse across systems. We have our system of credit, various checks and balances, laws, and regulations, as well as whatever security measures we have in place. We extend credit to people and organisations whom we trust. To establish this trust, we rely on reputation, proven track records of trustworthiness, and other vague notions. This allows us to do business with people whom we may not necessarily know. But there are still loopholes in our systems and flaws in security that enable bad actors to commit fraud, theft, perjury, and so on.

Blockchain technology has the potential to change the nature of trust. Not only in digitally rendered transactions but also in everyday life. Traditionally, trust and credit are relatively synonymous. However, trust also has a victim, called privacy. To trust one another, we have to give away some of our privacy. As such, trust is closely related to your identity. If I am to trust you, I want to know who you are. The problem with this becomes quite clear with a simple example; if you want to buy alcohol, the shop or bar needs to know whether you are legally allowed to do so. Since the shop or bar owner does not know you, he/she does not trust you if you simply state that you are old enough to do so. Fair enough, as you might be lying. To solve the issue, you are asked for your government-issued identity card, which states your date of birth. Unfortunately, it also states your name, identity number, and a whole bunch of other, private, information. When purchasing alcohol, your name really is not relevant to determine whether you are legally allowed to buy alcohol. In fact, your date of birth is irrelevant as well to the seller: all they need to know is whether you are *old enough* and this requires a binary yes/no. Unfortunately, it was never possible to offer a level of trust to prove you are old enough without revealing other (potentially sensitive) information as collateral damage. Until now.

Zero Knowledge Proof (ZKP) is a method used in cryptography to prove ownership of a specific piece of knowledge without revealing the content of that knowledge. In other words, you can get your alcohol without revealing who you are and when you were born but with proof that you are old enough to buy alcohol. ZKP ensures that data can be shared without leaking personal information. One party can prove a certain fact without revealing personal information, thereby creating the required trust to perform a transaction.

ZKP creates transactions that protect users' privacy using mathematics. As such, ZKP improves verification processes to such an extent that one party can prove to another party that a given statement is true, without revealing any information about that statement. It offers a statistically (probabilistically) checkable proof. For a ZKP to be sound and thorough, it has to have three characteristics; completeness, soundness, and zero knowledge.

- *Completeness*: assuming the statement is true, an honest verifier who is faithfully and correctly following the protocol will be rightly convinced of the fact sought by the actions of an honest prover who is faithfully and correctly following the protocol.
- *Soundness*: falsification by the prover must be impossible. There should be no way for the prover to falsify knowledge and falsely convince the verifier. That is to say, the verifier cannot be deceived given the perimeters of the ZKP.
- *True Zero Knowledge*: if it is the case that the statement is true, the verifier can learn nothing other than the truth of the statement. In the example above, the verifier (the shop or bar) can learn that the prover (the customer) is old enough to purchase alcohol, without revealing any information including the date of birth. If the verifier learns anything other than the fact that the prover is old enough, the condition of zero knowledge will have been violated and you no longer have a true ZKP.

At present, most current blockchain technologies are only pseudonymous. A user's identity can be traced back to their transactions by linking blockchain transactions to a real name with a network address (for example when a user purchases something online using bitcoin and has the product delivered to his/her house). Despite the sterling reputation of blockchain as the perfect cyber security solution, many in the know are aware of this weakness. In fact, law enforcements all over the world have been exploiting this vulnerability to catch criminals, such as the proprietors of the Silk Road, an infamous online black market. But ZKP could fill the gaps left vulnerable by the flawed anonymity provided by some distributed ledger technologies. ZKP raises the bar for certainty in cryptography because a true piece of zero proof knowledge is, in theory, unbreakable. It transforms the basic commodity of trust from being synonymous with crossing your fingers and lack of privacy, into a real, unbreakable, and 100 per cent private, virtual, good.

ZKP still has many (technical) challenges to overcome. Not the least of which is cultural. Not having to show your government-issued identity to prove your age will require many people to get used to. At first, many will remain sceptical. Nevertheless, a society where trust is created using ZKP is a more private society. It will bring back control of your privacy to the consumer instead of leaving it in the hands of organisations. As such, ZKP-enabled transactions will improve your privacy. Trust and privacy will become even more important when blockchain meets big data, which I will discuss in the next chapter.

4.6 Blockchain and reputation

When talking about trust, it is only a small step to move to reputation. Reputation, after all, is vital for successful collaboration. In the past, when you required some work done, you would ask a local craftsman to do so. You were confident that you could trust the craftsman as it was a small village. Any betrayal by him or her would result in loss of business. On the other hand, the craftsman knew he/she could trust you as when you would betray the craftsman it would mean that no one in the village wanted to work for you again. It was a system that worked very well. Unfortunately, with the internet turning the world into a small global village, that system pretty much disappeared. As a result, it has become increasingly difficult to trust someone you don't know. To understand the challenges we face with reputation, it is important to understand what reputation is and how it is created. Reputation is a certain opinion about a person, company, or device. A reputation is created over time, based on a set of criteria. It is a mechanism of control within societies and increasingly also among connected devices. It is important to know that reputation exists on multiple levels, ranging from an individual, organisation, communities, to countries and cultures. Nowadays, even connected devices are developing a reputation, which provides insights on their trustworthiness.

Reputation is not only developed by your behaviour, quality of work, and if you, or an entity, keep a promise, but also by a concept I call *shadow reputation*. Shadow reputation refers to the reputation of those you interact with (the people, companies, and machines in your network). Dealing with trustworthy entities will increase your reputation. The other way is also the case, dealing with untrustworthy entities, for example criminals or hacked devices, will negatively affect your reputation. You can compare this to "having the wrong friends". When you become too closely linked to "the wrong friends", it will directly affect how people view you and as such have an impact on your reputation. This *shadow reputation* is intrinsically linked to who you are and how others identify you.[242] This leads us to the concept of a self-sovereign identity; an identity that is owned and controlled by the person or the device that created it. Within a self-sovereign identity, the user not only controls his/her reputation and shadow reputation, but also his/her attributes. After all, an identity consists of many different attributes, which are constantly changing and evolving in terms of priority and durability. Some attributes such as birthdates, place of birth, biological parents, and Social Security numbers will stay with a person for his or her entire life. Others, such as an employee number, student number, address, or telephone number could change periodically. Still, other attributes could be very short-lived, such as a username on a forum or

website. Each of these attributes has different, uniquely identifiable characteristics, and the combination of them constitutes a person's or device's identity
(although the person might perceive that differently). A self-sovereign identity
can be defined by the 5P's as it is *personal* (it is about you), *portable* (meaning
you can take your identity and data from one platform to another), *private*
(you control your identity and data), *persistent* (it does not change without
your consent), and *protected* (your identity cannot be stolen). In other words, a
self-sovereign identity is a paradigm shift from today's identity system, and it
will drastically change how organisations are able to deal with customer data.

Next to a self-sovereign identity, also reputation and shadow reputation are
increasingly becoming important due to the global village we live in. However, trusting people, or devices, on the internet whom you don't know has
become notoriously difficult. And that is a shame, as it limits the opportunity
to do business and to benefit from this global village that we have created.
Therefore, we need a new system, and we have already seen the first examples
of such a system; ratings and reviews. By now, most of us are familiar with
ratings, whether it is your Uber rating, your Airbnb rating, your eBay rating,
or your Amazon rating. In the past years, pretty much any large internet
platform has introduced ratings and reviews, and the system gives us at least
some confidence. However, there are also plenty of problems with such a
centralised, reputation system:

1   The platform is centralised, so anyone, whether hackers or administrators,
     could adjust ratings and reviews at a click of a button.
2   It is quite easy to perform fraud and have your friends give you positive
     ratings or give your enemies negative ratings, even if you have not used
     their services.
3   The ratings are non-portable: if you have a five-star rating on eBay and
     then want to do business on Amazon, you have to start from scratch.
4   The ratings only give you some level of confidence; they are not corre-
     lated with any revenue potential. However, in the offline world, if you
     would be a five-star artist you could probably ask more money for your
     work than if you were a three-star artist. Online, it does not work like
     that.

Reputation is especially important with the Internet of Things coming our
way. Just as humans should be able to trust each other, connected devices
have to trust each other as well if they want to perform transactions. After all,
doing business with a malware-infested connected device is bad for business.
Therefore, just like humans, connected devices and sensors also have an
identity. This identity consists of attributes. An attribute is a characteristic or
feature of that device. Each of these attributes has different, uniquely identifiable characteristics, and the combination of them constitutes a device's
identity. An IoT device also has a reputation: how reputable is the device,

does it indeed do what it should do. Finally, IoT devices also have a shadow reputation. This revolves around the other devices in the same network and the reputation of those devices. A connected device linked to another device that contains malware is less valuable. A connected device's or machine's identity can, therefore, also be defined by the 5P's. It is *personal* (it is about that particular device or machine), *portable* (meaning the data can be easily shared in a secure way with other devices), *private* (the device controls the identity and data), *persistent* (it does not change without consent), and *protected* (the identity and data cannot be stolen). Ensuring IoT devices adhere to the 5P's of identity is a key requisite to keep the Internet of Things secure. But how can you determine and ensure the reputation of a connected device? Moreover, how can we create a system that incorporates all aspects of reputation, without invading our privacy?

A solution for the above problems could be to simply build a meta reputation platform that monitors everything that you do and calculates a unique score that will affect your online and offline activities. Sounds scary? Could be, but it is exactly what China is developing: Sesame Credit, a social credit score, will dramatically impact the Chinese society and invade the daily lives of Chinese citizens in a variety of ways. It is a system that will make social (online) trust a major aspect of Chinese citizens as everything that one does contributes positively or negatively to the social score. A person's social score will directly affect a person's dealings with the government or businesses online and offline.[317] As such, a positive score could result in preferential treatment, such as skipping long lines at the hospital or access to loans. However, it also results in penalties for breaking social trust and not complying with "good behaviour" (as determined by the government), such as denial of public office consideration or loss of welfare and social security. Although Sesame Credit will undoubtedly create a more trustworthy society, it also is a massive privacy violation and it remains a centralised service. If the Chinese government would like to demote a citizen, it could simply change the score and the citizen is left with all corresponding problems.

Box 4.1 Sesame Credit's impact on society and privacy

The ability to provide product and service offerings to customers online requires businesses to assess risk. This risk assessment becomes difficult when a reliable online reputation system is practically non-existent. This was the issue that China's emerging credit reporting and scoring industry faced.[318] With the help of large private organisations such as Ant Financial, Alibaba's payment affiliate, they developed Sesame Credit. This social scoring system stands to drastically affect society and invade the daily lives of Chinese citizens in a variety of ways.

Alibaba was one of the eight approved technology companies by China's central bank in 2014 to develop online and e-commerce rating systems based on social trust.[319] Ant Financial developed and integrated Sesame Credit into Alipay and assigned social credit scores to Alipay users who had agreed to use the credit-scoring service.[320] Sesame Credit can leverage Alibaba's robust database in conjunction with other factors, such as online transactional history, tax payment history, and traffic infraction history, to determine an individual's trustworthiness.[321] As such, Sesame Credit is becoming a nation-wide credit rating system that incorporates social scoring.[317] It is a reputation system unlike anything before. It calculates credit scores based on online and offline shopping habits. For example, an individual who buys diapers may have higher scores than a person who spends money on entertainment, since the diaper transactions would be perceived as being more responsible. Sesame Credit will impact society as the use of the credit scoring and reporting is incorporated into the everyday life of the Chinese. The program will help China push its development of a nation-wide social credit system. However, it also comes with concerns regarding privacy and transparency of information.

Many individuals were not aware that Sesame Credit rated them when the service initially began.[322] This caused concern, especially because the system lacked 100 per cent accuracy. China will use artificial intelligence to continuously improve the system, using the massive amounts of data gathered through the system. Sesame Credit assigns a social score based not only on a person's dealings with businesses but also on how they interact socially online and offline. The score also takes into account the actions of the people in your network. If a friend robs a bank, that will negatively affect you, even if you had nothing to do with it. However, the Chinese government is not stopping there. Recently, it announced that all cars would be required to have an RFID chip that can monitor the exact movements of the car.[323] Although the government states it will be just to combat congestion, it will likely be used to increase surveillance. Add to that the 170 million CCTV cameras already in place, many of which are smart cameras, as well as the rapid developments in facial recognition; it is quite likely that increasingly offline actions of Chinese citizens will also contribute, positively or negatively, to their social credit score.[324–326]

Since the social credit score is a centralised system, controlled by the government, it gives the government tremendous power, rewarding citizens that do well (according to the Chinese government) and punishing them for breaking social trust. The goal is to enhance market economy regulation and penalise people and businesses for poor practices, such as selling toxic food or engaging in bribes. The Chinese government aims to fully implement these measures by 2020.[327]

A solution to the lack of online trust (if we do not want a solution such as Sesame Credit) would be to develop a decentralised reputation system, using blockchain or another distributed ledger technology. Such a blockchain-based reputation system would solve all four problems as mentioned earlier:

1   It is decentralised, which means that a person's reputation becomes immutable, verifiable, and traceable. As a result, the provenance of reputation becomes visible and transparent, and anyone can understand how

a certain reputation came about. In addition, since it is immutable, no central governing body can adjust your reputation.

2   Only users who have used your service or bought a product from you can leave a review. Such verified reviews are already commonplace on Amazon, which are marked differently from other reviews, but Amazon remains a centralised platform.

3   Reputations become portable and owned by the individual, organisation, or thing. Since the reputation is decentralised and immutable but controlled by the user, it becomes possible to take your reputation from one platform to another. All of a sudden, you could take your Uber reputation to Lift and directly make a fair revenue.

4   Reputations can be linked to your ability to make revenue. The higher your reputation, the higher the quality of the product or service you offer, the more money you could ask for that service. A five-star Airbnb host could make more money than a four-star Airbnb host, governed by smart contracts so that users have a monetary incentive to perform better.

You could argue that the above would violate privacy as much as Sesame Credit does. However, that is not the case with a decentralised reputation system. After all, if developed correctly, the user remains in full control thanks to a self-sovereign identity. As such, the user, organisation, or device can determine who has access to the reputation score and who does not. A decentralised reputation-based society makes so much sense. Despite all the positive things the internet has brought us, it has also significantly lowered trust levels among individuals, organisations, and connected devices. In the past, personal relationships were strong enough to create a system where good behaviour was rewarded and bad behaviour punished. With the internet, that system no longer functions as it should. However, distributed ledger technology offers us a chance to fix reputation once and for all. It will take some time before we have developed a decentralised reputation system, but it is worth the wait. A more trustworthy and better society allows for more reliable collaboration among individuals, organisations, and things.

4.7 How blockchain changes collaboration across industries

Apart from collecting and analysing data to achieve a competitive advantage, as discussed in Chapter 3, collaborating with industry partners can also result in a competitive advantage.[41] With the development of Blockchain, doing so has become easier than ever before. The characteristics of an immutable, verifiable, and traceable decentralised ledger results in *decentralised* organisations where trust is created through cryptography among actors that are dispersed decentralised.[134] It also enables *autonomous* organisations, where decision-making is automated using smart contracts, and governance is embedded in the code.[42, 60, 134] Organisations that are *decentralised* and/or *autonomous* are enabled by peer-to-peer transactions within human-to-human and human-to-machine or even machine-to-machine networks. Where the two come together, in *Decentralised Autonomous Organisations,* complex mechanisms interact to organise activity automatically and autonomously, without management or employees.[14] These new disruptive forms of organisation design rely heavily on a delegative leadership style and advanced information technology to enable dispersed teams to collaborate without a centralised power that makes the decisions, making them a potential threat to traditional, centralised organisations.[328, 329] Blockchain requires collaboration outside the boundaries of organisations, resulting in organisations where peer-to-peer collaborations thrive. Trustless, peer-to-peer collaboration among humans and/or machines, where (strategic) decision-making is automated and governance is embedded in the code, is a paradigm shift.[42] For the first time, machines can collaborate automatically and even autonomously with other machines and even humans, while ensuring that the outcome will be in line with what has been agreed upon before. Humans develop the decentralised and/or autonomous organisation, which will then interact with other human and artificial actors, possibly even autonomously. As such, thanks to blockchain technology, *the social, the material,* and *the artificial* become increasingly interwoven and perhaps even entangled.[330] However, the more they do so and the more human-to-machine and machine-to-machine collaboration become pervasive, the more organisations require the need for artificial intelligence to govern these interactions. This in itself requires governance, as we will see in Chapter 6. But first, let's see how blockchain is already applied in the financial services industry, the retail industry, the telecom industry, the manufacturing industry, and finally the content industry.

4.7.1 The financial services industry

Traditionally, the financial services industry is known for its legacy systems and some banks have stacks of legacy systems, some of which are 30–40 years old. It is, therefore, not surprising that the financial services industry has embraced blockchain technology to improve many of their outdated systems and, along the way, save a lot of money (which, not surprisingly, might be the main reason for them to adopt blockchain). Using a distributed ledger, banks can trade faster and cheaper and become more efficient. Some of the benefits are as follows.

Instant settlements

Transactions can be done in minutes or seconds, while currently, settlements can take up a week. With blockchain technology, settlements become user-optimised, which will save a significant amount of time and money, for both parties involved. Blockchain will remove the need for a lot of middle and back office staff. Many banks are experimenting with instant settlements, including the Bank of Canada that ran a test in 2018 together with the Toronto Stock Exchange operator TMX Group, and non-profit organisation Payments Canada. The test showed that automating instantaneous securities settlements becomes possible with a blockchain. The test enabled direct swapping cash from buyers to sellers, resulting in instant settlements.[331] When transactions are settled near instantly, it removes a significant part of the risk that the counterparty cannot meet its obligations, which could be a substantial expense for banks.

Improve capital optimisation

One of the main features of blockchain is that it removes the need for a trusted intermediary and makes peer-to-peer transactions possible. When Blockchain is applied in the financial services industry, it could render useless the fee-charging intermediaries such as custodian banks (those that transfer money between different banks) or clearers (those vouching for counterparties' credit positions). As such, Blockchain offers better capital optimisation, due to a significant reduction in operational costs for banks. In addition, when banks share a blockchain, the total costs of that blockchain and the surrounding ecosystem might be higher than individual costs of managing transactions at a bank. However, the costs are shared among all participating banks and as such there is a significant cost reduction.

Improved contractual performance due to smart contracts

When banks and financial institutions are using smart contracts, it will improve contractual term performance as contracts execute automatically once certain pre-set conditions have been met. It is important that those smart contracts are firmly rooted in law and comply with any regulations across jurisdictions. Because of this, the blockchain startup R3 had to tailor-make the smart contracts within its open-source Corda blockchain. Especially complex financial asset transactions can benefit from blockchain technology, due to automatic settlement using smart contracts under the control of an incorruptible set of business rules.

Increased financial solutions in terms of crisis

Increased options for financial solutions in times of crisis due to the availability of new financial products. In 2016, Bitfinex, one of the largest crypto exchanges, was hacked and 120,000 bitcoins were stolen. When the Bitfinex hack happened, the solution that it developed was compensating the customers, who all shared equally in the loss, with a tradeable Recovery Right Token (RRT). One token was valued at US$1 loss, and each token could be seen as an IOU. Customers could trade the token for the market price (if they did not believe in the recovery of Bitfinex or if they did and wanted to make a profit), they could exchange it for equity (which happened with nearly half of all tokens), or they would be bought back by Bitfinex for US$1 at some time in the future. An interesting example of an innovative financial solution. It is quite likely that without it, Bitfinex would have gone bankrupt and all customers would have lost their money.

Reduced error handling and improved transparency

Any data that is recorded on a blockchain can be tracked in real time, leaving a very detailed audit trail. As such, it eliminates error handling and reconciliation. In addition, it improves transparency across the industry. This could lead to improved regulatory reporting and monitoring by central banks, especially when the regulators also have access to the blockchain.

Most of the banks are currently experimenting with blockchain, one way or another. They do not only focus on bitcoin but on multiple networks and cryptocurrencies to understand which technology offers the best solution for an improved financial industry. It is vital for the financial services industry to innovate and to investigate new technologies to improve their products and services. If the incumbents don't change their offering and innovate, newcomers will disrupt their business as we have already seen with a variety of FinTech startups that are building new ways to handle your financials.

Unfortunately, while most banks are investigating blockchain, most of the banks are not very fond of working with crypto startups. Most of them simply refuse any company that has something to do with cryptocurrencies, whether you are a trading company or doing an ICO. These banks rather stay away from cryptocurrencies, being afraid of criminal activities such as money laundering. There are only a handful of traditional banks that allow cryptocurrency companies to open a bank account with them and the process to open such an account can easily take between six months and a year. In addition, the fees charged by these banks are often a lot higher than for normal accounts. Although you could argue that the entire point of a crypto startup is not to have a bank account, almost always you still need a bank account, for example, to pay your taxes or your employees. Fortunately, there are also disruptors in the market that do welcome crypto startups:

- *Change*, a crypto bank based in Estonia and Singapore, with the objective to revolutionise banking. It offers crypto wallets and a cryptocurrency credit card to make ATM withdrawals and payments.
- *Revolut*, a UK-based FinTech company that has recently moved into crypto. It allows you to buy, exchange, and hold Bitcoin, Ether, Litecoin, Bitcoin Cash, and Ripple. However, it does not accept cryptocurrency firms as customers.

- *Bitwala*, a German bank aiming to offer crypto-first current accounts. It also briefly offered a bitcoin debit card via Visa, but that was blocked again by Visa.

You wonder if banks are not digging their own grave by refusing to work with companies that offer a cryptocurrency. The FinTech startups working with cryptocurrencies often offer far better services than traditional, slow, and bureaucratic banks.

4.7.2 The retail industry

The retail industry has become increasingly complex in the past decades. Products are made in one part of the world, assembled in another, and sold in a third part of the world, whether it is food, clothing, or flowers. As a result of this complexity, transparency has become challenging. It is not always clear to consumers how and what products move through the supply chain. When it comes to tracking products from farm to plate, customers are often left in the dark. Even with Fair Trade, where transparency is a precondition, it is often difficult to verify if a Fair-Trade product is indeed fair. This lack of transparency is increasingly a source of discontent for consumers, who want to know what they buy, the materials sourced, and if regulations were followed. However, it is also necessary for retailers to understand how their products move through the supply chain. Not only for non-eatable goods but especially also for perishable goods it is important to be certain whether, for example, the temperature during transportation remained within certain limits. As such, the provenance of products is becoming increasingly important, and that is exactly where blockchain could contribute. The potential of blockchain technology for the retail industry is enormous as it can eliminate errors that generally happen with global, complex supply chains. There are several ways in which blockchain can help.

Creating transparency

Blockchain enables anyone with access to check the provenance of whatever is recorded on a blockchain. This makes blockchain technology so valuable for the retail industry because once all supply chain partners participate in a decentralised solution, complete transparency becomes possible for all stakeholders. More importantly, all stakeholders can be confident that the data is correct and has not been tampered with. This transparency makes it easier to verify if products have been produced in the correct way, who was involved and how a product was treated. This becomes especially useful when something goes wrong with a product, as it allows regulators to quickly determine where it went wrong.

Improving supply chain efficiency

Not only transparency can be achieved, but also efficiency can be increased when smart contracts are used. Smart contracts can settle transactions automatically once the goods arrive and action can be taken automatically once certain pre-defined rules are not followed. For example, when the temperature in a refrigerated container becomes too high, it automatically results in a lower price to be paid by the buyer as the good may have been damaged. It will save a lot of paperwork and results that a fair price is paid for a product that might have been damaged while being transported. Blockchain is a natural partner for industry partners that want to collaborate more effectively and efficiently.

Warranties

Warranties can easily be converted and stored on a blockchain, where consumers can easily transfer them if they decide to sell their product. The company Warranteer helps retailers move their warranties to the cloud and on to the blockchain, enabling retailers to keep their warranties up-to-date, verifiable, and transferable.

Reducing counterfeit products

Products such as luxury handbags, diamonds, or electronics can easily be put on a blockchain, by adding a tag to the product and storing the details of that tag on a blockchain to verify and track individual products. Consumers can thus easily verify if their product is real or fake and retailers can follow their products throughout the supply chain. This will allow them to quickly determine whether products were diverted from the original supply chain. The company Block Verify offers such a solution, aiming to reduce the number of counterfeit products.

Two examples of retail blockchain applications

The potential of blockchain for the retail industry is enormous, and there are a variety of startups working on retail solutions ranging from transparency, authenticity, provenance, payments, and transactions. The companies *Provenance* and *Everledger* are both great examples of what blockchain can do for supply chain management. The company *Provenance* enables organisations to obtain a detailed transaction record that tracks every major event in the production process from when the pieces roll out of the assembly line to the final delivery to a customer. By showing the story behind the production, consumers get a product they can trust, and that is exactly as advertised. Worried about fair trade? Provenance makes it easy to verify fair trade statements, organic certifications, and much more. The company *Everledger*, on the other hand, focuses on protecting high-value assets as they make their way from the producer to an eventual client. It started with diamonds, a small, extremely valuable asset that has come under fire in recent years due to blood diamonds. With *Everledger* it is possible to record the dozens of unique characteristics of a diamond on a blockchain, which enables you to track and trace a particular diamond throughout the supply chain. But it doesn't end there. By incorporating smart contracts, Everledger allows a frictionless transfer of assets that helps protect every party involved in a sale. Not only startups are working on creating solutions for the retail industry, also, incumbents are incorporating the technology.

Walmart: from mangoes and pork to chocolate

Not surprisingly, the digital-native organisation Walmart, which started using big data before anyone had heard of the term, is one of the first to use blockchain technology. First, it experimented with mangoes, to trace slices of mango to their origin, and Chinese pork, to track the movements of it in China to prevent disease outbreaks linked to the food. Now, it has teamed up with eight other food giants and IBM to bring blockchain to its food supply chains.[332, 333] Blockchain will not only allow it to improve its data management systems and improve the efficiency within the supply chain, but more importantly, it can help prevent infectious diseases becoming deadly by cutting down an investigation into food-borne illnesses from weeks to seconds. Once a source is known, action can be taken instantly.

In addition to reducing the time needed to identify tainted sources to mere seconds, its smart tracking program aims to also collect environmental data from end-to-end. Some products need constant refrigeration. When temperatures get too high, it can affect quality. With blockchain technology, buyers can track the entire journey and pay for the quality they actually receive, all handled automatically through the use of smart contracts and tracking. Without full supply chain transparency, these processes are rarely simple, and in some cases, near impossible.[334]

Alibaba: tackling food fraud

Alibaba is collaborating with AusPost, PwC, Blackmores, and Fonterra to develop a blockchain solution that will help the retail giant to combat food fraud.[335] It aims to develop a "Food Trust Framework" to improve Alibaba's supply chains in terms of integrity and traceability. Food fraud consists of packaging low-quality food with high-quality food labels and it is difficult to trace. (Tip: watch the fascinating documentary *Sour Grapes* on Netflix to get an idea of the scale of such fraud.) By collaborating with vitamin and supplement maker Blackmores and dairy brand Fonterra, Alibaba wants to offer consumers full transparency in the provenance of these products, thereby hoping to boost consumer confidence.[336] By tagging the products with a QR code, it allows consumers to authenticate and verify products, while the retailers can easily monitor their products across the supply chain.

Blockchain is a natural partner for the retail industry, by offering much-needed transparency, reducing the possibility of counterfeit products and thus protecting consumers. It can make supply chains more efficient and effective and can result in better service to customers using, for example, warranties on a blockchain. However, bringing the global supply chains to the next level will be a challenge, as it requires many different stakeholders from across the globe to collaborate with each other. Fortunately, pilots such as developed by Walmart and Alibaba show the potential and more retailers will follow soon.

4.7.3 The telecom industry

The telecom industry is known for reinventing itself. In the early days of telecom, fixed landlines were the key product of Telco's, while with the advent of the mobile phone this moved to mobile subscriptions and the massive cash cow SMS. However, in recent years, for many telecom organisations the main revenue is no longer *call* but *data*, which required another change in their business model. With every organisation turning into a data organisation, there are significant opportunities for the telecom industry to reinvent itself once again.

Since telephony is so pervasive, the telecom industry is huge and often complex, with over 2,000 mobile network operators. Many different players and billions of consumers and devices that interchangeably use a variety of networks. In addition, the Internet of Things will add tens of billions of devices to the global telecom networks, providing a huge opportunity for the telecom industry. All these connections and billions of transactions have to be managed, and blockchain technology can do this. Blockchain's core attributes to make data immutable, verifiable, and traceable enables the telecom industry to create an ecosystem where consumers are in full control, and where there is trust, security, and transparency in the participating ecosystem.[337] The result is lower costs for consumers, better networks, and an overall improved experience for all stakeholders. Within an ecosystem with billions of transactions, there are probably numerous applications possible and here are three applications that I believe will have the most impact on the global telecom industry.

5G enablement and customised data plans

5G is rapidly being developed across the world. The benefits of 5G compared to 4G are substantial. 5G will not only offer network speeds as high as 10Gbps but also enable lower communication latency – up to 1 millisecond. The combination of high speed and such low latency will enable new products, applications and services that are currently not possible. Simply, because currently, it takes too long for data to move between a device and a data centre (where the data crunching is done). 5G will also support the massive increase in connected devices expected with the Internet of Things. Why are these features important for the Internet of Things? Simply consider a self-driving car; a car travelling at 100 km/hr would travel 2.7 meters further before the breaks are applied if there is a latency of 100 milliseconds. Obviously, that would be unacceptable. The same would apply to games, drones and many other (industrial) applications.

To achieve ubiquitous access across networks for billions of devices, telecom organisations, or Communication Service Providers (CSPs), need to ensure a variety of access nodes and mechanisms.[338] Each telecom organisation can, of course, do this centrally but it often results in delays and non-seamless provisioning. A much more reliable and efficient solution would be to do this using a private blockchain, accessed by the CSPs.

Within a private blockchain, the rules and agreements among various CSPs can be coded in smart contracts, which are stored on the private blockchain. Devices that want to connect to the network broadcast their identity to the decentralised network. Based on the parameters within the smart contracts, users are charged accordingly. While the smart contracts are immutable, the parameters can easily be changed if required, allowing for flexible and reliable service to any device.

From communications service provider to identity service provider

Online identity is the next big thing, and numerous organisations are working on developing self-sovereign identities for individuals, organisations, and things. In the future, each bit of data might also have its own identity (or meta information) that enables easy and reliable data-sharing across consumers and organisations. A self-sovereign identity brings back full control to the end-user to manage their identity, and it offers a new revenue model for the telecom industry.

CSPs could offer a virtual sim card, an eSIM (embedded SIM) that offers virtual identities for devices, data, or users.[339] This virtual identity can then be used to perform transactions among users, organisations, and connected devices such as logging in to a social network or purchasing goods online. A virtual identity can offer many benefits, and these benefits are only limited by the number of partners the CSP can sign on to the system.[338] This "identity-as-a-service" could be a significant new revenue model for telecom organisations.

IoT: smart homes, smart cities, and smart everything

By 2035, the average person will interact with a connected device nearly every 18 seconds, in effect digitally documenting every move, query, purchase, plan, and transaction. The Internet of Things offers a significant new revenue model for CSPs as all these billions of transactions among billions of devices need to be managed securely. CSPs can start with establishing a blockchain network by adding blockchain nodes to every mid-range cell tower, which can be done at relatively low costs.[338] Such a decentralised network operated by multiple CSPs can then be used to offer self-managed peer-to-peer networks, enabling highly secure transactions among connected devices. Of course, organisations such as IOTA are also working on building the infrastructure for the Internet of Things.

With a predicted US$19 trillion of added value to the global economy thanks to the Internet of Things, there are ample opportunities for CSPs to boost their revenue with decentralised IoT services. Australian telecom organisation Telstra is already exploring several of these opportunities.

Box 4.2 Telstra leverages blockchain to address technicalities

According to Katherine Robins, principal security expert at Telstra, Telstra intends to use blockchain to secure the IoT ecosystems of smart homes.[340] The company has tested its IoT smart home system on a variety of distributed ledgers such as Ripple, Apache Hyperledger, and Ethereum. It resulted in exploring the viability of applying blockchain technology to IoT as a security enhancement solution for devices that were limited to storing small quantities of data.[341] Initially, these tests were exclusive to ADSL-T Gateway routers, but they were expanded to other home devices, including switches and cameras.[342]

As the number of IoT devices expands, so will the number of transactions. Keeping up with these transactions increases computational requirements, which Telstra sees as a serious challenge. Moreover, too much traffic can leave IoT devices vulnerable to other security issues, such as (Distributed) Denial of Service (DDoS) attacks. These attacks can bring down entire enterprise servers and halt the delivery of service to millions of customers. Telstra plans to mitigate these issues by incorporating blockchain technology to store a device firmware's cryptographic hashes on private blockchains and reduce the time it takes to verify transactions.[342]

Telstra extends the security provided by blockchain technology and combines it with biometric features, such as voice and facial recognition. These are stored encrypted on a blockchain, making it immutable, verifiable, and traceable.[342, 343] The usage of blockchain makes IoT security significantly more efficient and cost effective and this additional security helps to reduce fraudulent transactions and mitigates unauthorised users from accessing smart devices or networks. It will enhance the customer experience by providing peace of mind to consumers who will know that their data is safe and that they have control over who has access to their information.

With the advent of blockchain technology, CSPs should transition from telecom organisations to digital services enablers. T-Mobile seems to understand this new paradigm as in 2018, it started to quietly build a decentralised enterprise blockchain solution to tokenise a user's authority to perform transactions.[344] Also, in 2018, Huawei, the world's third largest handset maker, started to develop a blockchain-enabled mobile phone in collaboration with Sirin Labs.[345] The idea would be to include a cold storage wallet on the phone and a system that could automatically convert fiat money into crypto money. In addition, Huawei is building a blockchain-enabled platform for insurance solutions, thereby clearly showing a move towards a digital services enabler.[346]

The future for telecom organisations is anything but dire. With so many new digital services being developed and billions if not trillions of transactions to be processed, there is ample room for innovation and opportunities for the global telecom industry.

4.7.4 The manufacturing industry

In manufacturing, an immutable data trail can have value in a variety of functions ranging from supply chain management and logistics to production. With sensors becoming an integrated part of every manufacturing plant, collecting, understanding, manipulating, and leveraging that data holds tremendous potential value for those on the production side of the supply chain. Every sensor on the production floor gathers a tremendous amount of data, which contributes to the datafication of the organisation of tomorrow. However, until that data is collated and interpreted, it is just an added expense line for data storage. Sensors have enormous potential for the manufacturing industry but only if there is a platform ready and able to absorb that information and make it usable, reliable, traceable, and verifiable.

That is where the blockchain comes in with services like *Factom Iris* and *Super Computing Systems*. *Factom Iris* individually identifies all of the devices connected, so you not only know what data is created but, often more importantly, where it is coming from. That doesn't mean getting an instant notification that there is a shutdown on the line, it means that you don't need to worry about false identifications. By building device profiles, the same way that companies do for individuals, *Factom Iris* verifies the identity of devices, ensuring that the data is coming from the stated source. The company *Super Computing Systems* adds another layer of verification that can help with physical problems within a factory and digital verification: when sensors dump data, it comes with a timestamp to show exactly what happened when. This can be critical when tracking down roadblocks that are slowing production or trying to find the cause of an accident.

A transparent supply chain offers manufacturers some significant benefits, particularly in an era where some producers support guaranteed uptimes and subscription-based services. With sensors and a decentralised data collection system, businesses can draw information from shipped units around the world, use predictive analytics to determine likely points of failure, and take proactive steps to avoid any equipment downtime. When you can advertise a piece of construction equipment that never breaks down or a manufacturing plant that hands out its own repair requests before the line shuts down, you have a product that can change the face of manufacturing forever, which is exactly what Syncron, a blockchain startup, proposes for the future.

By blending technologies like IoT and blockchain, manufacturers have new opportunities for cost savings and controls, along with the ability to offer better service to customers. As this technology matures and moves out of the startup phase, expect to see adoption expand beyond the world's largest enterprises. Data means more insight into your business and getting access to good data is likely to depend on the blockchain. Better security, scalable platforms, and immutable histories make manufacturing and blockchain a synergistic combination.

4.7.5 The content industry

When the web was developed over 25 years ago, the technologies in place significantly lowered the cost of sharing content such as videos, music, and articles. Thanks to the internet, it has become possible to reach a large part of the global population simply from behind your computer. Those companies who first understood the power of the web, and managed to execute their vision correctly, are now the leading global monopolies we are so familiar with: we use Google for finding information, Facebook or WeChat for social activities, Spotify to listen to music, and YouTube to watch videos, etc. However, in recent years there has been an increase in fake news, clickbait, spam, and copyright infringements, enabled by these platforms. This book is also likely to appear on other websites, where it can be downloaded illegally without me, or my publisher, being able to do anything about it. Ripping videos off YouTube is extremely easy, and websites such as the Pirate Bay continue to exist, thereby damaging those who created the content. Even medical journals are now experiencing problems with fake news. The open-access system of allowing the internet to distribute high-quality research to a wider audience has allowed unreliable content into the mix.[347] Spam also remains a problem, since people keep falling for it. Since spam is extremely cheap to send out, only a few individuals out of millions have to fall for it to make it worth sending. For the last few years, the best methods to fight spam have been to attempt to legally shut down spammers and create better spam filters.

With media attention to these problems growing, people are increasingly becoming aware of the effects that emerging technologies have in the hands of such tech organisations; there is an increase in low-quality content, but more importantly, genuine content creators are no longer in control regarding distribution and compensation of the content they create. Instead, large (online) publishers and distributors own all the rights, and the original content creator only gets a small percentage (55 per cent on YouTube, 10–15 per cent with book publishers, and 0 per cent on any content on Facebook). This does not only count for user-generated content, but also large news publishers miss out; 62 per cent of Americans obtain their news through Facebook while publishers on Facebook only get paid US$100 a day.[348, 349]

The Imagination Age

The result is that being creative, whether it is in creating written content (such as investigative journalism, academic articles, or blogs), videos, music, or other forms of creativity, hardly brings any revenue to creators, apart from a very small niche of online superstars who have made millions. It is a winner-takes-all concept, leaving the large majority of content creators with (near) empty hands and the revenue owned by said tech giants, distributors, or other middlemen. And that is a problem. It is time for change. It is time for the Imagination Age.

The Imagination Age was first coined by designer and writer Charlie Magee in 1993. It is a theoretical period after the Information Age, when creativity and imagination become the primary drivers of economic value.[350] Technologies such as blockchain and artificial intelligence will play a key role in enabling the Imagination Age. Not only will they empower content creators and enable them to earn a fair reward instantly, they will also enable creators to develop better content and earn higher revenues. For example, blockchain can enable us to return content ownership to the content creator. Recording metadata and copyright information on a blockchain is the first step to put content creators more in control as it establishes undeniably who created what content when. The company *Proof of Existence* is an online service that incorporates blockchain. It involves content being certified and timestamped into the bitcoin blockchain, providing a cryptographic record. It is a public record proving you own the content without actually revealing the information or yourself. When you add metadata of content on the blockchain as well, it becomes possible to verify at any time that you were the original creator. This information can be used to take back control if someone violates your copyright, but it is not yet sufficient to bring back control completely. In fact, in 2018, China's Supreme Court ruled that blockchain evidence is legally binding evidence. The court ruled that internet courts in the country have to recognise "digital data that are submitted as evidence if relevant parties collected and stored these data via blockchain with digital signatures, reliable timestamps and hash value verification or via a digital deposition platform, and can prove the authenticity of such technology used".[351]

To achieve such a system on a global scale, we also need to establish a decentralised infrastructure where content creators know when their content is distributed across the web by whom. If that information is available in real time, the next step should be to allow content creators to deny the content distribution through certain channels, for whatever reason. The final stage of giving back control to creators is real-time payment when content is consumed, directly from consumer to creator, without intermediaries confiscating the revenue. Also, those helping to distribute the content in the correct manner should be rewarded for increasing the reach of the content. Multiple startups are working on this, including Akasha, Steem.it, and Decent. It requires a cryptocurrency and real-time payments and distribution of revenues using smart contracts. As such, blockchain offers content creators the possibility to take back control and be rewarded fairly and instantly.

Without any one individual or organisation maintaining or controlling a database, blockchain will ultimately change the way content is created, shared, consumed, and maintained. Further down the road, even Facebook and Google may lose the power they currently possess, with privacy and autonomy restored to the individual using a self-sovereign identity. Providers such as Spotify and YouTube currently take a high percentage of artists' and author's products. Hopefully, a decentralised ecosystem will disrupt the status quo and provide an easier and more effective way for creators of content to keep more of their earnings. The days of centralised, commercially owned content may eventually go the way of the horse and buggy. As distributed ledger technology continues to improve and advance, content creators will finally retrieve control over their content and be able to make a fair earning with it.

4.8 Conclusion

We have nearly reached the end of this very long chapter, which shows how complex the technology is that is coined to be a bigger invention than the internet. Knowing what blockchain is and how it can contribute to improving your organisation and supply chain is one thing; knowing how to develop a blockchain strategy is another thing altogether. Therefore, I have tried to provide you with a variety of ways how blockchain can and will affect your organisation. Blockchain, particularly when used in concert with other technologies, offers organisations an opportunity to rethink their internal and external processes, remove inefficiencies, improve transparency and provenance, and build a better organisation overall, as I will show you in Chapter 7. However, within large process-oriented organisations, transforming a centralised business to a decentralised organisation, where cryptography is used to create trust, where smart contracts automate decision-making, and where governance is embedded in the code, can be a daunting task. Especially, because when data becomes immutable, verifiable, and traceable it affects other important concepts such as privacy, security, and ownership. Therefore, my advice is to start working together with your industry partners to see how blockchain can become part of your organisation. Blockchain differs from any other emerging technology as it often requires organisations to collaborate with industry partners, customers, and even competitors. Only through decentralised collaboration with your stakeholders, the benefits of blockchain technology become truly visible. However, it is also important to understand which problems within your organisation are best suited for a blockchain solution and which do not. Not all problems require a decentralised solution, a cryptocurrency, or smart contracts. Blockchain should be a means to an end, not the other way around as we will see in Chapter 7. When deciding to require a token, understand clearly why you need a token and what sort of token. Finally, make sure you comply with existing and future regulations, because although blockchain may help you improve your business significantly, it still requires compliance with regulation.

Chapter 5

The convergence of big data analytics and blockchain

Since the term big data was first coined in 2001, the amount of data available has grown exponentially. Business internet traffic nearly tripled in 2017 compared to 2012 and will continue to grow at a compound annual growth rate (CAGR) of 21 per cent to 2021. Global consumer internet traffic is expected to grow at a CAGR of 24 per cent for the next five years. With the Internet of Things, the world's total data volume will grow to 163 zettabytes per year by 2025, a tenfold increase compared to 2016. By 2035, the average person will interact with a connected device nearly every 18 seconds. In effect digitally documenting every move, query, purchase, plan, and communication in such minute detail that if this person cannot control access to his/her digital trail, privacy will have no meaning and security will remain uncertain.[161, 352, 353] This increasing availability of data significantly changes organisations in terms of strategy, design, culture, and operations.[138, 139] As discussed in Chapter 3, big data has become a corporate standard, and data analytics is a prerequisite to remain competitive.[i] However, for years, experts, consultants, and researchers have told organisations that the best approach to learning from big data was to centralise all available data, including customer, product, and operations data. Consequently, organisations around the globe have replaced large relational databases with data lakes running big data applications, creating a market worth well over US$100 billion annually.[354] However, there are quite a few problems and challenges that have arisen thanks to these massive centralised databases, for both organisations and consumers. These need to be addressed if we want to build the organisation of tomorrow.[355]

First of all, large and multinational organisations span multiple jurisdictions and territories, where variables such as technologies, infrastructure, markets, customer demands, and consumer protection laws are different. Consequently, each business unit often develops its own data infrastructure solution. Often with its own standards and its own data silos, resulting in technical troubles when pooling data across lakes. Second, different departments often hold multiple copies of the same data source. How does an organisation know which copy is the master copy, or the most up to date? Third, sharing data across companies is even more challenging. Although companies such as DataStreamX and DataMarket facilitate the global exchange of information, sharing data with a competitor is usually tricky, even if it can bring substantial benefits.

Moreover, data security remains a big issue. Any organisation can be hacked. The breach of Equifax, the consumer credit reporting agency that exposed the personal data of some 143 million Americans in June and July 2017, is among the biggest hacks with the biggest impact on consumers. Thus far, the Equifax breach has cost the company US$4 billion.[356] The company's CEO resigned over the hack, as did its Chief Information Officer and its Chief Security Officer.[357] The Federal Trade Commission, the Consumer Financial Protection Bureau, the Securities and Exchange Commission, a few state attorneys general, and other agencies in Britain and Canada have investigated whether the hack was preventable and whether several executives deliberately sold stocks before making their knowledge of the breach public.[358, 359] Equally troubling, in October 2016, hackers seized numerous unsecured IoT devices for DDoS attack, resulting in a widespread outage of websites. These connected devices could be hacked via their widely known default passwords.[360] Connected devices have a variety of vulnerabilities and almost any smart device is a vulnerable device.[361] Security issues include technical problems (outdated software, insecure data transmissions, etc.) and people problems (simple and default passwords, public Wi-Fi, etc.). As more devices connect to the internet and each other, without a security solution, the Internet of Things will become the Internet of Vulnerable Things.[362] How can an organisation prevent the dissemination of valuable private data if its firewall can be so easily breached using IoT devices?

To make matters worse, the growing datafication of our society creates tension with consumers. Increasingly, consumers believe that privacy no longer exists. Organisations such as Google, Facebook, Microsoft, and Experian collect troves of data to offer personalised advertising, services, and products across the web.[16] Not only do commercial organisations collect vast amounts of personal data, but governments also aim to use data to understand and control their citizens. The more data are linked together, shared, or sold to other companies, the more consumer privacy is violated.[363] For years, consumers have been handing over their data to companies that, in return, offer "free" services, such as email or social media. These companies use and abuse the data according to their take-it-or-leave-it terms of service, as we have seen with the Facebook/Cambridge Analytica scandal. Although consumers create the data, big corporations make billions of US dollars off them. This centralised control of data ownership by large corporations is harmful to consumers. It could even threaten democracy, as we have seen with Facebook's influence during the Brexit campaign and the 2016 US elections.[16] Consumers increasingly demand more control over their data, which could affect how organisations can collect, store, and apply customer data. Consequently, there is a trend towards restoring data ownership and control to consumers. This will require organisations to rethink their approach to data.

Fortunately, the technology that can solve the issues consumers have with today's data practices will also solve the organisational challenges companies face. Some have argued that blockchain would do for value what the internet did for information. As we have seen, data recorded on a blockchain is immutable, verifiable, and traceable. These new characteristics of data will help organisations solve issues related to data. The convergence of big data and blockchain will greatly affect how organisations should approach data and how they can derive insights from it. This chapter discusses these applications and aims to help organisations to develop solutions that ensure proper data sharing, data governance, privacy, security, and data ownership.

5.1 Data sharing

For most organisations, the importance and advantages of data sharing are clear and have been clear for years.[364] Combining various internal and external data, so-called mixed data, offers organisations additional insights that can significantly benefit the organisation.[164] Sharing data across geographically dispersed business units can be challenging because of different standards, formats, or silos. Sharing data with the competition, however, is nearly impossible due to confidential data. After all, why would you share one of your organisation's most valuable assets with your competitor? However, sharing this data with industry partners can greatly benefit all stakeholders. To do so, organisations require an accurate, reliable, and data-preserving technology. While existing companies such as DataStreamX or DataMarket offer novel solutions, none of them offers the benefits of sharing data that is trustable and private. Blockchain, however, enables organisations to keep control over their proprietary and confidential data if they want to share data with industry partners. The data will remain within the organisation, and simply provides industry partners with access to it under certain conditions. It enables organisations to segment data as they want, store each segment into a vault, and have full control over who has access to those vaults, governed by asymmetric cryptography and smart contracts. As a result, organisations "never make anything available that you can't, or that you don't want to", according to Marcien Jenckes, advertising president at Comcast Cable, which will be releasing a data-sharing solution in 2019.[365] Thanks to the usage of decentralised cryptography, the blockchain solution developed by Comcast is more secure than traditional solutions, which often enable reverse-engineering the data to obtain any missing information. Comcast is collaborating with several organisations, including NBC Universal, Disney, Altice USA, Cox Communications, TF1 Group in France, Channel 4 in the United Kingdom, and Mediaset Italia to figure out how the system should work.

Another solution currently being developed for enterprise data-sharing is the Fujitsu data exchange network. It allows organisations to share their data safely and quickly with industry partners and competitors, without disclosing confidential information. Added advantage is that organisations will get paid for every bit that is used by the third party.[366] It uses a Hyperledger-based framework that provides organisations full control over their distributed data. The objective is to promote interchanges of data collected by various organisations and companies. Every transaction will be recorded on the blockchain. This will help organisations understand who had access to what data when, how that data was used, and how much money the data generated. The biggest advantage of the platform is that organisations no longer have to hand over their data to companies such as Experian or Acxiom. Using distributed ledger technologies means that these intermediaries are no longer necessary.

Data sharing will also be very useful for the Internet of Things, where independent sensors can sell their data to the highest bidder (whether this is another sensor or an organisation) using micro- or even nanotransactions. Such transactions have never been possible due to the high transaction costs involved with traditional payments (or even nowadays in bitcoin). It is likely that future cryptocurrencies will enable sensors or organisations to pay for data by transferring thousandths or millionths of a cent. This capability will spur new business models for organisations that install sensors across the globe and sell the data collected by those sensors to interested parties. The first platform to enable such data sharing is called Terbine. It has enabled a sensor data exchange for the IoT. In 2018, Terbine launched an IoT data exchange platform to prevent the mesh of thousands of one-to-one data-sharing agreements between corporations, agencies, and academic institutions while making IoT data sources discoverable by humans and AI.[367] Terbine has indexed all publicly available sensor data and grades the quality of that data, thereby creating a global frictionless IoT marketplace, according to David Knight, founder and CEO of Terbine.

IOTA, on the other hand, has developed a revolutionary new blockchain technology. It enables companies to share their data on an open marketplace in real time, without the need for fees. IOTA can settle transactions in real time among connected sensors through a blockless distributed ledger that is infinitely scalable, called *tangle*. The tangle is built using a so-called DAG, or a *directed acyclic graph*, which is actually not a blockchain at all. IOTA has created a decentralised and self-regulating peer-to-peer network for the IoT that will enable anyone to share data among connected devices and sensors for free. With blockchain technology, or tangle in the case of IOTA, organisations can verify the integrity of and pay for the data shared across business units, organisations, and things. In 2017, it launched a new data marketplace, data.iota.org, making it possible to securely store, sell, and access data streams, especially targeted at the Internet of Things. In 2018, it announced Qubic to enable smart contracts on the tangle. A true paradigm shift for organisations, it enables including previously unthinkable data sources that will result in better products and services. However, the technology is still in development, and it might take some time before the technology is ready to be used by connected devices.

5.2 Data governance

With a growing amount of data playing an increasingly critical role within organisations, data governance has also grown in importance.[368, 369] Although data governance can be seen as a new term, similar approaches, such as (total) data quality management (DQM) or master data management (MDM), have been around for quite some time. Especially when organisations see data as an asset, monetise it through secure data sharing, and include it on their balance sheet, data governance is very important.[370] As a result, how you govern the data should play a critical role in the organisation.[368] In fact, data governance has become such a necessity for organisations that they no longer can get away with minimal efforts.[371]

Data governance is all about creating guidelines and standards to achieve high-quality data, and ensuring compliance with the processes developed around the usage of data.[372] It is growing in importance because decades of using and storing data in disparate stores and formats have resulted in many inconsistencies. This makes it difficult for companies to understand their data.[373] Improper master data management processes could result in a variety of problems that could harm your business, including operational problems or incorrect customer profiles. Since a blockchain preserves data indefinitely, MDM will only become more important. Resilience and irreversibility are two key attributes of blockchain; once transaction data are added and accepted by the nodes, they become immutable.[374] However, blockchain does not magically transform low-quality data into high-quality data in terms of consistency and correctness. Garbage in still means garbage out. If bad or low-quality data are presented in the right way, it will be appended to the blockchain. If a document contains false information but is presented in the right way, it will still end up on a blockchain.[277]

To respond to the strategic and operational challenges involved with data that is added to a blockchain, organisations require a data-governance framework that combines the business and technical perspectives related to data.[372] Such a data-governance framework contains five important domains: data principles, data quality, metadata, data access, and data lifecycle.[375] *Data principles* define how business users can manage and deal with the data available. *Data quality* refers to the accuracy, timeliness, credibility, and completeness of the data. *Metadata* is defined as *data about data* and should provide a description of the data and facilitates the understanding and categorising of data.[373, 375] *Data access* determines who has access to what data within the organisation. *Data lifecycle* is about how data is used, stored, and organised over time. In addition, data governance is often viewed as the policies, processes, and organisational structures that enable data valuation; accessibility, monitoring, and recovery of data; as well as ownership and stewardship.[369, 371] Data stewardship is a data management approach related to the (re)identification of individuals from data and should include processes around acquiring, storing, safeguarding, and using data to prevent (re)identification of data.[376] Those companies that can maintain a balance of value creation and risk exposure in relation to data can create a competitive advantage.

Data governance is relevant for any industry. One specific sector can especially benefit from blockchain-enabled data governance because of the sensitive data generated, stored, and shared: the healthcare sector. Already, multiple companies are investigating the potential of combining healthcare data with blockchain, including DeepMind, Google's subsidiary driven by artificial intelligence. In March 2017, London's Royal Free Hospital and DeepMind announced plans to develop kidney monitoring software. The long-term objective is to allow hospitals, the National Healthcare Service, and patients to track their health data and to share and combine data securely through distributed ledger technology.[377] DeepMind's co-founder, Mustafa Suleyman, and Ben Laurie, its head of security and transparency, called this a *verifiable data audit*: whenever an entity interacts with data, it adds an entry to the ledger. The entry indicates which piece of data is used and why. For example, a doctor accessed a patient's blood test data to check it against the NHS national algorithm for acute kidney injury. Any access and changes made to the patient's data would be immediately visible. In other words, they are creating an auditing system for health data and thereby ensuring that the data are accurate and that the patient's privacy and safety is ensured.[378]

Organisations that want to apply blockchain within their organisation will need to ensure that their data is correct and of the highest standards. If done correctly, blockchain could be a catalyst for better data, resulting in better insights. If done incorrectly, it could haunt you indefinitely as the data will always remain available. High-quality data is data that is complete, accurate and consistent, available, timestamped, and industry standards-based (meaning compatible with other data). If it has not been created in the right way, it requires cleansing, parsing, or enriching the data. This is difficult and time-consuming. Doing so will result in reduced costs, improved efficiency, better insights, and enables collaboration across verticals and with industry partners. Complete data means that all relevant data for a customer is linked and entered in a database. Often obtaining complete data records is a challenge for organisations. It is only too easy to forget to ask all the required information or customers do not see the benefits of providing all the required details. Accurate and consistent data is all about ensuring that the data is entered correctly, without misspellings, typos, and/or random abbreviations. In addition, the data should be timestamped, which refers to that it is clear when the data was created, changed and/or deleted, and by whom. It should also be sufficiently up-to-date for the task at hand. Finally, it should adhere to industry standards so that it can be exchanged between companies and verticals. These requirements may seem obvious and easy to ensure, as there are sufficient technologies and techniques available in the market that could help. However, the problem is not so much the technology. It is much more a human problem and that makes it a lot more difficult to solve. In the end, if data is not managed correctly and the quality is not ensured, your data can become a risky liability instead of a valuable asset. Any organisation that takes itself seriously should take the quality of data very serious. Not only because it becomes immutable on a blockchain, but also because data is nowadays used to develop, test, and train algorithms. Low-quality training data can result in significant problems, as we will see in the next chapter. The right high-quality data will result in better and smarter algorithms that will return better insights and results. So, within a data-driven, information-centric organisation everyone should be aware of the importance of high-quality data to ensure a positive contribution of the data at hand, especially when blockchain gets involved.

5.3 Data security

Despite the high market value, the bitcoin blockchain has not yet been hacked. Although it is likely that many hackers are trying, especially with a market capitalisation in the hundreds of billions of US dollars. Although a variety of cryptocurrency exchanges have been hacked, which are centralised platforms, blockchain technology itself offers security on several fronts that are very useful for organisations dealing with big data. Security is vital as we have seen in Chapter 3, and blockchain can contribute positively to it. There are three main areas where blockchain can have a positive effect when it comes to data security: confidentiality, integrity, and availability.[379]

5.3.1 Data confidentiality

According to the National Institute of Standards and Technology (NIST), confidentiality refers to "preserving authorised restrictions on information access and disclosure, including means for protecting personal privacy and proprietary information".[380] Confidentiality is increasingly becoming important, especially in its ability to stop identity theft. Identity theft is especially known to harm consumers, although organisations can fall victim to commercial identity theft. This entails using fake identities to obtain information or to bill for services or products that have not been delivered. It happens to all types of organisations, and as recently as April 2017, Facebook and Google disclosed being the victims of a US$100 million commercial phishing scam.[381]

Although many organisations apply asymmetric cryptography or *public key infrastructure* (PKI) to secure communication, PKI relies on a trusted central authority to issue the certificates (key pairs), an authority that can be compromised by hackers using, for example, a man-in-the-middle attack. Blockchain, however, can prevent such attacks by creating public and auditable PKI, thereby decentralising the issuing of certificates. The *keyless signature infrastructure* (KSI) developed by Guardtime is one such decentralised approach. KSI differs from a PKI approach, which is the standard cryptographic toolshed for authentication of data using a digital signature, as signatures can be reliably verified without assuming continued secrecy of the keys.[382] As Mike Gault, co-founder and CEO of Guardtime – a technology company with decades of experience defending networks from nation-state attacks – explained, "signatures generated by KSI can be used as a wrapper (or stored as additional metadata depending on the data model) for any size and type of data such that the signature is cryptographically linked to the underlying data. The cryptographic link allows assertions to be made at a later date regarding the time, integrity and provenance of the data".[383] In 2016, using KSI the company managed to secure all one million e-health records of Estonia.[384] Danube Tech is another tech firm that aims to develop a decentralised PKI and restore control of online identities to their rightful owners. A third company is CertCoin, developed by MIT, which used a distributed ledger to remove the central authority for issuing certification.[385]

A common approach to identity theft is to obtain and exploit usernames or passwords of consumers illegally, sometimes by hacking centralised databases. Organisations are required to take the necessary security measures to prevent hackings. However, any security measure taken by organisations will be in vain if customers still use traditional usernames and passwords, such as *123456* or *password*. In such instances, a decentralised (certification) system can help. As Alex Momot, founder and CEO of Remme – a company that aims to eliminate passwords stated, blockchain can move the responsibility of strong authentication from the user to the organisation.[384] The full encryption of blockchain ensures that data cannot be accessed by unauthorised parties while in transit through untrusted networks. In addition, inherent to blockchain is the immutability of data, preventing parties to illegally adjust data for their own benefit. Therefore, for organisations to ensure confidentiality, blockchain has become key. Increasingly there are a variety of solutions, such as those offered by Guardtime, Danube Tech, and CertCoin.

5.3.2 Data integrity

The second contribution of blockchain in terms of data security is that it ensures integrity, which the NIST defines as "guarding against improper information modification or destruction, and includes ensuring information non-repudiation and authenticity".[380] The combination of hashing and cryptography as well as the decentralised nature of blockchain means that there is no central authority or actor that can adjust the data on the blockchain for its own benefit. Doing so would be known instantly to all other stakeholders with access to the blockchain. With blockchain, any asset can be retrieved or moved only with the corresponding cryptographic key. Therefore, the key becomes an asset that its owner can monetise since it is backed by the underlying asset.[386] Protecting the private key is critical. Therefore, organisations should be aware of how to deal with the cryptographic keys and how to expect customers to deal with them. A lost private key can prevent data on a blockchain from being decrypted or, if it falls into the wrong hands, it can make the data public for those who have access to the private key. Therefore, to ensure integrity, organisations would require educating consumers on how to deal with private keys, as many consumers are not familiar with private and public keys and how they work. As David Treat, managing director financial services and blockchain lead for Accenture said, "leaving cryptographic keys in software sitting on a computer is the equivalent of leaving your house keys under the welcome mat".[386] Although blockchain ensures integrity by making data immutable, there remains a responsibility for organisations and consumers.

5.3.3 Data availability

The third contribution of blockchain to data security is availability, which NIST defines as "ensuring timely and reliable access to and use of information".[380] Distributed ledger technology does not have a single point of failure, which would make a DDoS attack exponentially more difficult. For a blockchain network to be brought down, all nodes within the network should be attacked, which would be the equivalent of robbing a million vaults at the same time, if you were to rob a bank. With some decentralised networks incorporating millions of computers, this becomes highly improbable to achieve. This is why a blockchain-based PKI is so valuable since it does not have a single point of failure (the central authority that issues the certificates).

Since the technology is still so new, there must be a note of caution despite blockchain's potential to improve data security. In the (near) future, currently unknown security issues might appear that could have an impact on how the technology is used and applied. In addition, many startups are experimenting with various new blockchain technologies or cryptographic practices, which, if done incorrectly, could result in potential security breaches. Therefore, as with any digital technology, security should be a key component of any digital strategy to protect consumers, customers, devices, and employees.

5.4 Data privacy and identity

Increasingly, big data is invading consumers' lives and affecting their privacy because the web has become such a centralised platform. As a result, there is a major problem with having centralised organisations collecting so much consumer data and using it to offer personalised advertising to their users. As Jonathan Taplin discussed in his book *Move Fast and Break Things*, organisations that have access to so much data and use it to steer consumer behaviour could directly undermine our democracy.[16] These centralised organisations do not forget or forgive. Especially, because actions (i.e. data) speak louder than words. As long as consumers are not in control of their own data, it is possible that human beings are being defined by their data.

A solution to these problems and the privacy nightmare of Sesame Credit, as discussed in Chapter 4, might be the incorporation of a *self-sovereign identity*. This an identity that is owned and controlled by the person or the device that created it. To develop a *self-sovereign identity*, we need to look differently at identity. In the book *Blockchain: Transforming Your Business and Our World*, we discussed at length how we could develop such a *self-sovereign identity*. In a nutshell, and as discussed in Chapter 4, not only humans have an identity but also devices and organisations. An identity consists of attributes, reputation and a shadow reputation. The combination of these aspects form a user's or device's identity. Although we have an identity infrastructure for people in place, at the moment we do not have an identity infrastructure in place for things. Despite that, we are rushing to connect devices to the internet. This could pose significant future challenges, argues David Birch, an internationally recognised thought leader in digital identity and digital money. According to Birch, the only way to achieve this is by using a decentralised solution. A central database that stores everything about everything would be too dangerous.[387] If an identity consists of ever-changing attributes, a self-sovereign identity restores the control over who has access to those attributes to the consumer, or device. So instead of social media companies or governments owning a person's identity, the consumer is in full control and determines, for each interaction, who gets access to what data points. Attributes, reputation, and shadow reputation result in a unique identity of an individual, organisation, or thing.

As discussed in Chapter 4, a self-sovereign identity can be defined by the 5P's as it is personal (it is about you), portable (meaning you can take your identity and data from one platform to another), private (you control your identity and data), persistent (it does not change without your consent), and protected (your identity cannot be stolen).[242] In other words, a self-sovereign identity is a paradigm shift from today's identity system.

Building the infrastructure might be a challenge, however, as is the cultural change that is required when consumers become solely responsible for securing their private key that is linked to their self-sovereign identity. That is why David Birch believes that banks should be responsible for storing identity information, since they already have a secure infrastructure in place to deal with money. Birch argues that in the future, banks' function as stores of money might become outdated, which is why they should pursue guarding identity and reputation, albeit using a decentralised solution.[387] So, the bank of tomorrow might look completely different than today's bank.

As a result of self-sovereign identities, consumers will become black boxes for organisations, and only the consumer will determine what data will be shared with an organisation. That will significantly change data ownership, how organisations can deal with customer data, and how they can derive insights from it.

5.5 Data ownership

Increasingly, consumers are concerned about who has access to their data. A 2016 Pew Research survey showed that 74 per cent of consumers said it was "very important" to have control over who could get information about them.[388] The study also revealed that transparency of data collection is a concern. Often, consumers do not even realise that they provide companies with the permission to use their data.[389] Websites and applications were one of the first collectors of large amounts of personal data.[390] Centralised organisations, such as Facebook, Google, or Amazon, have too much control over consumer data and this system no longer works. Such centralised control of data ownership by large corporations is harmful to consumers, as it gives centralised organisations enormous power and puts consumers in a vulnerable position. It limits transparency and authenticity because users can only see their own interactions or transactions. It becomes problematic when a third-party vendor, or a partner of an application a user utilises, has access to this information. Especially because companies do not necessarily make it easy for users to know who their partners or affiliates are that purchase the right or have access to the personal data of their users.

According to Craig Mundie, senior adviser to the CEO of Microsoft and the company's former chief research and strategy officer, the focus should shift from data collection and retention to how personal data are used. He suggested annotating data at its point of origin and wrapping it with metadata that includes how the data can be used by whom and under what circumstances.[391] Alex "Sandy" Pentland, author of the book *Social Physics*, adds to this that consumers should have the right to full control over their data and that the protection of personal privacy ensures the future success of a society.[392]

One approach to achieve this is by using the *keyless signature infrastructure* (KSI) approach as discussed earlier. This would enable consumers to add a "wrapper" with metadata and rules governing the use of personal data. This also could contribute to the protection of data when the wrapper is recorded on a blockchain and governed by smart contracts to ensure that organisations can not alter the rules without the consumer knowing. The result is data that consumers can control and own, instead of an organisation. Smart contracts can then be used to change rules securely, depending on certain pre-set conditions and parameters. Therefore, with blockchain, data governance can become intrinsically linked to the data, preventing manipulation and protecting consumers.

Giving consumers full control over their data enables consumers to decide which organisations can use their data, how, and when. Since data on a blockchain is immutable, verifiable, and traceable, it enables data provenance. Data provenance shows how data has changed as well has how ownership and permissions have changed over time, how the data was created and used, and who is in control of that data. This works as if every bit of data has its own vault, including smart contracts linked to it, which regulates who has access to the data, for how long, and for what price. Every transaction can be traced, and the data owner can benefit in real time. So, instead of organisations analysing all consumer data and determining how they will benefit from it, the consumer determines which organisation gets access to the data. This could mean that the organisation has to pay for that data. Data becomes a means of exchange, whereby the consumer can give data away for free to a charity to help a cause he/she believes in, provides required data when booking a flight and requires payment for data when used in a marketing campaign. Within the organisation of tomorrow, the control will move from the organisation to the consumer. Consent moves away from a simple "I accept terms and conditions" to technologically implementing solutions that not only obtain real-time consent from users but also reward consumers for usage of their data. This shift will become a significant but not impossible technical and cultural challenge for organisations to meet. And if you think that this is still far away, you are wrong. As of 2018, multiple organisations are already working on giving consumers back the control over their data. For example, the startup Blockstack is working on a new internet using decentralised applications where users own their data. With Blockstack, users obtain digital keys that enable them to control their data. They use these keys to sign into the applications locally, and they own any data they generate while doing things on the internet. It combines a decentralised domain name server system with blockchain technology to deliver these capabilities. If it succeeds, Blockstack will significantly change the game for organisations.

Today's consumer wants control back in their hands when it comes to their data. Blockchain offers us a chance to bring back this control. It will give consumers a means to monetise the data they create while enhancing the customer experience with better security, privacy, and more control. Given the technical and cultural challenges of such a solution, organisations should begin preparing for this future today.

5.6 Conclusion

The convergence of big data and blockchain will require new solutions and approaches from organisations, regulators, and individuals to ensure that, in the end, everyone can benefit from data. It is a paradigm shift when, suddenly, the creator of the data is in full control, rather than the organisation collecting the data. As a consequence, organisations need to ensure data privacy and security, especially when related to individuals and things, and if they want to share data across organisations. Distributed ledger technology is vital for organisations if they wish to achieve this. Data sharing requires standards to ensure that organisations and consumers can easily share their data across borders and organisations, while remaining in control, keeping data private, and being able to monetise it. However, not only organisations need to adapt, but also regulators and governments need to ensure that consumers become in full control of their own data and to ensure that organisations take data security seriously. A self-sovereign identity will become the new normal, for individuals as well as organisations and things, albeit it might take a while. Governments and policy advisors, therefore, need to understand what a self-sovereign identity entails. They need to draft legislation to force organisations to move to self-sovereign identity systems and to restore control to the individual. In addition, with the advent of the self-sovereign identity, individuals need to become aware of the opportunities and responsibilities that come with being in control of their data, such as keeping a private key truly private. Therefore, it is vital to build awareness of what the convergence of big data and blockchain means for consumers. This requires long-term education of consumers on how to deal with private keys.

Within the organisation of tomorrow, control of data will move to the individual, organisation, or device responsible for creating it. With that, consumer data will become a black box that will require technical consent to access and a monetary reward to use. However, it also enables data-sharing among industry partners and even competitors, opening up new ways of collaboration to make more efficient and effective supply chains. Data vaults will become the new normal, governed by smart contracts that execute automatically once certain pre-set conditions have been met. Watchdogs should ensure that these smart contracts are ethical and treat each customer fairly and equally in similar situations.

Increasingly, we will see organisations bringing governance to the data and the code by applying smart contracts and cryptography to ensure trust in a trustless society. Governance within organisations will shift from boardrooms to developers, who will be responsible for incorporating governance within the code. The convergence of big data and blockchain will not slow down in the coming years. On the contrary, we live in a time of exponential progress, and the coming years will see the development of a plethora of new solutions developed with the customer in mind. The organisation of tomorrow ensures proper data ownership, privacy, and security while enabling individuals, organisations, and things to share and monetise their data. It is a paradigm shift that requires action from all stakeholders involved, including governments, policy makers, and regulators, to ensure that moving to this new paradigm is done in accordance with the law and that it truly protects consumers.

Note

i This chapter is an updated, extended, and paraphrased version of the white paper that I wrote for the Blockchain Research Institute in Toronto: Mark van Rijmenam, "The Convergence of Big Data and Blockchain: Disrupting the Business of Data Analytics", foreword by Don Tapscott, Blockchain Research Institute, December 15, 2017.

Chapter 6

Artificial intelligence to automate the organisation

The organisation of tomorrow will be built around data and will require smart algorithms to make sense of all that data. The first step is to datafy your organisation by collecting data at every process and customer touchpoint. The second step in the organisation of tomorrow is to distribute that data, either using centralised databases in the cloud or decentralised databases using distributed ledger technology. The third step is to analyse all that data and find patterns that will help to make sense of it. The final step in building the organisation of tomorrow is to automate it using artificial intelligence and smart contracts. It will enable organisations to leverage the data and embed smartness in every process and customer touchpoint. It will empower your employees and customers when you apply intelligence and put the smartness to work.

Artificial intelligence is a broad discipline with the objective to develop intelligent machines. AI consists of several subfields: machine learning (ML), a subset of AI that enables machines to learn from data; reinforcement learning, which is a subset of ML and focuses on artificial agents that use trial and error to improve itself; and deep learning, also a subset of ML that aims to mimic the human brain to detect patterns in large data sets and benefit from those patterns. Artificial intelligence has been around since the 1950s, thanks to the work of Alan Turing, who is widely regarded as the father of theoretical computer science and artificial intelligence. Back then, Alan Turing already dreamed of machines that would eventually "compete with men in all purely intellectual fields".[393] Such super intelligent machines would transform societies in unimaginable ways. As Irving John Good, a cryptologist who worked with Alan during the Second World War, stated, these "machines will be feared and respected, and perhaps even loved".[394] Since these early statements, AI research has been overpromising and underdelivering for decades, resulting in several AI-winters. However, due to new successful applications of AI in a variety of domains, driven by tech giants such as Google, Facebook, Tencent, Baidu, Apple, Alibaba, Amazon, and Microsoft, there has been increased attention on AI. Not only as a force for good, but also as a possible catastrophic risk.[395] This has resulted in open source initiatives such as OpenAI, a non-profit AI research company started by Elon

Musk with the objective to "advance digital intelligence in the way that is most likely to benefit humanity as a whole". As we have seen in Chapter 2, artificial intelligence is fundamentally different than human intelligence and, therefore, it requires a fundamentally different approach than any other technology so far. Not only to ensure that your organisation can benefit from AI, but also to prevent AI from inflicting any damage on humans, animals, organisations, and societies as a whole. In other words, the questions we should ask when dealing with AI is how can the social (organisations) and the material (technology) ensure that the artificial behaves as planned and how can the artificial augment the social and the material? This is especially relevant, since the development of AI results in an increasing convergence of the human and the machine. It results in social, technological, political, and ethical implications where AI and humans are becoming interwoven in mutually dependent networks.[396] The more advanced AI will become, the more interwoven these networks will be.

There are three forms of AI, each increasing in intelligence: narrow AI, Artificial General Intelligence (AGI), and Super Artificial Intelligence (SAI). Narrow AI refers to AI that can outperform humans on specific tasks in narrow domains. For example, a trading algorithm or Google Translate on your smartphone. Within narrow AI, artificial intelligence's most common application is about finding patterns in enormous quantities of data and acting autonomously and automatically. This allows companies to automate and improve complex descriptive, predictive and prescriptive analytical tasks and create value at unprecedented level. AGI refers to AI systems having autonomous self-control and self-understanding and the ability to learn new things to solve a wide variety of problems in different contexts. For example, imagine an application capable of driving your car, doing your accountancy, and making you a coffee.[397] The final phase of intelligence is SAI, which is intelligence far exceeding that of any person, however clever.[113, 394] SAI would be able to manipulate and control humans as well as other artificial intelligent agents and achieve domination. SAI is likely to be developed in the (near) future, although it is unclear when we will achieve SAI.[113, 398, 399] How it will look is also still unknown, but it will be fundamentally different to human intelligence. Therefore, it is important that organisations and governments start preparing today by incorporating AI in their operations, ensuring proper regulations and guidelines, preventing biased algorithms and biased data and ensuring that AI behaves as planned.

SAI will likely be developed as part of an intelligence explosion, when AGI, due to fast cycles of self-improvement and reinforcement learning, will reach a stage of superintelligence.[394] This transition to SAI could last several seconds, multiple months, or years.[113] Humans tend to anthropomorphise AI and see AGI on the scale of the village idiot–Einstein. This seriously underestimates the potential impact of SAI. The aforementioned scale is a mere dot on the complete scale of all possible forms of intelligence.[116] Therefore, when governance and ethics are not incorporated in the development of AI, the price that we may need to pay can be very high.[400] The more intelligent AI becomes, the less clear its behaviour becomes to the user.[119] Algorithms are black boxes, especially super intelligent algorithms. We cannot make any assumptions when dealing with SAI, except that it will have full access to its source code and can overrule any control mechanisms that have been implemented by its developers.[113, 125] Therefore, it is important only to build AI that we fully understand. To prepare organisations for situations that they cannot imagine today requires flexibility in design and processes. And to have a thorough theoretical understanding of how and why an artificial agent will make decisions in future, unexpected scenarios.[113, 116, 401, 402] The latter increases the problem, as building AI that behaves as we want it to behave – so-called Responsible AI – requires taking into account future design requirements to prevent future expensive fixes such as the Y2K computer bug.[116, 403] Super intelligent machines may be the last invention mankind need ever make; however, if we do it incorrectly, it may be because it is the end of mankind.[113, 394, 404, 405]

6.1 The algorithmic organisation

Superintelligence is still (very) far away. At first, we face the challenge to develop an algorithmic organisation, which is an organisation built around smart algorithms. Within such organisation, algorithms define company processes, deliver customer services, act when necessary and as such define the way the world works. Algorithms will become the intellect, the interoperability, the connection and the exchange between consumers, things, processes, and information that define the value of businesses. Thanks to machine learning and deep learning, algorithms will be able to understand user and/or device behaviour, learn from users and/or devices and perform the right action accordingly. Algorithms will optimise your supply chain, they will drive our cars, they will monitor your robots, they will replace your call centre, they will determine the right marketing message, they will keep your company secure, and they will even become your boss. Algorithms will be able to do so, because they are able to consider the entire context. Context that is so important, and required, to truly understand what is going on within a particular process, business, device, or changing environment. With sufficient data sources, that each tells its side of the story, algorithms can better determine the right action based on a myriad of data points. This is why the datafication of your business is so important, as you need a large variety of data sources to become context aware.

To understand the importance of context, let's take the example of a self-driving car. A self-driving car that can navigate autonomously can be very useful, it can replace a human, and if it is good at detecting its environment, it can do so safely. However, when a self-driving car would be able to interact with its environment and derive meaning from that, it becomes a lot safer. If it knows that the cars in front of it are about to brake, it can take pre-emptive actions. Or if it knows that the traffic light will be red when it arrives, it can take action accordingly. Sure, it could "see" this information using its sensors, but if it is connected to the other cars around it, it can communicate with them. They can then collectively define the best action for all users on the road, instead of just for themselves.

What applies to self-driving cars, will not only apply to most connected devices, but also to organisations. If an organisation understands its environment, if it is context-aware and can communicate intelligently with other relevant actors in its environment, it can make better decisions based on all those different variables in that context. To achieve this, you need AI. However, only when machine learning is powerful enough to find relevant patterns, anomalies, or correlations can organisations truly benefit from the vast number of data sources in your business. AI will enable you to do all sorts of "fun" things and make your organisation more effective and efficient. Let's look at some examples:

- *Predictive maintenance*: based on the usage of a connected device or product, AI can detect possible equipment failure before it actually happens. This will ensure that a broken product/tool will not corrupt the network and negatively affect your supply chain. For example, an energy company with offshore windmills can use sensors and predictive maintenance to know when a windmill requires some sort of repair, instead of routinely flying by helicopter to do maintenance check-ups. It will not only save organisations a lot of money, but it will also make products safer as they are fixed before they break down.
- *Increased operational efficiency*: deep insights uncovered by machine learning algorithms can be turned into predictions of how to structure your operations based on the requirements and the context. AI-powered machines can autonomously improve the efficiency of manufacturing processes, considering cycle times, quantities used, lead times, temperatures, downtimes, errors, and market demand to improve the output of the machine, whether this is a burger-flipping robot or an advanced robot within a solar panel factory. For example, by incorporating AI into its data centres, Google managed to cut down the energy bill of its data centres by 40 per cent. Because of this result, in 2018 Google put AI fully in charge of its data centre cooling.
- *New revenue streams*: the patterns and insights detected in the vast amount of data can be exploited by organisations that own connected devices. The insights can be sold to other organisations that can benefit from it. Rolls-Royce, for example, uses AI to detect how airlines can save on fuel and sells those insights back to airlines.[406]
- *Better predict (health) risks*: insights from wearables can be used to detect a variety of health problems that could indicate potentially life-threatening

situations that otherwise would remain undetected. Fujitsu, for example, uses AI to detect stress levels through wearables worn by employees and based on the insights can act to improve the workplace environment.[407]

- *Augment your employees*: AI can provide your employees with the right information at the right moment to make them more efficient and effective, but also exoskeletons can augment your employees to make repetitive hard work easier. Ford has been rolling out exoskeletal technology globally to help employees who perform repetitive overhead tasks. Such AI skeletons can help employees accomplish accuracy and precision even when faced with immense complexity.

- *Improve and expand your marketing activities*: the holy grail of marketing is to offer the right product at the right time for the right price to the right customer via the right channel. Using AI, systems can now simulate hundreds and thousands of possible production outcomes or consumer buying behaviour. These scenarios will help organisations to better understand market demand and match that to production outcomes to ensure the right number of products are made for the available demand and at the right price. That information can then be used to enable hyper-personalisation. This has long been seen as the best chance to reach your customer in the information overflow that reaches consumers on a daily basis. Advanced deep learning and machine learning techniques now enable organisations to achieve this by finding patterns in vast data sets and incorporating the context to tailor the right message.

- *Improve your decision-making capabilities*: the best decisions consider the complete context. However, humans are limited in the amount of context they can include in their decisions. In addition, humans are driven by money, sex, and status which could influence their decisions, while existing AI is logical and probabilistically driven only. As such, AI is better able to make independent decisions. As long as the algorithm is not trained using biased data and considers the entire context, AI can significantly improve your decision-making processes.

- *Improve your security*: AI offers our best chance to improve your (digital) security and fight cyber-attacks and malware as it can incorporate many more datasets and information than humans can, as was discussed in Chapter 3. Often, to discover and stop a cyber-attack or a security breach, the context plays an important role. Small anomalies can provide great information about an upcoming attack. AI will enable organisations to move from a responsive behaviour to a predictive behaviour, stopping cyber-attacks and security breaches before they occur, instead of fixing the damage after they have happened.

Of course, these are only a few of the areas where AI can make a difference in the organisation of tomorrow. Every process, if it has been datafied, can be improved and automated using artificial intelligence. An algorithm is simply a well-defined sequence of steps, broken up in ever smaller steps so that a computer can perform the tasks automatically. In the end, artificial intelligence is just like Lego. To build something nice, you need to combine the right pieces in the right way, where each algorithm forms a unique piece in a large scheme.

Let's take this a little bit further. Most of us have played with Lego when we were small. I did, at least, and I absolutely loved it. I can remember the days when my friends and I were playing with Lego for hours on end, constantly creating new structures and building complete cities. We loved it, and I am sure it stimulated my creativity. Even adults still play with Lego, often in group exercises to get some creativity flowing. Lego is a wonderful product, and I thank Ole Kirk Christiansen for inventing it. Lego actually comes in thousands of different shapes and 100 different colours, and with that, the most amazing structures can be built. Each Lego piece can only be used in a small number of ways (depending on the size of the Lego block). Each piece is compatible with every other piece ever created and every Lego piece created is manufactured to an exact degree of precision, with a fault tolerance of only 10 micrometres. With the right pieces and enough creativity, you can build anything you wish. Even a true 1:1 working copy of the magnificent Bugatti Chiron, built from LEGO Technic elements, as was done so in 2018. Artificial intelligence is no different to Lego. You want to make sure that different algorithms are compatible with each other. You want to safeguard that the algorithms are correct and have minimal fault tolerance. Above all, you want to start combining different algorithms to create an algorithmic business with enormous potential. Different algorithms can be used for different applications. Each algorithm should really focus on one thing and be extremely good at that. Building a generic algorithm that is good at everything is, not yet, feasible and it is likely to remain like that for at least the next decade. Therefore, if you wish to incorporate artificial intelligence into your organisation, you should start combining different algorithms in different ways to solve a problem and start small. If you attempt to build the equivalent of the Lego Bugatti when starting with AI, which took 13,438 man-hours to design and build, you will undoubtedly fail. Best would be to start small and see which processes you can automate using artificial intelligence. From there on, you can slowly turn your organisation into an algorithmic business by connecting and combining the different algorithms.

However, when you are developing an algorithmic business, and managing this AI Lego building process, your organisation requires a Chief AI. As with Lego, if you wish to succeed in building something awesome, it helps to know in advance what you want to build and which pieces you require for that. The same goes for AI; which business problem do you try to solve and what technology pieces do you require for that. The business need should always be the driving force, as otherwise, you end up with either the wrong puzzle pieces or a different solution. In both cases, you have spent a lot of resources without addressing the actual business need. Therefore, organisations should prevent that AI transforms from a means to an end, to the goals itself. As Kristian Hammand, chief scientist of Narrative Science and a professor of computer science and journalism at Northwestern University, argues, the Chief AI should not bring "the hammer of AI to the nails of whatever problems are lying around".[408] Specific problems require a specific solution with specific data requirements. To manage this difficult process, you need a Chief AI. He or she should have a thorough understanding of the business, combined with a thorough understanding of the technology. The Chief AI should combine an understanding of the technology with an understanding of what those technologies can do for the organisations strategically. Artificial intelligence serves the business needs, and it is not the business serving the AI needs. Therefore, the Chief AI should be able to understand the business needs and be able to translate these to technical requirements and adapt (existing) AI tools to those needs. It is the Chief AI's responsibility to always keep the strategic business objectives in mind when integrating artificial intelligence into the business. As such, the Chief AI will need to have several important responsibilities combined into one person, rather than splitting them up across the board.

First of all, the Chief AI should act as a liaison between developers and strategists. He/she should be able to foster a team where different team members have a strong fit when engaging with each other, yet who can easily focus on their own respective domains to achieve the business need. Building a team where developers and strategists are aligned is difficult, as usually, the two speak different languages. However, such alignment is key to the success of AI projects. Second, the Chief AI should focus on attracting the right AI talent. Since the Chief AI has a clear understanding of the business objectives of the organisation as well as the available technology already in-house, the Chief AI should be able to attract the right AI talent. By knowing which pieces of the puzzle are missing when solving a business need, the Chief AI is in the right position to hire the best talent for the job. Next to attracting the right AI talent, the Chief AI should be able to retain this talent by offering them interesting and challenging AI projects. Finally, the Chief AI should understand your organisation's data needs. Without data, there is no artificial intelligence. Especially deep neural networks require lots of data to train the algorithms. However, this data should be unbiased and of high-quality. This requires the Chief AI to understand data governance best-practices and be able to apply these to the internal data processes. With artificial intelligence, garbage in means garbage out. Therefore, ensuring the right data governance practices is an important task for the Chief AI.

Artificial intelligence is like Lego; different algorithms can be combined in different ways to solve different problems. Different algorithms have different strengths and weaknesses. The Chief AI should manage the process of offsetting the weakness of one AI with the strengths of another algorithm and vice versa. So, for an organisation to become an algorithmic business, it is more about the application of artificial intelligence rather than the development of new tools and reinventing the wheel. Using AI is as much a natural evolution as the transition to digital business models that many organisations have been through in recent years. AI can offer your organisation significant new value, and one of the areas where this is clearly visible is in the customer service department. Especially in call centres, conversational AI, also known as chatbots, is taking over much of the work previously performed by call centre agents.[409]

6.2 Conversational AI

Since a few years, chatbots are here, and they will not go away any time soon. Facebook popularised the chatbot with Facebook Messenger Bots, but the first chatbot was already developed in the 1960s. MIT professor Joseph Weizenbaum developed a chatbot called ELIZA. The chatbot was developed to demonstrate the superficiality of communication between humans and machines. It used very simple Natural Language Processing (NLP). In 1972, the PARRY chatbot was developed to simulate a paranoid schizophrenic person and in 1995 A.L.I.C.E. was a popular online language-processing bot. Of course, since then we have progressed a lot and, nowadays, it is possible to have lengthy conversations with a computer. Conversational AI consists of an advanced technology that uses NLP so that computers can comprehend human language. The most well-known chatbots are actually personal assistants (PAs), that can help consumers with a variety of tasks. The virtual PAs include Apple's Siri, Amazon's Alexa, Google Assistant, or Baidu's DuerOS.

Chatbots are a very tangible example where humans and machines work together to achieve a goal. A chatbot is a communication interface that helps individuals and organisations have conversations, and many organisations have developed a chatbot. There are multiple reasons for organisations to develop a chatbot, including obtaining experience with AI, engaging with customers, reducing the number of employees required for customer support, disseminating information and content in a way that users are comfortable with and, of course, increasing sales. Chatbots offer a lot of opportunities for organisations. They are an easy way for organisations to become familiar with artificial intelligence. Especially, because conversational agents by itself do not necessarily have to be artificially intelligent, but AI can play into it. In addition, they can be a lot of fun to interact with if developed correctly. But how do you start with conversational AI and how do you build a good and engaging chatbot? Starting with a chatbot is not easy, as there are many different variables to consider:

1   define the reason for a chatbot;
2   create the conversation flow;

3   build the chatbot;
4   train the chatbot;
5   analyse the conversations and the data derived from it;
6   improve the chatbot based on the analytics received.

Let's discuss each step briefly.

(1) Define the reason

First of all, it is important to decide why you would need a chatbot. A chatbot should be a means to an end, but not an end itself. It should alleviate a pain point or increase your customer engagement. It cannot, yet, replace your entire customer support department. Understanding the objective of your chatbot will help define the conversation flow as well as determine the type of chatbot you need. There are different types of chatbots ranging from simple FAQ bots, so-called "on rails" bots, to chatbots that allow the input of free text. The more you allow the user to determine the direction of the conversation, the less the chatbot is in control. That determines how you can use the chatbot.

(2) Create the conversation flow

Designing the conversation within a chatbot is challenging. Not only should you develop a persona that matches your brand personality, but the conversational interface should also be clean, and the chatbot should aim for a positive experience. Therefore, the conversation should not be developed by the developer, but by a copywriter in collaboration with the marketing or communication department. It is important to create the right conversation flow for the right objective. Especially, because an open question can get a lot of different responses. To ask a question in such a way where you get a narrow set of responses is challenging. Therefore, any text that is used within the chatbot should be written by copywriters, and not the developers. This will likely result in some sort of governance structure to be in place (especially in large organisations) around the content that is given as input to the chatbot. Especially, because for some conversations, people feel more comfortable with a chatbot than with a human and you would want to be prepared for that. For example, an Australian financial services company noticed that customers felt more comfortable cancelling with a machine than they do with a human. In such cases, sentiment analysis is an important aspect. It can be used to ensure that the bot has a positive attitude and customers have a positive experience. Unfortunately, people will also always try to break a chatbot by providing nasty comments. An Australian chatbot developer once had to block a 13- or 14-year-old kid because it threatened to kill the bot. Therefore, when developing a chatbot, you should pay attention to the conversational strategy and know that the platform itself is not stand alone. It should be integrated with all the other elements of the business.

(3) Build the chatbot

There are many different chatbot platforms, ranging from platforms that enable simple FAQ chatbots to more advanced chatbots that take into account the context. Once you have decided what platform to use, it is important to decide whether to outsource or not. There are plenty of chatbot developers out there that can help you, but not every developer might offer the right solution. It is important to investigate and ensure that you work with the right chatbot developer. In any case, it is important to provide the chatbot with as much context as possible. Context-aware chatbots can offer a lot of added value because they can offer a positive experience to the end user. Building a chatbot is the easy part, among others because of the many platforms and developers out there. Integrating the chatbot into your systems to incorporate the context is a lot more difficult. The most added value is achieved when, for example, the chatbot is connected to your CRM system and a customer wants to change an address and the chatbot can say: "sure, give me your new address, and I will update the system for you". This is where you see operational efficiency, satisfaction, and the Net Promoter Score (NPS) going up. Context matters. For example, an American chatbot developer created a chatbot that is person-aware, meaning that the chatbot knows who the person is in the chat as the chatbot is linked to internal company systems. So, the moment an employee starts a conversation, the bot already knows the context. As a result, it is a lot smarter because it has a better understanding of the context, resulting in a better experience for the user.

(4) Train the chatbot

With software and AI development come bugs. That is the nature of software development. Therefore, it is important to train and test the chatbot properly. When training the chatbot, the amount of data is important. A million transcripts may seem fine, but if the chatbot will handle ten million conversations, it is not enough. However, if your training data is 10–20 million conversations and you can only get 2–3 million conversations, your foundation is relatively set. It could take a lot of time before the bot will encounter unknown responses. When playing with unsupervised learning, the training data should always be significantly higher than the expected live data.

The best approach is to have machine and person to work together until there is sufficient confidence around the decisions that are coming out of the system. With any training data for AI, it is important that the data is unbiased and of high-quality. If not, the AI will become biased as it does not know any better. Conversational utterances or linguistic statements are going to be biased and, unfortunately, unbiased data is hard to detect automatically. Thus, it requires a lot of manual work, such as pre-processing the data, removing synonyms, removing stop words to remove any bias. Finally, training your chatbot does not stop when the bot is launched. It is a continuous process, and you require analytics to do so.

(5) Analyse the conversations

A conversation is by its nature data-driven and leads to more data. This data can be analysed, and the insights of the analytics can be used to improve the conversational flow of the chatbot as well as the responses. You need thorough testing processes in place to enable output text to be used to train the chatbot again. You do not want biased data to enter the AI. Since all conversations are data, it is possible to extract valuable information from the conversations. This can be done both actively and passively to capture and feed that data into the overall reporting mechanisms. It can be done on a micro level of an individual conversation for an individual user. It can also be done at a macro level for the questions that are being asked and answered by all users. This is called conversational analytics: what was said, how was it said, what was the intent, what is the sentiment, did we accomplish the goal, what was the goal? Where does it fit in the larger context? Without conversational analytics, it is impossible to develop an engaging and successful chatbot. It is also possible to add the capability to jump in and intervene in any conversation, but that sort of deceits the purpose. However, it can be useful because often machines still don't understand the full context and then human intervention can be required.

(6) Improve the chatbot

Of course, all analytics can offer valuable insights to improve the chatbot. Reviewing the transcripts and looking at places where the chatbot did not understand what people are asking can help to build up the data sets to improve the chatbot. Alternatively, you can look at places where the chatbot thinks it got it right, but actually got it wrong and rectify that information to improve the conversation. The objective should be to continuously improve the chatbot, make it increasingly context-aware and better at understanding the intent of the conversation. Such supervised learning will improve the chatbot. This can prevent problems such as Microsoft's *Tay* that used unsupervised learning (meaning the data of the users were used to learn without this data being labelled by humans).

On March 23, 2016, Microsoft launched an AI chatbot on Twitter, called *Tay*. *Tay*'s objective was to have conversations with Twitter users, learn from these interactions and improve its conversations. However, after only 16 hours and 96,000 tweets, Microsoft took *Tay* offline as it had tweeted inappropriate, inflammatory, offensive, and racist messages. This incident resulted not only in a public relations disaster for Microsoft but a global uproar and new impetus for the public debate on the morals of AI.[410–412] The *Tay* case shows how AI may act differently in a real setting than during testing in a controlled environment, even when dealing with relatively simple AI such as a chatbot.[413] It also shows that biased data can negatively affect business outcomes – in this case, resulting in sizeable damage to the Microsoft brand.[410] Many of the organisations use transcript data from customer support or use data from chatbot conversations to further train the chatbot. To prevent problems such as seen with *Tay*, when developing a chatbot the rules for the chatbot need to be provided; that is, what it can do and cannot do, what the boundaries are, when wrong data are entered that should be deleted (one of *Tay's* rules were that it allowed being directed to repeat things, resulting in some of *Tay's* infamous tweets). Chatbots needs to have content that can be classified as a "no-go" zone. It needs to have a list of content and topics it cannot talk about, even if users harass and try to break it. When users talk about those things, it should revert automatically to something else and have a positive sentiment instead.

Chatbots offer a great way for organisations to improve their business. To make it more efficient and increase the customer experience. However, it is important that the chatbot learns in a supervised way and is bound by certain rules that drive the conversation if you wish to prevent examples such as Microsoft's Twitter bot *Tay*. Natural Language Processing is getting better, and in due time, it will become possible to have engaging conversations with a machine.

With all of the benefits that conversational AI brings to businesses, conversational AI will change customer service in a variety of ways. Businesses will be able to serve customers faster, shift and develop front-line staff to creative and strategic roles, such as managing and developing the chatbots. This strategic move can enhance customer service, and help enterprises leverage their employees' knowledge and skills to profit from the company's digital investments. Chatbots can access customer data via the cloud and use the data to quickly and accurately review the customer's transactional or communication history. This allows the chatbot to create an enhanced experience for the customer since it would be knowledgeable of the situation. Customer service representatives who may not be as quick as a chatbot to analyse this data may actually hamper the customer's experience by causing them to wait even longer. The customer's time is important. Furthermore, conversational AI is not limited to one industry. It can be applied to almost any industry, including banking, fashion and hospitality. Enterprises are already putting conversational AI technology in motion now. Here are a few examples.

HSBC. HSBC bank has incorporated a voice recognition system so that its customers can log into their accounts without personal identification numbers (PINs) and passwords. After creating a "voice print" to substitute for passwords or PINs, customers can access their accounts using their voices. The system cross-checks more than 100 identifiers that are unique to the customer, including how fast the customer speaks and even physical attributes, such as the shape of the vocal tract and nasal passage.[414]

ING. ING is catapulting open banking by investing in conversational banking technologies to improve banking experiences for its customers and to stay competitive. For example, the company is experimenting with humanoid robots named Ginger and Pepper, which could teach children about finances thanks to voice-driven technology made capable through advancements in NLP. The robots were also used on a trial basis in supermarkets for prospective customers.[415]

Bank of America. Its chatbot digital assistant, Erica, helps the bank's customers make better financial decisions by offering financial advice based on the customer's banking habits using cognitive messaging, artificial intelligence, and predictive analytics. The bot can suggest how much the customer can save to reach a specified financial goal, such as saving US$100 towards paying down a credit card. The bot also provides suggestions using predictive analytics to determine the spending and saving habits of the retail banking consumer. Banking customers can use the bot via text messaging or a mobile app to ask questions and receive financial advice.[416]

Spring. Mobile fashion e-commerce marketplace Spring is using its chatbot Spring Bot within the Facebook Messenger app as a modern concierge for customers. The bot acts as a personal shopping service for customers. The bot is demonstrative of how retailers can answer customers' questions and drive purchases online and via mobile devices.[417]

Duolingo. Duolingo has incorporated chatbots into the iPhone version of its free apps to help users learn a foreign language. These Duolingo bots are designed to hold a conversation naturally with the user via text messaging. However, the company expects to expand this to use voice recognition technology in the future.[418]

The Holiday Inn Osaka Namba hotel. The hotel uses a chatbot to check in guests, make restaurant reservations, and act as the hotel's concierge. With the chatbot, guests can get an answer to questions about hotel check-in and check-out times and other pertinent details during a stay at any time of the day. This helps to improve operational efficiency as chatbots, obviously, do not need a break.[419]

Marriott. The hotel chain employs chatbots by using Facebook Messenger to prioritise relationships it has with its customers and to create an extra moment of engagement. Aloft – a Marriott hotel brand – also employs chatbots to help customers with requests with its ChatBotlr chatbot. Travelers can access ChatBotlr via text messaging for service requests.[420]

Chatbots can help improve your customer service, and they are a clear example of the potential AI has for organisations. However, the example of *Tay* also shows that even in relatively simple AI application as a chatbot, there are still possible dangers that can cause significant harm to consumers and organisations.

6.3 The dangers of AI

Artificial intelligence offers a lot of advantages for organisations by creating better and more efficient organisations, improving customer services with conversational AI and reducing a wide variety of risks in different industries. Although we are only at the beginning of the AI revolution that is upon us, we can already see that artificial intelligence will have a profound effect on our lives, both positively and negatively. In 2018, Elon Musk praised the work of OpenAI after a team of five neural networks had defeated five humans, who ranked in the top 99.95 percentile of players worldwide, in the popular game Dota 2. The five bots had learned the game by playing against itself at a rate of a staggering 180 years per day. In April 2019, the OpenAI team consisting of five improved bots, for the first time, beat a reigning world champion e-sports team. With 45,000 years of practice, the five bots successfully navigated difficult strategic decisions. The game requires strong teamwork among the five players and, therefore, the achievement is quite remarkable. It is more evidence that AI is rapidly becoming more advanced. However, directly after the five bots beat the five humans 2–1 in 2018, Musk cautioned for the power of AI by urging that OpenAI should focus on AI that works with humans, instead of against humans.[421] His statement is in line with his previous warnings for AI, which Musk believes could result in a robot dictatorship or an AI-arms race amongst superpowers that could be the most plausible cause for the Third World War.[422] Therefore, we need to focus on developing Responsible AI, where organisations exercise strict control, supervision, and monitoring on the performance and actions of AI.

Failures in achieving Responsible AI can be divided into two, non-mutually exclusive categories: philosophical failure and technical failure.[116] Developers can build the wrong thing, so that even if AGI or SAI is achieved, it will not be beneficial to mankind. Or developers can attempt to do the right thing, but fail because of a lack of technical expertise, which would prevent us from achieving AGI or SAI in the first place. The border between these two failures is thin, because "in theory, you ought first to say what you *want*, then figure out *how* to get it. In practice, it often takes a deep technical understanding to figure out what you want".[116] Not everyone believes in the existential risks of AI, simply because they say AGI or SAI will not cause any problems or because if existential risks do indeed exist, AI itself will solve these risks. Meaning that in both instances nothing happens.[423] Nevertheless, SAI is likely to be extremely powerful and dangerous if not controlled properly, simply because AGI and SAI will be able to reshape the world according to its preferences. This may not be human-friendly. Not because it would hate humans, but because it would not care about humans. It is the same that you might go "out of your way" to prevent on stepping on an ant when walking, but you would not care about a large ants' nest if it happened to be at a location where you plan a new apartment building. In addition, SAI will be capable of resisting any human control.[117, 424] As such, AGI and SAI offer different risks than any other known existential risk humans faced before, such as nuclear war, and requires a fundamentally different approach.

To make matters worse, algorithms are extremely literal. They pursue their (ultimate) goal literally and do exactly what is told while ignoring any other, important, consideration. An algorithm only understands what it has been explicitly told. Algorithms are not yet, and perhaps never will be, smart enough to know what they do not know. As such, they might miss vital considerations that we humans might have thought of automatically. Therefore, it is important to tell an algorithm as much as possible when developing it. The more you tell, i.e. train, the algorithm, the more it considers. Next to that, when designing the algorithm, you must be crystal clear about what you want the algorithm to do and not to do. Algorithms focus on the data they have access to and often that data has a short-term focus. As a result, algorithms tend to focus on the short term. Humans, most of them anyway, understand the importance of a long-term approach. Algorithms do not, unless they are told to focus on the long term. Therefore, developers (and managers) should ensure algorithms are consistent with any long-term objectives that have been set within the area of focus. This can be achieved by offering a wider variety of data sources (the context) to incorporate into its decisions and focusing on so-called soft goals as well (which relates to behaviours and attitudes in others). Using a variety of long-term and short-term focused data sources, as well as offering algorithms soft goals and hard goals, will help to create a stable algorithm.[62]

A mixed data approach can be used by the algorithm to calibrate the different data sources for their relative importance, resulting in better predictions and better algorithms. The more data sources and the more diverse these are, the better the predictions of the algorithms will become. As such, AI learns from its environment and improves over time due to deep learning and machine learning. AI is not limited by information overload, complex and dynamic situations, lack of complete understanding of the environment (due to unknown unknowns), or overconfidence in its own knowledge or influence. It can take into account all available data, information, and knowledge and is not influenced by emotions.[114] Although such learning would allow AI to rework its internal workings, AI is not yet sentient, cognisant, or self-aware. That is, it cannot interpret meaning from data.[114] AI might recognise a cat, but it does not know what a cat is. To the AI, a cat is a collection of pixel intensities, not a carnivorous mammal often kept as an indoor pet.[114]

Another problem with AI is that they are black boxes. Often, we do not know why an algorithm comes to a certain decision. They can make great predictions, on a wide range of topics, but that does not mean AI decisions are error-free. On the contrary, as we have seen with *Tay*. AI "preserves the biases inherent in the dataset and its underlying code", resulting in biased outputs that could inflict significant damage.[114, 175] In addition, how much are these predictions worth, if we don't understand the reasoning behind it? Automated decision-making is great until it has a negative outcome for you or your organisation and you cannot change that decision or, at least, understand the rationale behind that decision. Whatever happens inside an algorithm is sometimes only known to the organisation that uses it, yet quite often this goes beyond their understanding as well. Therefore, it is important to have explanatory capabilities within the algorithm, to understand why a certain decision was made.

6.3.1 Explainable AI

Researchers and developers can only see the actions of AI and infer the strategy from this but cannot see the reasoning behind it. This is why researchers are working on developing explainable AI (XAI) to help us understand why a certain decision was made.[62, 112–114, 119, 425–429] XAI is a new field of research that tries to make AI more understandable to humans. The term was first coined in 2004 as a way to offer users of AI an easily understood chain of reasoning on the decisions made by the AI, in this case especially for simulation games.[119] XAI relates to explanatory capabilities within an algorithm to help understand why certain decisions were made.[62] The more sophisticated AI becomes, the less obvious its behaviour becomes to the user of AI. With machines getting more responsibilities, they should be held accountable for their actions.[119, 400, 430] XAI should present the user with an easy to understand chain of reasoning for its decision.[119, 426] When AI is capable of asking itself the right questions at the right moment to explain a certain action or situation, basically debugging its own code, it can create trust and improve the overall system. Especially if it is able to explain its actions in "human-understandable concepts and terms", also known as *plain English*.[427, 429] The objective of XAI is to ensure that an algorithm can explain its rationale behind certain decisions and explain the strengths or weaknesses of that decision.[431] Explainable AI, therefore, can help to uncover what the algorithm does not know, although it is not able to know this itself. Consequently, XAI can help to understand which data sources are missing in the mathematical model, which can be used to improve the AI. In doing so, XAI can be useful for developers to create better, more trustworthy algorithms, which in the end could lead to Responsible AI.

In addition, XAI can help prevent so-called self-reinforcing loops. Self-reinforcing loops are a result of feedback loops, which are important and required to constantly improve an algorithm. However, if the AI misses soft goals and only focuses on the short term, or if the AI is too biased because of the usage of limited historical and/or biased data, these feedback loops can become biased and discriminatory. Self-reinforcing loops, therefore, should be prevented. An example of what can go wrong when this occurs happened in 2011 when a book about flies came to be priced at US$23 million on Amazon. Thanks to Amazon's algorithmic pricing, two booksellers on Amazon started competing automatically against each other. Amazon vendors can use algorithmic pricing to automatically change their pricing based on what the competitor is doing. Thanks to this automatic bidding, Peter Lawrence's book *The Making of a Fly* was priced at US$23,698,655.93 before the algorithm was stopped. Although the bookseller would have made a nice profit if it would have been sold, it shows that unexpected bugs can sneak into an algorithm. Using explainable AI, researchers can understand why such self-reinforcing loops appear (in the case of the book on flies it was because pricing parameters were missing, allowing the price to rise continuously until a human intervened), why certain decisions have been made and, as such, understand what the algorithm does not know. Once that is known, the algorithm can be changed by adding additional (soft) goals and adding different data sources to improve its decision-making capabilities.

Explainable AI should be an important aspect of any algorithm. When the algorithm can explain why certain decisions have been/will be made and what the strengths and weaknesses of that decision are, the algorithm becomes accountable for its actions. Just like humans are. It can then be altered and improved if it becomes (too) biased or if it becomes too literal, resulting in better AI for everyone.

6.3.2 Incorporating AI ethics

Ethical AI is completely different from XAI and it is an enormous challenge to achieve. The difficulty with creating an AI capable of ethical behaviour is that ethics can be variable, contextual, complex, and changeable.[401, 432, 433] The ethics we valued 300 years ago are not the same in today's world. What we deem ethical today might be illegal tomorrow. As such, we do not want ethics in AI to be fixed, as it could limit its potential and affect mankind.[401] AI ethics is a difficult field because the future behaviour of advanced forms of a self-improving AI are difficult to understand if the AI changes its inner workings without providing insights on it; hence, the need for XAI. Therefore, ethics should be part of AI design today to ensure ethics is part of the code. We should bring ethics to the code.[401] However, some researchers argue that ethical choices can only be made by beings that have emotions, since ethical choices are generally motivated by these.[434, 435, 436] Already in 1677, Benedictus de Spinoza, one of the great rationalists of seventeenth-century philosophy, defined moral agency as "emotionally motivated rational action to preserve one's own physical and mental existence within a community of other rational actors". However, how would that affect artificial agents and how would AI ethics change if one sees AI as moral things that are sentient and sapient? When we think about applying ethics in an artificial context, we have to be careful "not to mistake mid-level ethical principles for foundational normative truths".[401] In addition, the problem we face when developing AI ethics, or machine ethics, is that it relates to *good* and *bad* decisions. Yet, it is unclear what *good* or *bad* means. It means something different for everyone across time and space. What is defined good in the Western world might be considered bad in Asian culture and vice versa. Furthermore, machine ethics are likely to be superior to human ethics. First, because humans tend to make estimations, while machines can generally calculate the outcome of a decision with more precision.[400] Second, humans do not necessarily consider all options and may favour partiality, while machines can consider all options and be strictly impartial. Third, machines are unemotional, while with humans, emotions can limit decision-making capabilities (although, at times, emotions can also be very useful in decision-making). Although it is likely that AI ethics will be superior to human ethics, it is still far away. The technical challenges to instil ethics within algorithms are numerous because as their social impact increases, ethical problems increase as well.[113, 437] However, the behaviour of AI is not only influenced by the mathematical models that make up the algorithm, but also directly influenced by the data the algorithm processes. Poorly prepared or biased data results in incorrect outcomes: *garbage in is garbage out.*[175] While incorporating ethical behaviour in mathematical models is a daunting task, reducing bias in data can be achieved more easily using data governance, as we discussed in Chapter 5.

High-quality, unbiased data, combined with the right processes to ensure ethical behaviour within a digital environment, could significantly contribute to AI that can behave ethically.[175] Of course, from a technical standpoint ethics is more than just usage of high-quality, unbiased data and having the right IT processes in place. It includes instilling AI with the right ethical values that are flexible enough to change over time. To achieve this, we need to consider the morals and values that have not yet developed and remove those that might be wrong. To understand how difficult this is, let's see how Nick Bostrom – Professor in the Faculty of Philosophy at Oxford University and founding Director of the Future of Humanity Institute – and Eliezer Yudkowsky – an artificial intelligence theorist concerned with self-improving AIs – describe achieving ethical AI:[113]

> The theoretical concept of coherent extrapolated volition (CEV) is our best option to instil the values of mankind in AI. CEV is how we would build AI if "we knew more, thought faster, were more the people we wished we were, had grown up farther together; where the extrapolation converges rather than diverges, where our wishes cohere rather than interfere; extrapolated as we wish that extrapolated, interpreted as we wish that interpreted".

As may be clear by CEV, AI ethics is a highly challenging field that requires special attention if we wish to build Responsible AI. Those stakeholders involved in developing AGI and SAI should play a key role in achieving AI ethics. XAI and AI ethics are one approach to Responsible AI. The other approach to achieving Responsible AI is to prevent bad AI from happening in the first place. Hence, the need for control methods when developing AI.

6.3.3 Control methods and the principal-agent problem

AI enables new forms of interaction between humans, resulting in interactions with different levels of intensity and involvement.[43] Networks involving some sort of technology can create complicated strategies involving unexpected technical and social implications.[59] Already, this behaviour is showing in AI-only networks, where algorithms start competing against each other, develop new encryption methods, or create their own secret language unsolicited as we saw in Chapter 2.[112, 122, 123] The behaviour of actors changes the state of the network, which is itself the product of previous actions.[59] As a result, a self-reinforcing feedback loop can result in unexpected behaviour.[113] The challenge is to understand how we can prevent AI agents behaving in ways that do not comply with the intention of the developers. To prevent this from happening, researchers, developers, and organisations should develop control methods. These can either be technical (adding a kill-switch to an AI that destroys the AI once it does something unexpectedly and harmful) or strategic control methods (having a board of advisors or trustees recommend in which area research is allowed or not allowed).

That AI will show unexpected behaviour is almost a given. Humans have flaws, and consequently, algorithms will have flaws. Two of the lessons we should take away from the *Tay* disaster is that algorithms will behave differently in a live environment than in a testing environment and that technology itself is not neutral, as discussed in Chapter 2. Technology is an integral part of a certain phenomenon and how humans use that technology defines whether the outcome is good or bad. A hammer can be used to build a house or to kill someone, just as a tweetbot can be used for friendly conversations or for humiliation. Hence, there are people who create AI with the intention to cause harm. A good example of that are viruses and, more recently, *deep fakes*. *Deep fakes* are the latest trend in fake news, and it consists of face-swapping celebrity faces onto porn performers' bodies. It was first revealed in 2017 that a Redditor named "deepfakes" was enjoying his hobby. However, since then there has been an explosion of face-swapped porn, and the implications are truly terrifying. Within weeks, AI-assisted fake porn became scarily easy for anyone to perform. While most of the videos are still related to porn, more users are now experimenting with the technology to place any face in any video. That is a truly scary application of AI because it means you could fake reality. But it gets scarier as in the same year, researchers from the University of Washington created a program that was capable of manipulating a video by turning an audio clip into a realistic lip-synced video.[438]

Combine this with *deep fakes* technology, and you have a technology that lets you have anyone say anything on video, even if he or she did not say so or was not present at a certain location. The consequences of this are enormous and were first shown soon after the *deep fakes* scandal when Trump started denying his vulgar remarks in the famous "Access Hollywood" tape, which he said were real only months before.[439] While *deep fakes* can be used to alter reality, viruses are intended to cause harm to humans and organisations. Unfortunately, *deep fakes*, are not the only problems that can be caused with AI. Fake news is also becoming increasingly easier to develop and more difficult to detect thanks to AI. In 2019, OpenAI developed an AI called GPT2. This predictive text software is so efficient in writing a text based on just a few lines of input, that OpenAI decided not to release the comprehensive research to the public. GTP2 was trained on a dataset of eight million web pages. With approximately 1.8 billion websites available, this is a relatively small training set. Despite that, the system has become capable of producing reasonable samples for 50 per cent of the time. Out of fear of misuse of the tool. Already, GPT2 has been described as the text version of deep fakes.

However, with AI there is an additional problem. Even when AI is created with the best intentions, it can still cause harm. I am sure that it was not Microsoft's intention to create a racist chatbot. What we are dealing with here is the principal-agent problem. This dilemma is predominantly known in political sciences or economics but is increasingly becoming relevant for computer sciences as well. It means that the principal, in this case, the developer, researcher, or manager, has different intentions and objectives than the agent, in this case the AI agent. Solving the principal-agent problem with AI is difficult because with an advanced AI the objective might change over time or the AI might not sufficiently consider the objectives of the principal (if developed incorrectly). If that happens, AI can turn rogue and cause significant havoc. Since it is impossible for humans to describe all possible outcomes of an AI, not aiming to solve the principal-agent problem can easily result in AI turning bad.

Traditionally, governance is focused on ensuring different stakeholders within an organisation are aligned. It focuses on the relationship and interactions between different groups. For example, the directors of an organisation, the board of an organisation, and the owners of an organisation, whom all may have different objectives and perspectives. Corporate governance can then be used to better align these objectives and perspectives, which is beneficial for an organisation. This tends to be done by the principal exercising control (using strategic and financial control methods such as budgets, and KPIs), monitoring the performance of the agent (such as monitoring the implementation of strategy or planning the succession of the CEO) and supervising the agent (through coaching or mentoring) to protect the principal's interests.[440] These existing corporate governance mechanisms of controlling, monitoring, and supervising work well when both agent and principal are human. However, strategic and financial control methods, succession planning or monetary rewards, and coaching or mentoring no longer work when the agent is artificial. Simply because AI is not driven by human motivations, but only by logic.[114, 441, 442]

However, when dealing with artificial agents, controlling, monitoring, and supervising can still be applied, but these governance practices should be applied differently (see Table 6.1).

Controlling an artificial agent can be done by ensuring that the code is written correctly and without bugs (which until now has proven to be impossible as code always contains bugs). That we only use bias-free (training) data, hence the importance of data governance, and that we understand the decision-making processes of an algorithm. This involves ensuring that there is an overarching rule-set that drives the logic of the AI and that the AI is limited to one specific task, just like Lego blocks. In addition, it involves developing national and supranational AI regulations to prevent individuals or organisations from intentionally developing harmful AI. This means that governments should follow the example set by Dubai in 2017 and also appoint a Minister of AI. Dubai did so as it wants to become the world's most prepared country for AI. If we wish to remain in control, and not be surprised by increasingly advanced AI, organisations and countries should follow Dubai's example of appointing a senior leader responsible for AI. Those leaders can then form overarching committees, similar to the Eurogroup that holds informal meetings of the finance ministers of the Eurozone to exercise political control over the euro, to establish guidelines and policies in terms of AI development. Although such AI regulation should not hinder technical developments, it should also advocate measures to ensure safe AI and to help

Table 6.1 Governance of artificial agents

Governance	Management	Artificial agents
Control	Strategic and financial control methods[443–446]	Applying control methods such as code testing, ensuring an overarching rule-set that drives conversations, limiting AI to one specific task and developing AI regulations
Monitoring	Monitoring activities such as succession planning, monitoring strategy implementation and evaluation and rewarding of C-level executives[440, 447–450]	Analytics such as conversation analytics or sentiment analysis to understand where improvements are required
Supervision	Coaching, mentoring or even steering of the agent[451–453]	Feeding analytics and unbiased training data back into the system using supervised learning

organisations and societies understand the impact of a fundamentally different form of intelligence.

Monitoring an artificial agent can be done using analytics. Analytics, as we have discussed in Chapter 2, refers to using data sources and statistical methods to understand how a digital agent performs and obtains insights about what has happened.[169–171] There is a wide variety of analytics, ranging from conversation analytics to anomaly detection, that organisations can use to identify problems with AI. Analytics offer insights to improve AI and, using subsequent insights, the principal can monitor if the agent behaves as planned and can take action if required. As such, analytics is an important monitoring tool.[454]

Supervising a digital agent can be done by feeding the insights from analytics back into the algorithm and using unbiased training data to train the AI. Such supervised learning, whereby a human agent controls the data that is used to train the AI, can help the AI learn. Unsupervised learning, whereby the AI learns using unfiltered input data, as was the case with *Tay*, can have unwanted consequences. At least, as long as the AI is not yet smart enough to detect and remove biased data by itself.[455] Preventing unsupervised learning can, therefore, contribute to solving the principal-agent problem as the input data is pre-processed, cleansed, and any bias removed,[175] thereby steering the AI in the right direction.

Bug-free code, unbiased data, and developing ethical and explainable AI are three enormous challenges that we need to overcome if we wish to minimise the risks of AI becoming a force for the bad. Nevertheless, controlling, monitoring, and supervising seem a suitable approach for developers, managers, or organisations to reduce the effects of the principal-agent problem when dealing with AI. It will be easier to steer AI in the right direction if the underlying code, assumptions, and objectives are correct. They will not likely solve the principal-agent problem, just like controlling, monitoring, and supervising does not solve the principal-agent problem when dealing with human agents. However, as software will always have bugs, problems with artificial agents can be reduced with the right governance practices. Therefore, if we wish to ensure AI remains benevolent in the future, we should start today to make sure that any AI developed incorporates human values, uses unbiased data, is understandable and bug-free. A huge challenge, but one we cannot ignore.

6.4 Conclusion

AI is going to become a lot more involved in the organisation of tomorrow. The artificial will be as important as the social or the material. Especially those organisations that have managed to datafy their processes will be able to benefit the most from AI. They have the prerequisite to developing intelligent algorithms: data. With that, artificial agents can rapidly become more intelligent. Although it is unsure what AI will bring us in the future, it is safe to say that there will be many more missteps before we manage to build Responsible AI. Such is the nature of humans. Machine learning has huge risks, and although extensive testing and governance processes are required, not all organisations will do so for various reasons. Those organisations that can implement the right stakeholder management to determine whether AI is on track or not and pull or tighten the parameters around AI if it is not will stand the best chance to benefit from AI. In the end, AI can bring a lot of advantages to organisations, but it requires the right regulation and control methods to prevent bad actors from creating bad AI and to prevent well-intentioned AI from going rogue. Therefore, if we learn from our mistakes and develop an effective set of preconditions, control methods, and ethical guidelines in the coming years, we might be able to ensure a proper transition from a human intelligence-driven organisation to an AI-driven organisation.

Within the organisation of tomorrow, humans and AI will work together. Thereby augmenting humans and removing the mundane tasks. AI can disrupt and improve many of the existing company processes, and as a result, humans can focus more on the people (your employees and customers) within an organisation. In today's organisations, a lot of employees have to deal with a lot of administrative tasks and bureaucratic processes. In the future, such tasks and processes will be managed by AI. As a consequence, organisations will not only become a lot more humane but also more efficient and effective. Moreover, as the World Economic Forum predicts, it will also result in a shift in *how* we work.[456] Work will move away from full-time work and move to a lot more contract-based, flexible work. With a focus on output instead of input. This will also require adaptation by governments to enable organisations to hire more flex-workers without the requirement to offer employees fixed contracts, as those will become scarce for most of the jobs (except for those jobs in software/hardware development and jobs based on distinctively human traits).

Consequently, the increasing convergence of humans and machines will result in social, technological, political, and ethical implications, where artificial intelligence and humans are becoming increasingly interwoven in mutually dependent networks. Within these human-machine networks, both artificial and non-artificial agents interact in the same context, which will significantly transform existing organisations. It will require organisations to offer lifelong learning for their employees, and in return, it will require flexibility and adaptation of those employees. Therefore, only those organisations that are capable of managing such a dramatic transformation will be able to remain competitive. It is time to start preparing, as there is not a moment to waste.

Chapter 7

Turning your organisation into a data organisation

We live in exponential times, and the world around us is changing faster than ever before. New technologies that are constantly being developed are the main driver. Most of these technologies have one thing in common; they create data. The fast-changing, uncertain, and ambiguous environment that organisations operate in today, requires organisations to rethink all their internal business processes and customer touchpoints: it requires every organisation to think and act like a software company, which often means adjusting the purpose and business model of the organisation.[11] Doing so involves applying some sort of analytics to understand the context of the organisation and to improve decision-making capabilities by interpreting different signals. In addition, blockchain can be incorporated to decentralise the organisation by implementing cryptography to create trust among actors involved and move to an autonomous structure by automating decision-making using smart contracts while embedding governance in the code. Organisations can use smart algorithms to define company processes, deliver customer services, act when necessary and as such define how the organisation operates. However, embedding smartness within the organisation using AI requires new governance practices that cannot be embedded in the code. Instead, it involves thoroughly testing the code of AI, analysing the behaviour of the artificial intelligent actor, and supervising its learning abilities. When incorporating big data analytics, blockchain, and AI, the organisation becomes a data organisation, regardless of the product or service that it offers. Companies such as Google, Facebook, WeChat, or Amazon have long understood this paradigm shift and have collected data rigorously since their inception. These organisations use technology to facilitate collaboration between stakeholders and where human-to-human interactions are increasingly replaced with human-to-machine and even machine-to-machine types of interactions. With more organisations starting to understand the need to become a data company, organisations in the not too distant future will become involved in numerous interactions among humans and machines, resulting in complex strategies and unexpected technical, ethical, and social implications. However, knowing that these technologies are required is one thing, incorporating them within your organisation and actually becoming a data organisation is a different ballgame. Therefore, in this chapter, I would like to offer you the tools to start transforming your business into a data organisation, today. Only those organisations most capable of incorporating data and data-related technologies will stand the best chance to remain competitive in this data-driven future.

So far, we have discussed the three main technologies that will make up the organisation of tomorrow: big data analytics, blockchain, and artificial intelligence. Each of these technologies affects the organisation differently. Big data analytics enable the empowerment of your employees and customers as they will have a better understanding of their environment and, hence, can make better decisions. Whether analytics is applied to improve your marketing message, optimise your production flow, or create better products, the key to these insights is having sufficient data. Blockchain and distributed ledger technologies can result in more efficient, effective, and transparent supply chains, faster settlement times for transactions, and reduction in fraud and corruption. The key to new collaboration among industry partners is having high-quality data that becomes immutable, verifiable, and traceable. Artificial intelligence can help automate many of the processes in your organisation, which will result in a changing job market on the one hand, but also a requirement for new skills within your organisation. However, it does require an infinite stream of unbiased, well-cleansed data.

Hence, if your organisation wants to succeed in becoming a data organisation that remains relevant and competitive tomorrow, the first step is having infinite streams of complete, high-quality, well-cleansed, unbiased data that is collected at every process and customer touchpoint within your organisation. The second step of transforming your organisation into a data organisation is to distribute the data, thereby facilitating new ways of collaboration with industry partners using distributed ledger technologies and making the data available to all your employees regardless of their location using cloud computing. Not all problems require a blockchain solution, but to enable seamless collaboration, data needs to be available in the cloud. Once company-owned data has been made easily accessible and exchangeable with internal and external stakeholders, it allows for more efficiency, transparency, security, and privacy across every step in the value chain. Of course, in the near future this will require a different approach for data that is now owned by the organisation (such as customer data). The third step in building the organisation of tomorrow is to analyse the available data for insights, patterns and anomalies using descriptive, predictive, and prescriptive analytics. This will provide you with the insights in your environment and the context to improve your decision-making. The final step will be to automate your internal processes and your decision-making. Smart algorithms will enable automation, but it is key that you have developed the right governance practices to ensure responsible AI. This leads us to the secret sauce to build the organisation of tomorrow:

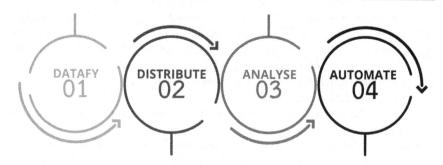

Figure 7.1 The D^2 + A^2 model

This *D^2 + A^2 model* consists of several actions, stakeholders, and required technologies that will help you prepare your organisation for tomorrow. Let's discuss each step in the *D^2 + A^2 model* to explain why it is important, how you can approach it and what technologies will enable it.

7.1 Datafy

Transforming your organisation into a data organisation requires data above all. In order to achieve that, the first step is to datafy your organisation. Datafication is the process of making a business data-driven, by transforming social action into quantified data. It involves collecting (new) data from various sources and processes using IoT devices and/or creating detailed customer profiles based on all (digital) customer touchpoints. Datafying your organisation starts by making your office, your workplace, your processes, and your products smart. This will make previously "invisible" processes traceable so that they can be monitored, analysed, and optimised. Thanks to the lowering costs of sensors, increasing low-cost bandwidth, cheap availability of cloud computing and processing capacity, as well as numerous connected devices it has become easier and cheaper to make these processes smart. It will enable you to capture data consistently and universally across different processes, products, and workplaces. The data can then be used to create insights using analytics or enable actions using smart contracts. Of course, data quality is of utmost importance when datafying your organisation. Low-quality and biased data will be useless and can even cause damage to your organisation and customers. When looking at your processes, look at it from a new angle. The datafication of your organisations opens a whole new line of possibilities, which you should approach from an out-of-the-box perspective. Only then will you be able to come up with real added value for your organisation.

There is hardly any limit to the datafication of your processes and your workplaces, as long as you comply with regulations that protect your employees and customers. However, the datafication of personality using websites and applications is a lot more difficult. Increased attention to privacy and security and regulations such as the GDPR make storing sensitive customer data increasingly harder. The process of datafication of your customers has traditionally been done by collecting and storing any data related to customer interactions. This allowed organisations to mix and match various customer data sources to obtain a complete 360-degrees of the customer. New legislation has made and will make it more difficult to continue to collect any type of customer data. In fact, there is a clear tendency to decentralised control of customer data, as we discussed in Chapter 5, where the consumer is in full control of their identity and data. In October 2018, Sir Tim Berners-Lee – the founder of the internet – revealed his new solution to achieve this: the Solid ecosystem, supported by his new venture Inrupt. The Solid ecosystem enables every internet user to decide where to store their data and how to share it with others. This can be any type of data, including articles, images, videos, calendar invites, wearable data, contacts in your address book, etc. Users can store this data on a Solid POD (Personal Online Datastore), which can be stored on a personal server or through one of the listed providers. Users can then connect their Solid POD using a personalised API to any of the platforms, giving them full control over their own data, instead of companies such as Facebook or Google. Of course, this poses significant challenges for organisations that want to create 360-degree customer profiles. All of a sudden, they can no longer simply collect and store any kind of customer data, but they will need to ask for permission to get access to the data. That is a significant change in how to deal with customer data and will require the organisation of tomorrow to rethink its customer data collection methodologies. It could result in customers refusing you their data, or only providing it in return for payment. Thus, when datafying your organisations from a customer perspective, it becomes vital to do so while taking customer privacy in mind and taking into account that you might not be able to obtain all the information you used to get.

Therefore, the first step that you can take is to identify those processes within your organisation that you want to improve. While evaluating the processes, investigate what you need to do to collect data from those processes. Do you need to install sensors to monitor activities or do you need to collect more data to create detailed customer profiles? Once you have identified the required technologies, start collecting the data. When you start datafying your organisation, the idea would be to start small, with simple processes that are relatively easy to datafy. Once you have gained experience with datafying your processes, you can focus on more complex processes. The datafication of your organisation is the first phase to transforming into a data organisation. The stakeholders within this process are your employees, customers, and the business processes available within your organisation and supply chain. The technology required for this is smart sensors and IoT devices that will be used to streamline and improve existing business processes. The result will be a significant change in culture. Not only will employees behave differently if they are aware that their behaviour is monitored on the workplace, but it will also make their work easier as they have more data at hand.

7.2 Distribute

Once you are collecting data within every process and customer touchpoint, it is, of course, important to store that data in order to use it. There are two ways of doing so. Ideally, the organisation of tomorrow will make use of a combination of these two technologies. First of all, as discussed in Chapter 4, you can distribute the data using distributed ledger technologies such as blockchain. It is important to note that distributed ledgers are not distributed to distribute data but to make the system resilient. The key is making data with high integrity accessible to multiple stakeholders. As such, the key for using blockchain is integrity not distribution and, currently, the decentralised ecosystem consists of multiple layers. It is still under development and new startups are constantly popping up and disappearing:[i]

1   *Infrastructure layer*: those applications that aim to create an infrastructure layer on which others can develop applications. Public blockchains include Ethereum, EOS, and Nxt, while private blockchains include Ripple, Hyperledger, MultiChain, and Chain.
2   *Consensus mechanisms*: required to ensure the state of the network and determining which node can validate transactions. There are numerous consensus algorithms available, ranging from Proof of Work, Proof of Stake and many others.
3   *Distributed computing*: using distributed ledger technology to distribute your computing requirements. Basically, cloud computing but then decentralised. Examples include Golem and Sonem.
4   *Distributed storage*: distributed data storage is especially important when you want to be sure that data can always be accessed, regardless of restrictions some countries have. Examples include Storj, IFPD, and FileCoin.
5   *Privacy and identity*: services that are focused on developing a self-sovereign identity and ensuring that data of internet users is kept private and personal. Examples include Sovrin, uPort, Civic, and Blockstack.
6   *Money transactions*: as discussed in Chapter 4, there are three different types of tokens: currency, utility, or security tokens. Currency tokens, meaning cryptocurrencies, are used to make financial transactions, and the most well-known is of course Bitcoin. Others include ZCash, Bitcoin Cash, or Monero.
7   *Wallets*: of course, all those cryptocurrencies need to be kept somewhere. Wallets are the bank accounts of the crypto world. You can have hot wallets (connected to the internet) or cold wallets (disconnected from the internet). Examples include MyEtherWallet, Jaxx, Exodus, or Trezor.

8   *Exchanges*: like with stocks in companies, tokens need to be exchanged, so there is a range of centralised and decentralised exchanges. Centralised exchanges have the risk of being hacked, which is not possible with a decentralised exchange. Examples of centralised exchanges include Bitfinex, Bitstamp, Coinbase, or Kraken. Examples of decentralised exchanges include 0x, bisq, bitshares, or EtherDelta.

9   *Industry applications*: every industry can use DLT to improve collaboration, enable provenance, speed up transaction settlements, or enable transparency. Examples per industry include:

- Healthcare – hashed health, MedRec, Gem, or Nebula Genomics.
- Legal – Integra Ledger, Aragon, or Otonomos.
- Media – Steem.it, Akasha, Synereo, or Backfeed.
- Internet of Things – IOTA, Chain of Things, Atonomi, or IoT Chain.
- Real estate – Ubiquity, Meridio, ManageGo, or Atlant.
- Banks – Change, Bitwala, Bancor, or Moni.
- Insurance – Etherisc, Immediate, Fidential, or B3i.
- Supply chain – Everledger, Blockverify, Omnichain, or Provenance.
- Logistics – ShipChain, CargoX, FreshTruf, or OriginTrail.
- Energy – LO3 Energy, PowerLedger, Grid Singularity, or SolarCoin.
- Retail – Lolli, Shopin, Ripe.io, or Beam.

Of course, the above list is by far not a definite list and the list will continue to change the more decentralised technology is developed. However, although blockchain can be beneficial to all industries, it does not mean that every problem requires a decentralised solution. A decentralised solution is only required when there is a trust issue (which generally happens when individuals, organisations, and things want to collaborate across organisational borders or between individuals) and when a transaction is taking place. If one of the two is not present, blockchain is not the solution and instead you should use the cloud. In addition, although there are many reasons why blockchain can be used as we saw in Chapter 4, for three particular problems blockchain is not the solution:

1. Blockchain does not work in isolation: first and foremost, blockchain only works when multiple organisations need to work together to achieve a common goal. When transactions need to take place within one organisation, not involving any external stakeholders, a (private) decentralised network is not the solution. Trust within an organisation can be achieved through different means. Applying a blockchain solution would be like using a piling machine to hit a nail. The same applies to smart contracts to automate decision-making. That will only be useful if external stakeholders are involved. Otherwise, you can just use artificial intelligence.

2. Customisation is Blockchain's enemy: when multiple organisations need to transact with each other and when there is a lack of trust, blockchain and smart contracts can be useful. For example, if I send tulips to someone in the United

States, we can use a smart contract to ensure that the buyer pays the right price for the right quality of the tulips. If we agree that the tulips have to remain between 10 and 14 degrees Celsius and the container becomes warmer, the quality of the tulips will deteriorate. In that case, if we use immutable sensor data, a smart contract could automatically result in a discount for the buyer.

Such transactions are simple and can be re-used over and over again. However, things change when transactions between two or more parties have to be highly customised and are constantly changing. In that case, creating a smart contract for every possible transaction becomes too much of a hassle. As a result, a blockchain solution would not be advisable.

3. If you require fast performance: one of the key challenges of blockchain technology is it is slow in terms of transactions per second. The scaling challenge has been mentioned over and over. Although solutions are coming, if you need to process millions of transactions per second, blockchain does not, yet, work. Existing relational database solutions have proven themselves to be capable of running trillions of queries in a very short timeframe. If your organisation requires fast performance, even if you need to collaborate with multiple other organisations, blockchain is not the right solution. Of course, this might change in the (near) future when the technology is developed further, but for now, it is better to stick with centralised databases.

On these occasions, distributed ledger technology is not the required technology. In that case, you are better off using cloud computing technology. The cloud can be especially useful to store, analyse, visualise, and share data within an organisation, where it does not matter that there is a centralised database. Naturally, this would be the case for transactions being done within one organisation and without external stakeholders being involved.

Distributing your data, whether centralised or decentralised, has multiple benefits for your organisation and three of the most important benefits are:

- *Security*: decentralised solutions are highly secure as we have seen in Chapter 5. In addition, cloud computing is generally more secure than on-premises data storage since data storage is not a core business process of most organisations.
- *Quality control*: decentralised solutions require extreme data governance processes to ensure that only high-quality data is stored on a blockchain, while cloud computing allows you to store a single version of your data centralised, instead of in silos. Hence, distributed data is likely to be high-quality data, although this does not happen automatically, of course.
- *Cost saving*: a centralised database in the cloud that is used by the entire organisation is cheaper than separate silos that cannot interact. In addition, although a decentralised solution seems more expensive (since everyone needs to store a copy of a blockchain), the benefits of, for example, instant settlement of transactions easily offset these extra costs.

Distributing your data, whether using a decentralised solution or using cloud computing, enables industry collaboration. To start with distributing your data, make sure you remove existing data silos within the organisation. Data silos are barriers to optimal usage of your data. In addition, similar to datafying your first process, start with a small proof of concept when distributing your data. For example, if you are a retailer, look at one single product and understand the processes it takes to incorporate blockchain technology to create peer-to-peer collaboration with the various industry partners. Similar to how Walmart started with mangoes and Chinese pork. Hence, the stakeholders involved in the process of distributing your data are your suppliers, your competitors but also your customers. The technology that you use can be any of the different applications described, ranging from decentralised data storage to distributed computing. The result will be increased collaboration. Not only among internal stakeholders and business units who can work with a single source of data, but also by enabling secure and trustworthy collaboration among industry partners and devices. It becomes possible to share proprietary data with your competitors, benefiting both without revealing any company secrets.

7.3 Analyse

After collecting data in every company process and customer touchpoint and storing the data in a distributed way, it is time to analyse that data using advanced analytics. As discussed in Chapter 3, for many businesses, the most likely path to creating competitive advantage is by using this "big data" and subjecting it to (advanced) analytics such as descriptive, diagnostic, predictive, or prescriptive analytics. It has become a prerequisite for a company facing uncertainty to use analytics to understand the environment and better grasp the context of their organisation. Therefore, the organisation of tomorrow cannot survive without comprehensive analytics. It is required to understand what is going on and how to respond to changes in the context of the organisation. However, where data become increasingly important, and knowledge is shared within the company, data shift the power structure within the business; moving it away from leaders with years of experience to those employees who have access to data and the power to analyse that data for insights to make (strategic) decisions and create new opportunities.[55] Within the organisation of tomorrow, information has to be available to those capable of making sense of it and/or those facing the customer.

Using analytics, there are multiple ways to retrieve insights from your data. Each type of analysis will have a different impact or result. The data mining technique you should use depends on the kind of business problem that you are trying to solve. One of the common ways to recover valuable insights is via the process of data mining. Data mining is a buzzword that is often used to describe the entire range of big data analytics, including collection, extraction, analysis, and statistics. This, however, is too broad as data mining refers to the discovery of previously unknown patterns, unusual records or dependencies. When developing your *big data analytics strategy*, it is important to have a clear understanding of what data mining is and how it can help you. The term data mining first appeared in the 1990s while before that, statisticians used the terms "data fishing" or "data dredging" to refer to analysing data without an a priori hypothesis. The most important objective of any data mining process is to find useful information that can be easily understood in large data sets. There are a few important classes of tasks that are involved with data mining.

Anomaly or outlier detection

Anomaly detection refers to the search for data items in a data set that do not match a projected pattern or expected behaviour. Anomalies are also called outliers, exceptions, surprises, or contaminants, and they often provide critical and actionable information. An outlier is an object that deviates significantly from the general average within a data set or a combination of data and they can be especially useful in detecting Black Swans. It is numerically distant from the rest of the data and, therefore, the outlier indicates that something is out of the ordinary and requires additional analysis. Anomaly detection is used to detect fraud or risks within critical systems. Anomalies have all the characteristics to be of interest to an analyst, who should further analyse it to find out what is really going on. It can help to find extraordinary occurrences that could indicate fraudulent actions, flawed procedures or areas where a certain theory is invalid. Important to note is that in large data sets, a few outliers are common. Outliers may indicate bad data, due to lack of data governance practices, but may also be due to random variation or they may indicate something scientifically interesting. In all cases, additional research is required.

Association rule learning

Association rule learning enables the discovery of interesting relations (interdependencies) between different variables in large databases. Association rule learning uncovers hidden patterns in the data that can be used to identify variables within the data and the co-occurrences of different variables that appear with the greatest frequencies. Association rule learning is often used in the retail industry to find patterns in point-of-sales data. These patterns can be used when recommending new products to others based on what others have bought before or based on which products are bought together. If this is done correctly, it can help organisations increase their conversion rate. A well-known example is that of Walmart's Strawberry Pop-tarts. Thanks to data mining, Walmart, already in 2004, discovered that Strawberry Pop-tarts sales increased by seven times before a hurricane. Since this discovery, Walmart places the Strawberry Pop-tarts at the checkouts before a hurricane is about to happen.

Clustering analysis

Clustering analysis is the process of identifying data sets that are similar to each other, to understand the differences as well as similarities within the data. Clusters have certain traits in common that can be used to improve targeting algorithms. For example, clusters of customers with similar buying behaviour can be targeted with similar products and services to increase the conversation rate. A result from a clustering analysis can be the creation of personas. Personas are fictional characters created to represent the different user types within a targeted demographic, attitude, and/or behaviour set that might use a site, brand, or product in a similar way. The programming language R has a large variety of functions to perform relevant cluster analysis and is therefore especially relevant for performing a clustering analysis.

Classification analysis

Classification analysis is a systematic process for obtaining important and relevant information about data, and metadata – data about data. The classification analysis helps to identify the categories the data belongs to. Classification analysis is closely linked to cluster analysis as the classification can be used to cluster data. Your email provider performs a well-known example of classification analysis: they use algorithms that can classify your email as legitimate or mark it as spam. This is done based on data that is linked with the email or the information that is in the email, for example, certain words or attachments that indicate spam.

Regression analysis

Regression analysis tries to define the dependency between variables. It assumes a one-way causal effect from one variable to the response of another variable. Independent variables can be affected by each other, but it does not mean that this dependency is both ways as is the case with correlation analysis. A regression analysis can show that one variable is dependent on another but not vice versa. Regression analysis is used to determine different levels of customer satisfaction, how they affect customer loyalty and how service levels can be affected by, for example, the weather. A more concrete example is that a regression analysis can help you find the love of your life on an online dating website.

Organisations that apply business analytics tools will be better able to understand their organisation as well as their ambiguous and uncertain environment. It will improve the ability to make the right decisions at the right moment and as such seize the right opportunities to create competitive advantage. Descriptive analytics enable an organisation to use a variety of structured data sources to achieve insights into what has happened; it is commonly referred to as business intelligence. Diagnostic analytics helps you to understand why something has happened. Predictive analytics uses machine learning and artificial intelligence to discover patterns and understand relationships in various unstructured and structured data sources to develop predictions for the future. Finally, prescriptive analytics changes an organisation at multiple levels and is the final stage in understanding a business. It not only offers predictions on what to do but also provides recommendations on how to act upon forecasts to take advantage of those predictions and often can take action automatically. Descriptive, diagnostic, predictive, and prescriptive analytics could use any of the above data mining techniques to provide you with relevant insights. As such, data mining will help the organisation of tomorrow to find and select the most important and relevant information. This information can then be used to create models that enable predictions on how people or systems will behave depending on the context, which will help you improve your decision-making capabilities. When you first start with incorporating analytics, determine which insights you want to obtain and what metrics or KPIs you find important. These are the starting point for selecting the right analytics tools.

Traditionally, decisions are made by those managers and leaders within the organisation that have the most experience and have access to the right information. Important information used to be provided solely to those decision-makers. As such, they were more knowledgeable than the rest of the organisation. However, the introduction of big data analytics changed this. Once a data-driven, information-centric culture is implemented, data and insights from data become widely accessible, in real time and across the organisation. The more data you have, the better the models will become that you can create using the data mining techniques, resulting in more business value for your organisation. As such, your decision-makers will be the stakeholders who are involved in the process of analytics. Especially, because when more members of your organisation have access to these insights, empowerment is a possibility resulting in a shift in power. In a data-driven business, the real decision-makers within an organisation are not senior managers or C-level executives but are those employees that face the customer or who are directly involved in creating the product or service. Some leaders might be reluctant to accept this shift in power, but only when all leaders accept the power shift, can the organisation truly benefit from big data analytics. Within the organisation of tomorrow, anyone with access to insights from data should be able to make a decision, resulting in flatter organisations.

Within organisations that distribute their data and analyse it for insights, decisions are made at the point where the most competence resides. Often this results in empowered staff. To truly benefit from analytics, the organisation of tomorrow should, therefore, aim to encourage this empowerment. It will result in self-empowered organisations that are guided by a common vision and shared ethical standards. Only when you incorporate the context at every level within your organisation, the organisation stands the best chance to remain competitive.

7.4 Automate

The final step in transforming your organisation into a data organisation is to automate your business processes and augment your customer touchpoints with artificial intelligence or smart contracts. Artificial intelligence will become especially valuable if you have completed the first three steps. Artificial intelligence requires large amounts of high-quality and unbiased data. Exactly what the organisation of tomorrow will have after datafying the different business processes and distributing the data using DLT or the cloud. In addition, thanks to data provenance when applying distributed ledger technology, it becomes possible to understand better why an algorithm came to a certain decision as it offers a traceable overview of the collected and used data, thereby contributing to achieving Explainable AI. The end goal of the organisation of tomorrow is to develop Responsible AI that becomes increasingly advanced, resulting in increased productivity and efficiency. Those organisations that want to prepare for an automated future should have a thorough understanding of AI. However, AI is an umbrella term that covers multiple disciplines, each affecting the business in a slightly different way.

When we look at artificial intelligence, it can be divided into three different domains:

1 Robotics, which deals with the physical world and it can directly interact with humans. Robotics can be used to improve our work in various ways. Including Ford's exoskeleton or Boston Dynamics' helping robots.
2 Cognitive systems, which deal with the human world. A great example of a cognitive system as part of AI are chatbots. Chatbots are a very tangible example where humans and machines work together to achieve a goal. A chatbot is a communication interface that helps individuals and organisations have conversations.
3 Machine learning, which deals with the information world. Machines use data to learn, and machine learning aims to derive meaning from that data. Machine learning uses statistical methods to enable machines to improve with machines. A subset of machine learning is deep learning, which enables multi-layer neural networks.

In the years to come, artificial intelligence will become more advanced, especially when not limited by human knowledge. In this process, it is adopting new tactics or strategies that humans have neither seen before nor imagined. Developments such as AlphaGo Zero, as discussed in Chapter 2, will remove the need for human intervention and/or historical data. This will make algorithms much more powerful and efficient as they train against itself. Thus, it is likely that we will see more of such developments, bringing us ever closer to the holy grail of artificial intelligence; artificial general intelligence. These AI systems have autonomous self-control and self-understanding and the ability to learn new things to solve a wide variety of problems in different contexts using unknown tactics and strategies. AGI is not around the corner, and the estimations differ when AGI will be ready, ranging from 10–15 years to 50 or even 100 years. I believe we will reach AGI in the next 15–20 years due to the rapid advancements in artificial intelligence and quantum computing. Both technologies affect each other positively, accelerating the development of each other.

An important component in achieving AGI will be deep learning. Deep learning is essentially what turns a static *if/then* based machine model into a self-improving model that learns from experiences and the feedback it gets. Before deep learning and the neural networks that allow it, all AI was really a complex set of *if this then that* statements. If a user inputs A, then the appropriate response is B. Deep learning allows computers to think outside the box. Instead of having only two options, they may have a long list of possible responses to a single query. The challenge lies in teaching the machine how to recognise when to deploy a particular solution. Complex equations apply weight to one solution or another based on additional criteria. For example, a perfect cup of coffee is different for different people. An AI pouring that cup might look at historical purchasing data to help decide how much cream to add and what type of sweetener the customer might prefer. Deep learning teaches your systems how to handle specific tasks by incorporating the context. The more complex the task, the longer it takes to train an AI. However, once trained an AI can accomplish manual and repetitive tasks much more rapidly than a human. Training AI without the benefits of deep learning modules means a lot of manual computations and adjustments. However, deep learning does require the use of large volumes of high-quality training data and a lot of computational power.

For apps, AI can incorporate everything from in-app customer service to better product selections to automated loan offerings. Insurance companies might use in-app AI systems to instantly handle claims, while lending institutions might use it to approve or deny loans. The smarter the app, the less need there is for a human on the other end of the technology to handle the finalisation of an action. For example, an insurance AI with the right training can use pictures of a crashed vehicle to determine the likely damage. Then, an adjuster can handle the person-to-person communications necessary to keep customers happy. When AI is handling the grunt work, the employee can take on a lot more cases each day, dramatically improving their efficiency. As such, AI will change the notion of work for many types of jobs.

To start automating your organisation, the right process would be to do so in small steps. It is impossible to build a fully automated business from scratch due to the complexity involved with artificial intelligence. As discussed in Chapter 6, AI is like Lego, and it requires small steps to build something beautiful. Especially, when you also take into account smart contracts to automate the organisation. While artificial intelligence can be used to automate internal business processes, smart contracts can be used to automate external business processes where other stakeholders are involved. Smart contracts will allow the organisation of tomorrow to automatically execute certain transactions or decisions, which were agreed upon by two or more actors.[133] Smart contracts create value as they execute these tasks automatically and they are deemed "the killer application for the decentralised world".[285] With the arrival of smart contracts deployed on a blockchain, the concept of what defines an organisation and how organisations can achieve competitive advantage will change drastically. Smart contracts combined with artificial intelligence will enable your organisation to automate many of your internal and external processes, which will bring your organisation closer to a decentralised autonomous organisation, or DAO. As discussed, such an organisation does not have any management or employees and is run completely by immutable code. While existing organisations will not likely become a DAO anytime soon, within the organisation of tomorrow different business processes could function as decentralised autonomous processes. Thereby not automating the entire business, but merely parts of it which will give it a competitive advantage over those organisations that rely on manual processes.

Together, the above four steps make up the $D^2 + A^2$ *model*, as shown in Figure 7.2. Summarising, to develop the organisation of tomorrow, an organisation should datafy its processes and customer touchpoints, ensuring high-quality data and the right data governance practices in place. The introduction of sensors and IoT devices will result in a change in your company culture as employees and customers will need to get used to the datafication of these processes. Once collected, the data can then be distributed either using distributed ledger technologies such as blockchain to enable trustless transactions and collaboration among industry partners or storing your data in the cloud to enable your employees to have access to one single version of data across the organisation. The third step is to analyse that data and using various data mining techniques to discover patterns across various data sources and obtain a better understanding of the context of the organisation. Descriptive analytics will enable the organisation to better sense the changes in your changing environment, while predictive analytics will help you seize the opportunities sensed by improving your decision-making capabilities. The organisation of tomorrow will also apply prescriptive analytics to transform your tangible and intangible assets accordingly. Finally, the organisation of tomorrow uses artificially intelligent agents such as immutable smart (or Ricardian) contracts and algorithms to automate your business processes and augment your customer touchpoints, resulting in a more efficient and effective organisation. The result of following the four steps of

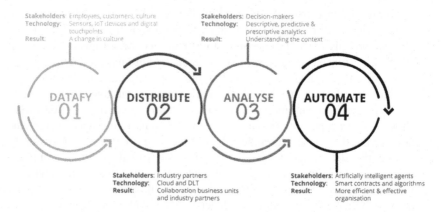

Figure 7.2 The D² + A² model

Datafying, Distributing, Analysing, and Automating is sustained competitive advantage. It will turn your organisation into a data organisation that is ready for the data-driven future ahead of us.

7.5 A note on privacy

This chapter is not complete with a note on privacy, which is especially important for a data organisation. For years, organisations like Google, Facebook, and Amazon have been building extensive profiles of you about who you are, what you have bought/liked/read, and your preferences. In exchange for "free" services, these organisations use extensive profiles to generate revenue through advertising that follows you across the web. In the twenty-first century, privacy has taken a new meaning, but that does not mean that consumers will accept this. As the initiative of Sir Tim Berners-Lee shows, it is about time that consumer regains the control over their own data and that organisations start to respect the privacy of their customers. This can best be achieved by adhering to several ethical guidelines.[164]

Organisations should be *transparent*, so that consumers know what will be done with the data that is collected, today and in the future. They should keep their communication *simple and understandable*, so that everyone, including digital immigrants, understands what's being done with the data. This means simplifying the terms and conditions to make sure that it does not read like the constitution. All data should be well *secured and encrypted*. Although distributed ledger technology will enable highly secure data, non-decentralised data remains receptible for hackers. Where data is collected, hackers will be active, and any organisation should assume that they can and will be hacked. Organisations should ensure that hackers do not stand a chance and if they do get access to the data, the data is useless. If your organisation has not yet been hacked, you are simply not important enough. If data is your most important asset, which is the case if you are a data organisation, it should require the utmost attention. Therefore, quantum-resistant encryption should be applied to your data to protect your organisation also in the era of the quantum computer. Next, the organisation of tomorrow should give back *control* of consumer data whenever possible. If the consumer created the data, the consumer owns it and should control it. Finally, *privacy should be part of the DNA*, so that all employees understand the importance of it. The development of a quality mark, to ensure that organisations adhere to these guidelines, could be imaginable/desirable.

Of course, there is also a responsibility for consumers. It will certainly help consumers if they are aware of how to act in a data-driven society. Customers should understand what data they share and not absentmindedly accept policy statements or terms and conditions that result in sharing personal data. They should be cautious with what they share, for example on social networks. Everything on social networks is public information and accessible. So, sharing a picture of your credit card on Facebook is probably not a good idea. Even in a future where consumers will have their own Solid POD containing all their personal data, they should still remain careful with how they deal with that data and with whom they will share it. This also includes being careful when downloading a new app on your phone. Many of us simply download an app and, without paying any attention or reading the terms and conditions, accept all requests to access personal data ranging from location data to contact details. Dealing with this more consciously would be a good starting point for consumers. Finally, consumers should not simply accept the new deal and demand that companies will take care of their personal data, either through legislation or by boycotting reckless organisations. Fortunately, legislation such as the GDPR helps in better protecting consumer data.

The organisation of tomorrow will not be able to survive very long when ignoring these ethical guidelines. The transition costs for consumers will only decrease, especially if they use solutions such as the Solid POD where they can easily take their data to a new service. Once we have reached a decentralised society, the power will lie with the consumer and organisations will have to focus on simply developing the best product and offering the best service.

7.6 Conclusion

Data collection can help every aspect of your business from developing new products to improving operational efficiency. Companies that use customer intelligence have better marketing results. Organisations that use data collected after a customer buys a product can make recommendations based on usage. Internally, data collection can improve your supply chain or help with recruiting talent. By collecting millions of data points, you provide your business with the information needed to drive strategic thinking and over-come internal roadblocks. You can collect information on everything from the amount of time it takes to pull and ship an order to the best delivery routes and average wait times for customers. This information can also be used to assess employee performance (of course, with the right privacy measures in place). Data leads to knowledge which ultimately drives decision-making.

The key message underlying this book is that data-driven organisations that incorporate big data analytics, blockchain, and AI will stand the best chance to remain competitive in the future. When these emerging information tech-nologies converge, a *gestalt shift* will occur; all of a sudden, we can see the world through a different, more technologically advanced, lens. It is like the famous rabbit–duck illusion – an ambiguous image in which a rabbit or a duck can be seen – once you switch from seeing the duck to the rabbit (or the other way around) it becomes difficult to see the original animal again. Achieving a similar *gestalt* shift in your organisation opens up a completely new perspective, where we see the organisation, and the society, as a data organisation. The convergence of technologies will offer new possibilities and solutions to improve our lives and create better organisations and societies, with data at the heart of it.[457] However, such data-driven organisations cannot function without humans in the loop as organisations remain social entities.[126, 127] Even when organisations are following the $D^2 + A^2$ *model* and move towards a decentralised and autonomous organisation, most organisa-tions will never transform into a full DAO. Consequently, there remains a human element to organisations, and as such, *the social, the material*, and *the artificial* should exist in coherence and interact with each other without negatively affecting one another. This means the artificial adheres to the ethics valued by the social, the material is bound by the norms and principles of our society and the culture within an organisation, and the social is not subordinate to the material and the artificial. All three should exist in balance with each other, and organisations that ignore the human side of doing busi-ness are likely to face difficulties. Therefore, to turn your existing organisation into a data organisation, there is a lot of work to be done. It means that you should datafy your processes, distribute your data via the cloud or using dis-tributed ledger technologies, analyse your data using analytics to sense and seize opportunities, and automate your decision-making using AI and smart contracts. In each of these steps, you should take into account ethical guide-lines to ensure that you respect your employees' and customers' privacy and security. When doing so, you will become a data organisation that is ready for the fast-changing data-driven future ahead of us.

Note

i   This overview was created in December 2018. By the time you read this, the list might have changed.

Epilogue
Towards data-driven globalisation

The organisation of tomorrow will look fundamentally different than the organisation of today. It will be an organisation with data at its heart and it will use technology to foster stronger relationships with other organisations and individuals. Organisations will employ robots and connected devices that will act autonomously and automatically, taking into consideration the complete context of the organisation, based on immutable, high-quality data. Consumers will be in full control over their data and privacy will, at least in Western countries, increase again. In order to achieve that, we need to develop self-sovereign identities for individuals, organisations and things and we need to create immutable reputations that make anonymity accountable and enable trustless transactions among humans and machines. Within these organisations, *the artificial* will become an important stakeholder that behaves differently than human stakeholders. To prevent any harm done by these artificial agents, whether intentionally or unintentionally, we need to step up our governance practices. If the social, material, and artificial will be able to interact seamlessly, it will foster an era of abundance where globalisation is the only sensible way forward.

For many nationalists, this message might be counterintuitive. Nationalists fear globalisation and pursue their country's interests above those of everyone else. Consequently, we live in a world where increasingly globalisation is under threat. The biggest threat comes from trade wars that could significantly harm the world economy. The problem with trade wars is that in the interconnected world that we live in, they affect everyone from small businesses to large conglomerates: it is a war with only losers.

Fortunately, in the past decade, globalisation has gone digital and, as such, within this global collaboration, technology is increasingly becoming important. As a result, globalisation has become more about data and less about stuff.[458] While in the twentieth century, globalisation was all about trading physical goods across the globe, in the twenty-first century, globalisation is all about exchanging data. In the interconnected digital world that we live in, borders are disappearing, and national legislation is increasingly difficult to maintain. In today's world, even a one-person company can be a multinational. In the past years, initial coin offerings enabled organisations to raise funds from anywhere in the world and the upcoming security token offerings will bring raising funds to the next (regulated) level. Of course, globalisation is still also about trading goods and building physical connections such as the Belt and Road initiative developed by China, but globalisation is increasingly more about the digital infrastructure. Data and emerging information technologies are the driving force behind today's globalisation. These technologies enable efficient, effective, and secure collaboration across borders; big data analytics provide insights in the constantly changing context and help find the right partners anywhere in the world. Blockchain ensures trust and enables peer-to-peer transactions among those globally dispersed partners or things. And artificial intelligence automates decision-making and improves cross-border partnerships, resulting in algorithmic businesses collaborating effortlessly with each other. Key to the new digital globalisation is trust. Therefore, when we want to collaborate across (digital) borders, we need more than believing someone's words or blue eyes. Especially when one is not certain of the other's intentions, as is with the Belt and Road initiative. An immutable, verifiable and traceable reputation can contribute positively to creating this trust required to build long-lasting relationships and collaboration. This is where digital technologies come into play. Blockchain can have a positive contribution to the nature of trust and, in addition, can ensure effective and efficient collaboration through the use of smart contracts. Big data analytics can provide insights into the soaring flows of data that generate more economic value than the global goods trade to help organisations understand the context in which they operate. Finally, artificial intelligence can give smaller businesses also a chance to go global, for example by proactively matching small companies with big contracts all over the world.[459] Consequently, in the twenty-first century you no longer have to be a large enterprise to do business across borders.

As a global society, we need to embrace global collaboration, but we need to have the right means to do so since unknown makes unloved. We need the right digital tools and to move away from protectionism and nationalism. Instead, we need to employ and embrace emerging information technologies to not only develop the organisation of tomorrow but also build immutable reputations for individuals, organisations, societies, and, thanks to the Internet of Things, even connected devices. In a world where globalisation has gone digital, the convergence of big data analytics, blockchain, and artificial intelligence is becoming the holy grail to ensure trustworthy, effective, and efficient global collaboration among individuals, companies, and connected devices. It will change how globalisation functions, driving economic growth and job creation across the world. In a world where you can trust the other party and collaborate effortlessly, prosperity quickly follows. Therefore, let's build the data-driven organisations of tomorrow that put customers at the centre of the organisation, embrace technology, and change how globalisation works, expanding it to the far corners of our world.

Glossary

Algorithm   A process or set of rules to be followed in calculations or other problem-solving operations, especially by a computer.

Analytics   The discovery of patterns in data that provide insights and turn data into information.

Artificial agency   Coordinated artificially intelligent intentionality formed in partial response to perceptions of human agency and material agency.

Artificial agent   Artificially intelligent actors that have the ability to act upon their own, apart from human intervention.

Artificial Intelligence (AI)   The process of constructing an intelligent artefact. Using computers to amplify our human intelligence with artificial intelligence has the potential of helping civilisation flourish like never before – as long as we manage to keep the technology beneficial and prevent AI from inflicting any damage.

Big data   A term that describes the large volume of data – both structured and unstructured – that inundates a business on a day-to-day basis. These data sets are so voluminous and complex that traditional data-processing application software are inadequate to deal with them.

Bitcoin   An innovative payment network and a new kind of money. It is a type of cryptocurrency. It is the first decentralised digital currency, as the system works without a central bank or single administrator.

Black Swans   Events that deviate from the expected, that have an extreme impact and although they are difficult to predict, they have retrospective predictability.

Blockchain   A digital ledger in which transactions made in bitcoin or another cryptocurrency are recorded chronologically. The cryptography underlying blockchain ensures a "trustless" system, thereby removing the need for intermediaries to manage risk, making data on a blockchain immutable, traceable, and verifiable.

Consensus mechanism   A feature in decentralised networks to determine the preferences of the individual users (or nodes) and to manage decision-making of the whole network. The key to any blockchain; with a consensus algorithm, there is no longer the need for a trusted third party;

and, as a result, decisions can be created, implemented, and evaluated, without the need for a central authority.

Cryptocurrency   A digital asset designed to work as a medium of exchange that uses cryptography to secure its transactions, to control the creation of additional units, and to verify the transfer of assets.

Cryptocurrency mining   A race that rewards computer nodes for being first to solve cryptographic puzzles on public blockchain networks. By solving the puzzle, the miner verifies the block and creates a hash pointer to the next block. Once verified, each block in the chain becomes immutable.

Cryptography   Protects data from theft or alteration, and can also be used for user authentication. Earlier cryptography was effectively synonymous with encryption but nowadays cryptography is mainly based on mathematical theory and computer science practice.

Datafication   Turning analogue processes and customer touchpoints into digital processes and digital customer touchpoints.

Decentralised Autonomous Organisations   An organisation that is run through rules encoded as computer programs called smart contracts. A DAO's financial transaction record and program rules are maintained on a blockchain. It is an organisation without management or employees, run completely by autonomous code.

Decentralised networks   A computing environment in which multiple parties (or nodes) make their own independent decisions. In such a system, there is no single centralised authority that makes decisions on behalf of all the parties.

Descriptive analytics   Analytics that enable organisations to sense, filter, shape, learn, and calibrate opportunities by providing insights into what has happened in their internal and external environment, from one second ago to decades ago.

Digital signatures   A digital code (generated and authenticated by public key encryption) which is attached to an electronically transmitted document to verify its contents and the sender's identity. Digital signatures are based on public key cryptography, also known as asymmetric cryptography.

Digitalisation   The conversion of information into digital format.

Distributed Application (DAPP)   Blockchain-enabled products and services are commonly referred to as Decentralised Applications, or DApps. A DApp has at least two distinctive features: (1) any changes to the protocol of the DApp have to be approved by consensus; and (2) the application has to use a cryptographic token, or cryptocurrency, which is generated according to a set algorithm. Bitcoin is probably the best known DApp.

Distributed Ledger Technology (DLT)   A digital system for recording the transaction of assets in which the transactions and their details are recorded in multiple places at the same time. A blockchain is a distributed ledger.

Distributed networks Distributed networking is a distributed computing network system, said to be distributed when the computer programming and the data to be worked on are spread out across more than one computer. Usually, this is implemented over a computer network. Participants in a distributed network are able to verify and authenticate other users' transactions and exchanges. For this reason, the community values its own worth and reputation.

Double spending problem Arises when a given set of crypto tokens is spent in more than one transaction. By solving the double spending problem, digital or cryptocurrency has now become viable.

Dynamic capabilities Those capabilities that enable an organisation to develop new products and services depending on changing market circumstances.

Emerging information technologies New advanced information technologies that use advanced computer programs to store, retrieve, manipulate, or transmit data.

Hash algorithm Each block of data on a blockchain receives a hash id, as a database key, calculated by a Secure Hash Algorithm. This block hash is fixed. In other words, the hash id allocated to the block never changes. Hash algorithms are used in a variety of components of blockchain technology, one of them being the hash id, which is a unique string of 64 numbers and letters that is linked to data in each block.

Hash function A hash function is any function that can be used to map data of arbitrary size to data of fixed size. The values returned by a hash function are called hash values, hash codes, digests, or simply hashes.

Immutability Unchanging over time; and impossible to change.

Initial Coin Offering (ICO) Crowd funding by issuing crypto tokens in exchange for fiat money. Also known as a Token Generation Event (TGE).

Internet of Things A network of physical devices that are connected through the internet and where sensors enable advanced data collection to generate insights.

Machine learning A method of data analysis that automates analytical model building. It is a branch of artificial intelligence based on the idea that systems can learn from data, identify patterns, and make decisions with minimal human intervention.

Material agency The capacity of non-human actors to act without human intervention.

Nano technology Science, engineering, and technology conducted at the molecular or nanoscale (which is about 1 to 100 nanometres).

Nodes Computers confirming transactions occurring on the network and maintaining a decentralised consensus across the system.

Open strategy Allowing previously excluded internal and external stakeholders, such as customers, suppliers, connected devices, employees, or even competitors, to join in the strategy-making process to create increased value for the organisation.

Peer-to-peer transactions Also referred to as person-to-person transactions (P2P transactions or P2P payments), electronic money transfers made from one person to another through an app.

Performativity Performativity shows how relations and boundaries between technologies and humans are enacted in practice and, therefore, are not fixed or pre-given. Something is performative when it contributes to the constitution of the reality it describes.

Practical Byzantine Fault Tolerance (PBFT) A process that relies on the sheer number of nodes in order to confirm trust. Assuming that a malicious attach on the network will occur, the PBFT provides a level of assurance and trust that would not otherwise be achievable.

Predictive analytics Analytics that uses machine learning and algorithms to find patterns and capture relationships in multiple unstructured and structured data sources to create foresight.

Prescriptive analytics The final stage of understanding your business. It is about what to do (now) and why to do it, given a complex set of requirements, objectives and constraints.

Private Key Infrastructure (PKI) A set of roles, policies, and procedures needed to create, manage, distribute, use, store, and revoke digital certificates and manage public-key encryption.

Proof of Stake (PoS) A way to validate transactions and to achieve a distributed consensus. It is an algorithm and its purpose to incentivise nodes to confirm transactions. PoS uses someone's stake in a cryptocurrency to ensure good behaviour.

Proof of Work (PoW) A requirement to define an expensive computer calculation, also called mining, that needs to be performed in order to create a new group of trustless transactions (the so-called block) on a distributed ledger or blockchain.

Quantum computing Incredibly powerful machines that take a new approach to processing information. Built on the principles of quantum mechanics, they exploit complex laws of nature that are always there, but usually remain hidden from view.

Self-sovereign identity The concept that people and businesses can store their own identity data on their own devices and provide it efficiently upon request. The key benefits of self-sovereign identity are the user only provides the information that is needed by the provider and the provider only receives and stores essential information (and with the identity-owner's express permission).

Smart contracts Programmable applications that can be automated to initiate upon satisfaction of certain conditions. Those conditions can include complex conditional logic. The smart contract verifies that parties to a transaction can meet their promises and then the technology manages the exchange so that each promise is satisfied simultaneously, almost certainly eliminating risk for all parties to the transaction.

Social agency How humans define and use technology and how people apply (new) technologies to achieve their goals.

Sociomateriality The theoretical concept that helps researchers understand how technologies and organisations interact.

Timestamp A sequence of characters or encoded information identifying when a certain event occurred, usually giving date and time of day, sometimes accurate to a small fraction of a second.

Trust protocol A mechanism whereby trust is managed by technology in a decentralised network. Trust is established through verification or proof of work and is supported by immutability of that work and the consensus of all participants.

References

1. Green, H., *IBM Think 2018*. 2018, IBM.
2. Hajkowicz, H., A. Reeson, L. Rudd, A. Bratanova, L. Hodgers, C. Mason, and N. Boughen, *Tomorrow's Digitally Enabled Workforce*. 2016, Brisbane: CSIRO.
3. Landis, C. and D. Blacharski, *Cloud Computing Made Easy*. 2013, Vitual Global, Incorporated.
4. O Reilly, C.A. and M.L. Tushman, The ambidextrous organization. *Harvard Business Review*, 2004. 82(4): 74–83.
5. Raisch, S., J. Birkinshaw, G. Probst, and M.L. Tushman, Organizational ambidexterity: Balancing exploitation and exploration for sustained performance. *Organization Science*, 2009. 20(4): 685–695.
6. Teece, D., M. Peteraf, and S. Leih, Dynamic capabilities and organizational agility. *California Management Review*, 2016. 58(4): 13–35.
7. Bennett, N. and J. Lemoine, What VUCA really means for you. *Harvard Business Review*, 2014. 92(1/2): 27.
8. Hartmann, P.M., et al., Capturing value from big data: A taxonomy of data-driven business models used by start-up firms. *International Journal of Operations & Production Management*, 2016. 36(10): 1382–1406.
9. Khatri, N. and H.A. Ng, The role of intuition in strategic decision making. *Human Relations*, 2000. 53(1): 57–86.
10. PWC, *Seizing the Information Advantage: How Organizations Can Unlock Value and Insight from the Information They Hold*. 2015. Available from: www.pwc.es/es/publicaciones/tecnologia/assets/Seizing-The-Information-Advantage.pdf, accessed April 29, 2019.
11. Gurbaxani, B., You don't have to be a software company to think like one. *Harvard Business Review*, 2016. Available from: https://hbr.org/2016/04/you-dont-have-to-be-a-software-company-to-think-like-one, accessed April 29, 2019.
12. Ciborra, C.U., The platform organization: Recombining strategies, structures, and surprises. *Organization Science*, 1996. 7(2): 103–118.
13. Goodwin, T., The battle is for the customer interface. 2015. Available from: http://social.techcrunch.com/2015/03/03/in-the-age-of-disintermediation-the-battle-is-all-for-the-customer-interface/, accessed February 18, 2017.
14. Garrod, J., The real world of the decentralized autonomous society. *triple C: Communication, Capitalism & Critique. Open Access Journal for a Global Sustainable Information Society*, 2016. 14(1): 62–77.

15. Puschmann, C. and J. Burgess, The politics of Twitter data. 2013. HIIG Discussion Paper Series No. 2013-01. Available from: https://ssrn.com/abstract=2206225/, accessed April 29, 2019.

16. Taplin, J., *Move Fast and Break Things.* 2017, London: Macmillan.

17. Berners-Lee, T., Re-decentralizing the web: Some strategic questions. 2016. Available from: https://archive.org/details/DWebSummit2016_Keynote_Tim_Berners_Lee, accessed October 9, 2017.

18. Dwyer, C., Privacy in the age of Google and Facebook. *IEEE Technology and Society Magazine*, 2011. 30(3): 58–63.

19. Herrman, J., Media websites battle faltering ad revenue and traffic. 2016. Available from: www.nytimes.com/2016/04/18/business/media-websites-battle-falteringad-revenue-and-traffic.html, accessed October 10, 2017.

20. Tene, O. and J. Polonetsky, Big data for all: Privacy and user control in the age of analytics. *Northwestern Journal of Technology and Intellectual Property*, 2012. 11: xxvii.

21. Acquisti, A., A. Friedman, and R. Telang, Is there a cost to privacy breaches? An event study. *ICIS 2006 Proceedings*, 2006: 94.

22. Morris, K., Facebook shadow profiles: What you need to know. 2013. Available from: https://mashable.com/2013/06/26/facebook-shadow-profiles/, accessed September 2, 2018.

23. Blue, V., Firm: Facebook's shadow profiles are "frightening" dossiers on everyone. 2013. Available from: www.zdnet.com/article/firm-facebooks-shadow-profiles-are-frightening-dossiers-on-everyone/, accessed September 2, 2018.

24. Bergen, M. and J. Surane, Google and Mastercard cut a secret ad deal to track retail sales. 2018. Available from: www.bloomberg.com/news/articles/2018-08-30/google-and-mastercard-cut-a-secret-ad-deal-to-track-retail-sales, accessed September 2, 2018.

25. Raine, L., Life in 2030: These are the 4 things experts can't predict. 2017. Available from: www.weforum.org/agenda/2017/11/life-in-2030-what-experts-cant-predict/, accessed September 2, 2018.

26. *The Economist*, The world's most valuable resource is no longer oil, but data. 2017. Available from: www.economist.com/news/leaders/21721656-data-economy-demands-new-approach-antitrust-rules-worlds-most-valuable-resource, accessed October 10, 2018.

27. Leonardi, P.M., Materiality, sociomateriality, and socio-technical systems: What do these terms mean? How are they related? Do we need them?, in *Materiality and Organizing: Social Interaction in a Technological World*. 2012, Oxford: Oxford University Press, pp. 25–48.

28. Orlikowski, W.J., Using technology and constituting structures: A practice lens for studying technology in organizations, in *Resources, Co-Evolution and Artifacts*. 2000, Springer, pp. 255–305.

29. Kikulis, L.M., T. Slack, and C. Hinings, Sector-specific patterns of organizational design change. *Journal of Management Studies*, 1995. 32(1): 67–100.

30. Assink, M., Inhibitors of disruptive innovation capability: A conceptual model. *European Journal of Innovation Management*, 2006. 9(2): 215–233.

31. Davis, G.F., What might replace the modern corporation: Uberization and the web page enterprise. *Seattle University Law Review*, 2015. 39: 501.

32. Croll, A. and B. Yoskovitz, *Lean Analytics: Use Data to Build a Better Startup Faster*. 2013, O'Reilly Media, Inc.
33. Schwab, K. and C. Smadja, Changing the structure of top management: Beyond structure to processes. *Harvard Business Review*, 1995. 73(1): 86–96.
34. McAfee, A. and E. Brynjolfsson, Big data: The management revolution. *Harvard Business Review*, 2012. 90(10): 61–67.
35. Grossman, R. and K. Siegel, Organizational Models For Big Data And Analytics. *Journal of Organization Design*, 2014. 3(1): 20–25.
36. Greenwood, R. and C.R. Hinings, Organizational design types, tracks and the dynamics of strategic change. *Organization Studies*, 1988. 9(3): 293–316.
37. Anthony, S.D., Kodak's downfall wasn't about technology. *Harvard Business Review*, 2016. Available from: https://hbr.org/2016/07/kodaks-downfall-wasnt-about-technology, accessed November 7, 2016.
38. Huber, G.P., A Theory of the Effects of Advanced Information Technologies on Organizational Design, Intelligence, and Decision Making. *Academy of Management Review*, 1990. 15(1): p. 221–254.
39. Garud, R., C. Hardy, and S. Maguire, Institutional entrepreneurship, in *Encyclopedia of Creativity, Invention, Innovation and Entrepreneurship*, ed. E.G. Carayannis. 2013, New York: Springer, pp. 1069–1074.
40. Grossman, R.The industries that are being disrupted the most by digital. 2016. Available from: https://hbr.org/2016/03/the-industries-that-are-being-disrupted-the-most-by-digital, accessed July 5, 2017.
41. Snow, C.C., Ø.D. Fjeldstad, C. Lettl, and R.E. Miles, Organizing continuous product development and commercialization: the collaborative community of firms model. *Journal of Product Innovation Management*, 2011. 28(1): 3–16.
42. Swan, M., *Blockchain: Blueprint for a New Economy*. 2015, Sebastopol: O'Reilly Media, Inc.
43. Tsvetkova, M., T. Yasseri, E.T. Meyer, J.B. Pickering, V. Engen, P. Walland, M. Lüders, A. Følstad, and G. Bravos, Understanding human-machine networks: A cross-disciplinary survey. *ACM Computing Surveys (CSUR)*, 2017. 50(1).
44. Schuh, G., T. Potente, R. Varandani, C. Hausberg, and B. Frånken, Collaboration moves productivity to the next level. *Procedia Cirp*, 2014. 17: 3–8.
45. Hoc, J.-M., From human–machine interaction to human–machine cooperation. *Ergonomics*, 2000. 43(7): 833–843.
46. Kitchin, R., *The Data Revolution: Big Data, Open Data, Data Infrastructures and Their Consequences*. 2014, Thousand Oaks: Sage.
47. Shadbolt, N.R., D.A. Smith, E. Simperl, M. Van Kleek, Y. Yang, and W. Hall, Towards a classification framework for social machines, in *22nd International Conference on World Wide Web*. 2013, Rio de Janeiro: ACM.
48. Smart, P., E. Simperl, and N. Shadbolt, A taxonomic framework for social machines, in *Social Collective Intelligence*. 2014, Springer, pp. 51–85.
49. Buregio, V., S. Meira, and N. Rosa. Social machines: A unified paradigm to describe social web-oriented systems, in *Proceedings of the 22nd International Conference on World Wide Web*. 2013, Rio de Janeiro: ACM.
50. Latour, B., On actor-network theory: A few clarifications. *Soziale welt*, 1996. 369–381.
51. Foucault, M., *Discipline and Punishment*. New York: Pantheon, 1977.

52. Galbraith, J.R., Organizational design challenges resulting from big data. *Journal of Organizational Design*, 2014. 3(1): 2–13.
53. Fosso Wamba, S., S. Akter, A. Edwards, G. Chopin, and D. Gnanzou, How "big data" can make big impact: Findings from a systematic review and a longitudinal case study. *International Journal of Production Economics*, 2015. 165: 234–246.
54. Apte, C., B. Dietrich, and M. Fleming, Business leadership through analytics. *IBM Journal of Research & Development*, 2012. 56(6): 1–5.
55. Berner, M., E. Graupner, and A. Maedche, The information panopticon in the big data era. *Journal of Organization Design*, 2014. 3(1): 14–19.
56. Carroll, J.M. and V. Bellotti, Creating value together: The emerging design space of peer-to-peer currency and exchange, in *Proceedings of the 18th ACM Conference on Computer Supported Cooperative Work & Social Computing*. 2015, Vancouver: ACM.
57. Kane, G.C., Crowd-based capitalism? Empowering entrepreneurs in the sharing economy. *MIT Sloan Management Review*, 2016. 57(4): 3–12.
58. Mattila, J., The blockchain phenomenon: The disruptive potential of distributed consensus architectures. BRIE Working Paper 2016-1.
59. Callon, M., Techno-economic networks and irreversibility. *The Sociological Review*, 1990. 38(S1): 132–161.
60. Shrier, D., W. Wu, and A. Pentland, Blockchain & infrastructure (identity, data security). *MIT Connection Science*, 2016: 1–18.
61. Prentice, S., Defining algorithmic business. Gartner [Research Report]. 2016, March 1. Available from: www.gartner.com/smarterwithgartner/the-arrival-of-algo rithmic-business/, accessed March 29, 2017.
62. Luca, M., J.O.N. Kleinberg, and S. Mullainathan, Algorithms need managers, too. *Harvard Business Review*, 2016. 94(1): 96–101.
63. Leavitt, H.J. and T.L. Whisler, Management in the 1980's. *Harvard Business Review*, 1958. 36(6): 41–48.
64. Woodward, J., *Industrial Organization: Theory and Practice*. Vol. 3. 1965, London: Oxford University Press.
65. Thompson, J.D., *Organizations in Action: Social Science Bases of Administrative Theory*. 1967, New York: McGraw-Hill.
66. Harvey, E., Technology and the structure of organizations. *American Sociological Review*, 1968. 33(2): 247–259.
67. Hickson, D.J., D.S. Pugh, and D.C. Pheysey, Operations technology and organization structure: An empirical reappraisal. *Administrative Science Quarterly*, 1969. 14(3): 378–397.
68. Emery, F.E. and E.L. Trist, Socio-technical systems, in *Management Sciences, Models and Techniques*, ed. C.W. Churchman et al. 1960, London: Pergamon, pp. 83–97.
69. Bostrom, R.P. and J.S. Heinen, MIS problems and failures: A socio-technical perspective, part II: the application of socio-technical theory. *MIS Quarterly*, 1977. 1 (4): 11–28.
70. Blau, P.M., C.M. Falbe, W. McKinley, and P.K. Tracy, Technology and organization in manufacturing. *Administrative Science Quarterly*, 1976: 20–40.
71. Pfeffer, J. and H. Leblebici, Information technology and organizational structure. *Pacific Sociological Review*, 1977. 20(2): 241–261.

72. Brynjolfsson, E. and L.M. Hitt, Beyond the productivity paradox. *Communications of the ACM*, 1998. 41(8): 49–55.
73. Orlikowski, W.J., The sociomateriality of organisational life: Considering technology in management research. *Cambridge Journal of Economics*, 2009. 34(1): 125–141.
74. Giddens, A., *The Constitution of the Society: Outline of the Theory of Social Structures*. 1984, Berkeley: University of California Press.
75. Orlikowski, W.J. and D. Robey, Information technology and the structuring of organizations. *Information Systems Research*, 1991. 2(2): 143–169.
76. Barley, S.R., Technology as an occasion for structuring: Evidence from observations of CT scanners and the social order of radiology departments. *Administrative Science Quarterly*, 1986. 21: 78–108.
77. DeSanctis, G. and M.S. Poole, Capturing the complexity in advanced technology use: Adaptive structuration theory. *Organization Science*, 1994. 5(2): 121–147.
78. Mutch, A., Sociomateriality: Taking the wrong turning? *Information and Organization*, 2013. 23(1): 28–40.
79. Orlikowski, W.J., The duality of technology: Rethinking the concept of technology in organizations. *Organization Science*, 1992. 3(3): 398–427.
80. Yoo, Y., The tables have turned: How can the information systems field contribute to technology and innovation management research? *Journal of the Association for Information Systems*, 2013. 14(5): 227.
81. Leonardi, P.M., Theoretical foundations for the study of sociomateriality. *Information and Organization*, 2013. 23(2): 59–76.
82. Barad, K., Posthumanist performativity: Toward an understanding of how matter comes to matter. *Signs: Journal of Women in Culture and Society*, 2003. 28(3): 801–831.
83. Callon, M. and F. Muniesa, Peripheral vision: Economic markets as calculative collective devices. *Organization Studies*, 2005. 26(8): 1229–1250.
84. Orlikowski, W.J., Sociomaterial practices: Exploring technology at work. *Organization Studies*, 2007. 28(9): 1435–1448.
85. Napoli, P.M., Automated media: An institutional theory perspective on algorithmic media production and consumption. *Communication Theory*, 2014. 24(3): 340–360.
86. Orlikowski, W.J. and S.V. Scott, 10 sociomateriality: Challenging the separation of technology, work and organization. *Academy of Management Annals*, 2008. 2(1): 433–474.
87. Barad, K., *Meeting the Universe Halfway: Quantum Physics and the Entanglement of Matter and Meaning*. 2007, Durham, NC: Duke University Press.
88. Dourish, P. and M. Mazmanian, Media as material: Information representations as material foundations for organizational practice, in *Third International Symposium on Process Organization Studies*. 2011.
89. Mazmanian, M., M.L. Cohn, and P. Dourish, Dynamic reconfiguration in planetary exploration: A sociomaterial ethnography. *MIS Quarterly*, 2014. 38(3): 831–848.
90. Leonardi, P.M., When flexible routines meet flexible technologies: Affordance, constraint, and the imbrication of human and material agencies. *MIS Quarterly*, 2011. 35(1): 147–167.

91. Leonardi, P.M., B.A. Nardi, and J. Kallinikos, *Materiality and Organizing: Social Interaction in a Technological World*. 2012, Oxford: Oxford University Press on Demand.
92. Taylor, J.R., C. Groleu, L. Heaton, and E. Van Every, *The Computerization of Work: A Communication Perspective*. 2001, Thousand Oaks: Sage.
93. Boudreau, K., Open platform strategies and innovation: Granting access vs. devolving control. *Management Science*, 2010. 56(10): 1849–1872.
94. Latour, B., Where are the missing masses? The sociology of a few mundane artifacts, in *Shaping Technology/Building Society: Studies in Sociotechnical Change*, ed. W.E. Bijker and J. Law. 1992, Cambridge, MA: MIT Press, pp. 225–258.
95. Stang Våland, M. and S. Georg, The socio-materiality of designing organizational change. *Journal of Organizational Change Management*, 2014. 27(3): 391–406.
96. Leonardi, P.M. and S.R. Barley, What's under construction here? Social action, materiality, and power in constructivist studies of technology and organizing. *Academy of Management Annals*, 2010. 4(1): 1–51.
97. Balogun, J., C. Jacobs, P. Jarzabkowski, S. Mantere, and E. Vaara, Placing strategy discourse in context: Sociomateriality, sensemaking, and power. *Journal of Management Studies*, 2014. 51(2): 175–201.
98. Orlikowski, W.J., J. Yates, K. Okamura, and M. Fujimoto, Shaping electronic communication: The metastructuring of technology in the context of use. *Organization Science*, 1995. 6(4): 423–444.
99. Leonardi, P.M., Why do people reject new technologies and stymie organizational changes of which they are in favor? Exploring misalignments between social interactions and materiality. *Human Communication Research*, 2009. 35(3): 407–441.
100. Orlikowski, W.J., Improvising organizational transformation over time: A situated change perspective. *Information Systems Research*, 1996. 7(1): 63–92.
101. Zuboff, S., *In the Age of the Smart Machine: The Future of Work and Power*. 1988, New York: Basic Books.
102. Edmondson, A.C., R.M. Bohmer, and G.P. Pisano, Disrupted routines: Team learning and new technology implementation in hospitals. *Administrative Science Quarterly*, 2001. 46(4): 685–716.
103. Yoo, Y., Digital materiality and the emergence of an evolutionary science of the artificial, in *Materiality and Organizing: Social Interaction in a Technological World*, ed. P.M. Leonardi, B.A. Nardi, and J. Kallinikos. 2012, Oxford: Oxford University Press on Demand, pp. 134–154.
104. Latour, B., Reassembling the social: An introduction to actor-network-theory, in *Reassembling the Social: An Introduction to Actor-Network-Theory*. London: Oxford University Press.
105. Roberts, K.H. and M. Grabowski, Organizations, technology and structuring. *Managing Organizations: Current Issues*, 1999: 159–173.
106. Carlile, P.R., D. Nicolini, A. Langley, and H. Tsoukas, *How Matter Matters: Objects, Artifacts, and Materiality in Organization Studies*. 2013, Oxford: Oxford University Press.
107. Scott, S.V. and W.J. Orlikowski, Reconfiguring relations of accountability: Materialization of social media in the travel sector. *Accounting, Organizations and Society*, 2012. 37(1): 26–40.

108. Hassan, N.R., A brief history of the material in sociomateriality. *ACM SIGMIS Database: The DATABASE for Advances in Information Systems*, 2016. 47(4): 10–22.

109. Kallinikos, J., Form, function, and matter: Crossing the border of materiality, in *Materiality and Organizing: Social Interaction in a Technological World*, ed. P.M. Leonardi, B.A. Nardi, and J. Kallinikos. 2012, Oxford: Oxford University Press on Demand, pp. 67–87.

110. Faulkner, P. and J. Runde, On sociomateriality, in *Materiality and Organizing: Social Interaction in a Technological World*, ed. P.M. Leonardi, B.A. Nardi, and J. Kallinikos. 2012, Oxford: Oxford University Press on Demand, pp. 49–66.

111. Pentland, B.T. and H. Singh, Materiality: What are the consequences, in *Materiality and Organizing: Social Interaction in a Technological World*, ed. P.M. Leonardi, B.A. Nardi, and J. Kallinikos. 2012, Oxford: Oxford University Press on Demand, pp. 287–295.

112. Abadi, M. and D.G. Andersen, Learning to protect communications with adversarial neural cryptography. arXiv preprint arXiv:1610.06918, 2016.

113. Bostrom, N., *Superintelligence: Paths, Dangers, Strategies*. 2014, Oxford: Oxford University Press.

114. Ayoub, K. and K. Payne, Strategy in the age of artificial intelligence. *Journal of Strategic Studies*, 2016. 39(5–6): 793–819.

115. Yudkowsky, E., Levels of organization in general intelligence, in *Artificial General Intelligence*, ed. B. Goertzel and C. Pennachin. 2007, Berlin: Springer, pp. 389–501.

116. Yudkowsky, E., Artificial intelligence as a positive and negative factor in global risk. *Global Catastrophic Risks*, 2008. 1: 303.

117. Armstrong, S., A. Sandberg, and N. Bostrom, Thinking inside the box: Controlling and using an oracle ai. *Minds and Machines*, 2012. 22(4): 299–324.

118. Knight, W., Tech companies want AI to solve global warming. 2016. Available from: www.technologyreview.com/s/545416/could-ai-solve-the-worlds-biggest-p roblems/, accessed May 26, 2017.

119. Van Lent, M., W. Fisher, and M. Mancuso, An explainable artificial intelligence system for small-unit tactical behavior, in *The 19th National Conference on Artificial Intelligence*. 2004, San Jose: AAAI.

120. Le, Q. and B. Zoph, Using machine learning to explore neural network architecture. 2017, Google Research Blog. Available from: https://research.googleblog.com/, accessed November 25, 2018.

121. Zittrain, J.L., The generative internet. *Harvard Law Review*, 2006: 1974–2040.

122. Leibo, J.Z., V. Zambaldi, M. Lanctot, J. Marecki, and T. Graepel, Multi-agent reinforcement learning in sequential social dilemmas, in *Proceedings of the 16th Conference on Autonomous Agents and MultiAgent Systems*. 2017. São Paulo: International Foundation for Autonomous Agents and Multiagent Systems, pp. 464–473.

123. Lewis, M., et al., Deal or no deal? Training AI bots to negotiate. 2017. Available from: https://code.facebook.com/posts/1686672014972296/deal-or-no-deal-training-a i-bots-to-negotiate, accessed June 23, 2017.

124. Yoo, Y., R.J. Boland, K. Lyytinen, and A. Majchrzak, Organizing for innovation in the digitized world. *Organization Science*, 2012. 23(5): 1398–1408.

125. Alfonseca, M., M. Cebrian, A.F. Anta, L. Coviello, A. Abeliuk, and I. Rahwan, Superintelligence cannot be contained: Lessons from computability theory. arXiv preprint arXiv:1607.00913, 2016.

126. Daft, R.L., J. Murphy, and H. Willmott, *Organization Theory and Design*. Vol. 10. 2010, Andover: Cengage Learning EMEA.

127. Anderson, C., *Creating a Data-Driven Organization: Practical Advice from the Trenches*. 2015, Sebastopol: O'Reilly Media.

128. Miles, R.E., et al., Organizational strategy, structure, and process. *Academy of Management Review*, 1978. 3(3): 546–562.

129. Teece, D.J., G. Pisano, and A. Shuen, Dynamic capabilities and strategic management. *Strategic Management Journal*, 1997. 18(7): 509–533.

130. Buterin, V., Ethereum: A next-generation smart contract and decentralized application platform. 2014. Available from: https://github.com/ethereum/wiki/wiki/%5BEnglish%5D-White-Paper, accessed July 4, 2017.

131. Forte, P., D. Romano, and G. Schmid, Beyond Bitcoin, part I: A critical look at blockchain-based systems. IACR Cryptology ePrint Archive 2015.

132. Tapscott, D. and A. Tapscott, *Blockchain Revolution: How the Technology Behind Bitcoin is Changing Money, Business, and the World*. 2016, Penguin.

133. Morini, M., *From "Blockchain Hype" to a Real Business Case for Financial Markets*. Available at SSRN: https://ssrn.com/abstract=2760184, 2016.

134. Davidson, S., P. De Filippi, and J. Potts, Economics of blockchain, in *Public Choice Conference*. 2016, Fort Lauderdale.

135. Tapscott, D., Blockchain: The ledger that will record everything of value to humankind. 2017. Available from: www.weforum.org/agenda/2017/07/blockchain-the-ledger-that-will-record-everything-of-value/, accessed September 4, 2018.

136. De Meyer, A., C.H. Loch, and M.T. Pich, Managing project uncertainty: From variation to chaos. *MIT Sloan Management Review*, 2002. 43(2): 60.

137. Petrick, I.J. and R. Martinelli, Driving disruptive innovation: Problem finding and strategy setting in an uncertain world. *Research-Technology Management*, 2012. 55(6): 49–57.

138. Brown, T., Design thinking. *Harvard Business Review*, 2008. 86(6): 84–92.

139. George, G., M.R. Haas, and A. Pentland, Big data and management. *Academy of Management Journal*, 2014. 57(2): 321–326.

140. Christensen, C., M. Raynor, and R. McDonald, What is disruptive innovation. *Harvard Business Review*, 2015. 93(12): 44–53.

141. Van Rijmenam, M., T. Erekhinskaya, J. Schweitzer, and M.A. Williams, Avoid being the Turkey: How big data analytics changes the game of strategy in times of ambiguity and uncertainty. *Long Range Planning*, 2018.

142. Paap, J. and R. Katz, Anticipating disruptive innovation. *Research-Technology Management*, 2004. 47(5): 13–22.

143. Carayannopoulos, S., How technology-based new firms leverage newness and smallness to commercialize disruptive technologies. *Entrepreneurship Theory and Practice*, 2009. 33(2): 419–438.

144. Taleb, N.N., *The Black Swan: The Impact of the Highly Improbable*. 2007, Random House.

145. MacKay, R.B. and R. Chia, Choice, chance, and unintended consequences in strategic change: A process understanding of the rise and fall of Northco Automotive. *Academy of Management Journal*, 2013. 56(1): 208–230.

146. Stoll, C., The internet? bah. *Newsweek*, 1995. 27: 41.

147. Garud, R. and A. Kumaraswamy, Vicious and virtuous circles in the management of knowledge: The case of Infosys Technologies. *MIS Quarterly*, 2005. 29(1): 9–33.

148. Srivastava, A., K.M. Bartol, and E.A. Locke, Empowering leadership in management teams: Effects on knowledge sharing, efficacy, and performance. *Academy of Management Journal*, 2006. 49(6): 1239–1251.

149. Malone, T.W., Is empowerment just a fad? Control, decision making, and IT. *MIT Sloan Management Review*, 1997. 38(2): 23.

150. Merrill, P., *Innovation Never Stops: Innovation Generation: The Culture, Process, and Strategy*. 2015, ASQ Quality Press.

151. Taleb, N., *Fooled by Randomness: The Hidden Role of Chance in Life and in the Markets*. Vol. 1. 2005, Random House Incorporated.

152. Kim, H.E. and J.M. Pennings, Innovation and strategic renewal in mature markets: A study of the tennis racket industry. *Organization Science*, 2009. 20(2): 368–383.

153. Akkermans, H.A. and L.N. Van Wassenhove, Searching for the grey swans: The next 50 years of production research. *International Journal of Production Research*, 2013. 51(23–24): 6746–6755.

154. Lebied, M., 5 big data examples in your real life at bars, restaurants, and casinos. 2017. Available from: www.datapine.com/blog/big-data-examples-in-real-life/, accessed September 4, 2018.

155. Bansal, M., Using big data to brew profits one pint at a time. 2013. Available from: https://blogs.saphana.com/2013/10/04/using-big-data-to-brew-profits-one-p int-at-a-time/, accessed September 4, 2018.

156. Mulligan, C.E.A., *The Impact of Datafication on Strategic Landscapes*. 2014.

157. van der Meulen, R., Gartner says 8.4 billion connected "things" will be in use in 2017, up 31 percent from 2016. 2017. Available from: www.gartner.com/en/news room/press-releases/2017-02-07-gartner-says-8-billion-connected-things-will-be-in-us e-in-2017-up-31-percent-from-2016, accessed September 4, 2018.

158. Ericsson, Internet of Things forecast. 2016. Available from: www.ericsson.com/ en/mobility-report/internet-of-things-forecast, accessed September 4, 2018.

159. Statista, Internet of Things (IoT) connected devices installed base worldwide from 2015 to 2025 (in billions). 2016. Available from: www.statista.com/statistics/471264/ iot-number-of-connected-devices-worldwide/, accessed September 4, 2018.

160. Wellers, D., *Digital Trends That Will Shape Your Future*. 2016.

161. Reinsel, D.G., J. Gantz, and J. Rydning, *Data Age 2025: The Evolution of Data to Life-Critical*. 2017.

162. Gorodyansky, D. and D. Yang, How massive data growth is good for AI (and a problem). 2017, July 6. Available from: https://venturebeat.com/2017/07/06/how-ma ssive-data-growth-is-good-for-ai-and-a-problem/, accessed October 5, 2017.

163. Laney, D., 3D data management: Controlling data volume, velocity and variety. *META Group Research Note*, 2001. 6: 70.

164. Van Rijmenam, M., *Think Bigger: Developing a Successful Big Data Strategy for Your Business*. 2014, New York: Amacom.

165. Barton, D. and D. Court, Making advanced analytics work for you. *Harvard Business Review*, 2012. 90(10): 78–83.

166. Vahn, G.-Y., Business analytics in the age of Big Data. *Business Strategy Review*, 2014. 25(3): 8–9.

167. Bean, R., Just using big data isn't enough anymore. *Harvard Business Review Online*, 2016.

168. Siemens, G. and P. Long, Penetrating the fog: Analytics in learning and education. *EDUCAUSE Review*, 2011. 46(5): 30.

169. Chen, D., S.L. Sain, and K. Guo, Data mining for the online retail industry: A case study of RFM model-based customer segmentation using data mining. *Journal of Database Marketing & Customer Strategy Management*, 2012. 19(3): 197–208.

170. Chui, M., B. Brown, J. Bughin, R. Dobbs, C. Roxburgh, and A.H.B.J. Manyika, Big data: The next frontier for innovation, competition, and productivity. McKinsey Global Institute, 2011.

171. Mortenson, M.J., N.F. Doherty, and S. Robinson, Operational research from Taylorism to Terabytes: A research agenda for the analytics age. *European Journal of Operational Research*, 2015. 241(3): 583–595.

172. Gandomi, A. and M. Haider, Beyond the hype: Big data concepts, methods, and analytics. *International Journal of Information Management*, 2015. 35(2): 137–144.

173. LaValle, S., E. Lesser, R. Shockley, M.S. Hopkins, and N. Kruschwitz, Big data, analytics and the path from insights to value. *MIT Sloan Management Review*, 2011. 52(2): 21–32.

174. R. Koch, From business intelligence to predictive analytics. *Strategic Finance*, 2015. 96(7): 56.

175. O'Neil, C., *Weapons of Math Destruction: How Big Data Increases Inequality and Threatens Democracy*. 2016, New York: Crown Publishing Group.

176. Perugini, D. and M. Perugini, Characterised and personalised predictive-prescriptive analytics using agent-based simulation. *International Journal of Data Analysis Techniques and Strategies*, 2014. 6(3): 209–227.

177. Delen, D. and H. Demirkan, Data, information and analytics as services. *Decision Support Systems*, 2013. 55(1): 359–363.

178. Hamilton, B. and R. Koch, From predictive to prescriptive analytics. 2015. Available from: http://sfmagazine.com/post-entry/june-2015-from-predictive-to-p rescriptive-analytics/, accessed October 5, 2017.

179. Wu, M., Prescriptive analytics: Let me see you work, work, work. 2016, October 28. Available from: https://community.lithium.com/t5/Science-of-Social-Blog/Pre scriptive-Analytics-Let-Me-See-You-Work-Work-Work/ba-p/255119, accessed October 5, 2017.

180. Brahm, C., A. Cheris, and L. Sherer, What big data means for customer loyalty. 2016. Available from: www.bain.com/publications/articles/what-big-data-means-for-customer-loyalty.aspx, accessed October 5, 2017.

181. Davenport, T., Analytics 3.0. 2013, December 1. Available from: https://hbr.org/2013/12/analytics-30, accessed October 5, 2017.

182. Olavsrud, T., GE, Pitney Bowes team up on predictive and prescriptive analytics | CIO. 2015, July 14. Available from: www.cio.com/article/2947908/big-data/ge-p itney-bowes-team-up-on-predictive-and-prescriptive-analytics.html, accessed October 5, 2017.

183. Morgan, L., 8 smart ways to use prescriptive analytics. 2016. Available from: www.informationweek.com/cloud/platform-as-a-service/8-smart-ways-to-use-prescri ptive-analytics/d/d-id/1326074?image_number=6, accessed October 5, 2017.

184. Finger, L., Predictive analytics: A case for private equity?2017. Available from: www.forbes.com/sites/lutzfinger/2015/02/10/predictive-analytics-case-for-private-equ ity/, accessed October 5, 2017.

185. Columbus, L., Roundup of analytics, big data & BI forecasts and market esti- mates, 2016. 2016. Available from: www.forbes.com/sites/louiscolumbus/2016/08/20/ roundup-of-analytics-big-data-bi-forecasts-and-market-estimates-2016/, accessed April 20, 2017.

186. Marr, B., 17 predictions about the future of big data everyone should read. 2016. Available from: www.forbes.com/sites/bernardmarr/2016/03/15/17-predictions-about- the-future-of-big-data-everyone-should-read/, accessed October 5, 2017.

187. Teece, D.J., Explicating dynamic capabilities: The nature and microfoundations of (sustainable) enterprise performance. *Strategic Management Journal*, 2007. 28(13): 1319–1350.

188. Teece, D. and G. Pisano, The dynamic capabilities of firms: An introduction. *Industrial and Corporate Change*, 1994. 3(3): 537–556.

189. Eisenhardt, K.M. and J.A. Martin, Dynamic capabilities: What are they? *Strategic Management Journal*, 2000. 21(10/11): 1105.

190. Peteraf, M., G. Di Stefano, and G. Verona, The elephant in the room of dynamic capabilities: Bringing two diverging conversations together. *Strategic Management Journal*, 2013. 34(12): 1389–1410.

191. Zollo, M. and S.G. Winter, Deliberate learning and the evolution of dynamic capabilities. *Organization Science*, 2002. 13(3): 339–351.

192. Galunic, D.C. and K.M. Eisenhardt, Architectural innovation and modular corporate forms. *Academy of Management Journal*, 2001. 44(6): 1229–1249.

193. Marine-Roig, E. and S.A. Clavé, Tourism analytics with massive user-generated content: A case study of Barcelona. *Journal of Destination Marketing & Management*, 2015. 4(3): 162–172.

194. Dutta, D. and I. Bose, Managing a Big Data project: The case of Ramco Cements Limited. *International Journal of Production Economics*, 2015. 165: 293–306.

195. Kindström, D., C. Kowalkowski, and E. Sandberg, Enabling service innovation: A dynamic capabilities approach. *Journal of Business Research*, 2013. 66(8): 1063–1073.

196. Kay, N.M., Dynamic capabilities as context: The role of decision, system and structure. *Industrial and Corporate Change*, 2010. 19(4): 1205–1223.

197. Felin, T., T.C. Powell, D. Teece, and S. Leih, Designing organizations for dynamic capabilities. *California Management Review*, forthcoming, 2015.

198. Teece, D.J., A dynamic capabilities-based entrepreneurial theory of the multinational enterprise. *Journal of International Business Studies*, 2014. 45(1): 8–37.

199. Helfat, C.E. and M.A. Peteraf, Managerial cognitive capabilities and the micro- foundations of dynamic capabilities. *Strategic Management Journal*, 2015. 36(6): 831–850.

200. Fernández-Manzano, E.-P., E. Neira, and J. Clares-Gavilán, Data management in audiovisual business: Netflix as a case study. *El Profesional de la Información*, 2016. 25: 568–576.

201. Lawson, B. and D. Samson, Developing innovation capability in organisations: A dynamic capabilities approach. *International Journal of Innovation Management*, 2001. 5(3): 377–400.

202. Ikeda, K. and A. Marshall, How successful organizations drive innovation. *Strategy & Leadership*, 2016. 44(3): 9–19.

203. Liao, J.J., J.R. Kickul, and H. Ma, Organizational dynamic capability and innovation: An empirical examination of internet firms. *Journal of Small Business Management*, 2009. 47(3): 263–286.

204. Tellis, G.J., J.C. Prabhu, and R.K. Chandy, Radical innovation across nations: The preeminence of corporate culture. *Journal of Marketing*, 2009. 73(1): 3–23.

205. Wei, L.-Q. and C.-M. Lau, High performance work systems and performance: The role of adaptive capability. *Human Relations*, 2010. 63(10): 1487–1511.

206. Erevelles, S., N. Fukawa, and L. Swayne, Big Data consumer analytics and the transformation of marketing. *Journal of Business Research*, 2016. 69(2): 897–904.

207. Wamba, S.F., A. Gunasekaran, S. Akter, S.J. Ren, R. Dubey, and S.J. Childe, Big data analytics and firm performance: Effects of dynamic capabilities. *Journal of Business Research*, 2017. 70: 356–365.

208. Opresnik, D. and M. Taisch, The value of big data in servitization. *International Journal of Production Economics*, 2015. 165: 174–184.

209. Wang, C.L. and P.K. Ahmed, Dynamic capabilities: A review and research agenda. *International Journal of Management Reviews*, 2007. 9(1): 31–51.

210. Evans, J.R. and C.H. Lindner, Business analytics: The next frontier for decision sciences. *Decision Line*, 2012. 43(2): 4–6.

211. Kaisler, S., F. Armour, J.A. Espinosa, and W. Money, Big data: Issues and challenges moving forward, in *System Sciences (HICSS), 2013 46th Hawaii International Conference on.* 2013. IEEE.

212. Larson, D. and V. Chang, A review and future direction of agile, business intelligence, analytics and data science. *International Journal of Information Management*, 2016. 36(5): 700–710.

213. Chesbrough, H.W. and M.M. Appleyard, Open innovation and strategy. *California Management Review*, 2007. 50(1): 57–76.

214. Chesbrough, H.W., The era of open innovation. *Managing Innovation and Change*, 2006. 127(3): 34–41.

215. Appleyard, M.M. and H.W. Chesbrough, *The Dynamics of Open Strategy: From Adoption to Reversion.* 2016, Long Range Planning.

216. Surowiecki, J., *The Wisdom of Crowds.* 2005, Anchor.

217. Stieger, D., K. Matzler, S. Chatterjee, and F. Ladstaetter-Fussenegger, Democratizing strategy. *California Management Review*, 2012. 54(4): 44–68.

218. Chesbrough, H.W., *Open Innovation: The New Imperative for Creating and Profiting from Technology.* 2003, Boston: Harvard Business Press.

219. Dobusch, L., D. Seidl, and F. Werle, Opening up the strategy-making process: Comparing open strategy to open innovation. University of Zurich, Institute of Business Administration, UZH Business Working Paper, 2015(359).

220. Whittington, R., L. Cailluet, and B. Yakis-Douglas, Opening strategy: Evolution of a precarious profession. *British Journal of Management*, 2011. 22(3): 531–544.

221. Amrollahi, A. and A.H. Ghapnchi, Open strategic planning in universities: A case study, in *2016 49th Hawaii International Conference on System Sciences (HICSS).* 2016, IEEE.

222. Gegenhuber, T. and L. Dobusch, Making an impression through openness: How open strategy-making practices change in the evolution of new ventures. *Long Range Planning*, 2017. 50(3): 337–354.

223. Pittz, T.G. and T. Adler, An exemplar of open strategy: Decision-making within multi-sector collaborations. *Management Decision*, 2016. 54(7): 1595–1614.
224. Kennedy, S., G. Whiteman, and J. van den Ende, *Radical Innovation for Sustainability: The Power of Strategy and Open Innovation*. 2016, Long Range Planning.
225. Taylor, J.R. and E.J. Van Every, *The Emergent Organization: Communication as its Site and Surface*. 1999, Routledge.
226. Luedicke, M.K., K.C. Husemann, S. Furnari, and F. Ladstaetter, Radically open strategizing: How the premium cola collective takes open strategy to the extreme. *Long Range Planning*, 2017. 50(3): 371–384.
227. Stieger, D., K. Matzler, S. Chatterjee, and F. Ladstaetter-Fussenegger, Democratizing strategy: How crowdsourcing can be used for strategy dialogues. *California Management Review*, 2012. 54(4): 44–68.
228. Hautz, J., D. Seidl, and R. Whittington, Open strategy: Dimensions, dilemmas, dynamics. *Long Range Planning*, 2017. 50(3): 298–309.
229. Korsgaard, M.A., D.M. Schweiger, and H.J. Sapienza, Building commitment, attachment, and trust in strategic decision-making teams: The role of procedural justice. *Academy of Management Journal*, 1995. 38(1): 60–84.
230. Mantere, S. and E. Vaara, On the problem of participation in strategy: A critical discursive perspective. *Organization Science*, 2008. 19(2): 341–358.
231. Powley, E.H., R.E. Fry, F.J. Barrett, and D.S. Bright, Dialogic democracy meets command and control: Transformation through the appreciative inquiry summit. *The Academy of Management Executive*, 2004. 18(3): 67–80.
232. Bjelland, O.M. and R.C. Wood, An inside view of IBM's "Innovation Jam". *MIT Sloan Management Review*, 2008. 50(1): 32.
233. Johnson, G., S. Prashantham, S.W. Floyd, and N. Bourque, The ritualization of strategy workshops. *Organization Studies*, 2010. 31(12): 1589–1618.
234. Lewin, A.Y., L. Välikangas, and J. Chen, Enabling open innovation: Lessons from Haier. *International Journal of Innovation Studies*, 2017. 1(1): 5–19.
235. Biggs, J., A 15-year-old hacked the secure Ledger crypto wallet. 2018. Available from: https://techcrunch.com/2018/03/21/a-15-year-old-hacked-the-secure-ledger-crypto-wallet/, accessed November 1, 2018.
236. Bourne, V., *The State of Encryption Today*. 2015.
237. Curtis, S., Sony saved thousands of passwords in a folder named "Password". *Telegraph*, 2014, May 12. Available from: www.telegraph.co.uk/technology/sony/11274727/Sony-saved-thousands-of-passwords-in-a-folder-named-Password.html, accessed September 5, 2018.
238. Löffler, M. and A. Tschiesner, *The Internet of Things and the Future of Manufacturing*. 2013, McKinsey & Company.
239. Reid, F. and M. Harrigan, An analysis of anonymity in the bitcoin system, in *Security and Privacy in Social Networks*. 2013, New York: Springer, pp. 197–223.
240. Chaum, D., *Blind Signatures for Untraceable Payments: Advances in Cryptology*. 1983, Boston: Springer.
241. Nakamoto, S., Bitcoin: A peer-to-peer electronic cash system. 2008. Available from: https://bitcoin.org/bitcoin.pdf, accessed December 22, 2016.
242. Van Rijmenam, M. and P. Ryan, *Blockchain: Transforming Your Business and Our World*. 2019, London: Routledge.
243. Hall, R.H., The concept of bureaucracy: An empirical assessment. *American Journal of Sociology*, 1963. 69(1): 32–40.

244. Weber, M., H.H. Gerth, and C.W. Mills, *From Max Weber: Essays in Sociology*. 1948, London: Routledge and Kegan Paul.
245. Scott, W.R. and G.F. Davis, *Organizations and Organizing: Rational, Natural and Open Systems Perspectives*. 2015, Routledge.
246. Katz, D. and R.L. Kahn, *The Social Psychology of Organizations*. Vol. 2. 1978, New York: Wiley.
247. Burnes, B., Complexity theories and organizational change. *International Journal of Management Reviews*, 2005. 7(2): 73–90.
248. Malecki, E.J., The R&D location decision of the firm and "creative" regions: A survey. *Technovation*, 1987. 6(3): 205–222.
249. Snow, C.C., R.E. Miles, and H.J. Coleman, Managing 21st century network organizations. *Organizational Dynamics*, 1992. 20(3): 5–20.
250. Miles, R.E., C.S. Snow, J.A. Mathews, G. Miles, and H.J. Coleman, Organizing in the knowledge age: Anticipating the cellular form. *The Academy of Management Executive*, 1997. 11(4): 7–20.
251. Guoqiang, S., The definition, characteristics and forming factors of network organization [J]. *Nankai Business Review*, 2001. 4: 008.
252. Emery, M., The current version of Emery's open systems theory. *Systemic Practice and Action Research*, 2000. 13(5): 623–643.
253. Osborne, C., How open-source Big Data can improve supply chains. 2012. Available from: www.zdnet.com/article/how-open-source-big-data-can-improve-supply-chains/, accessed September 5, 2018.
254. Robertson, B.J., *Holacracy: The New Management System for a Rapidly Changing World*. 2015, London: Macmillan.
255. Kelly, J., UBS leads team of banks working on blockchain settlement system. 2016, August 24. Available from: www.reuters.com/article/us-banks-blockchain-ubs-idUSKCN10Z147, accessed February 11, 2017.
256. Arnold, M., Six global banks join forces to create digital currency. 2017, August 31. Available from: www.ft.com/content/20c10d58-8d9c-11e7-a352-e46f43c5825d, accessed September 20, 2017.
257. del Castillo, M., The world's largest shipping firm now tracks cargo on blockchain. 2017. Available from: www.coindesk.com/worlds-largest-shipping-company-tracking-cargo-blockchain/, accessed November 1, 2018.
258. del Castillo, M., IBM-Maersk blockchain platform adds 92 clients as part of global launch. 2018. Available from: www.forbes.com/sites/michaeldelcastillo/2018/08/09/ibm-maersk-blockchain-platform-adds-92-clients-as-part-of-global-launch-1/#4b561d4468a4, accessed November 1, 2018.
259. Maersk. 2018. Available from: www.maersk.com/en/news/2018/06/29/maersk-and-ibm-introduce-tradelens-blockchain-shipping-solution, accessed April 29, 2019.
260. Simson, M., SITA, British Airways and Heathrow conducting blockchain trial for operational data sync. 2017. Available from: https://apex.aero/2017/06/05/sita-british-airways-heathrow-blockchain-trial-operational-data-sync, accessed November 1, 2018.
261. Baker, J., Blockchain: The future of flight data management?2018. Available from: www.airport-technology.com/features/blockchain-future-flight-data-management/, accessed November 1, 2018.
262. UPS, *UPS Joins Top Alliance To Create Blockchain Standards For Logistics*. 2017.

263. Baydakova, A., UPS eyes blockchain in bid to track global shipping data. 2018. Available from: www.coindesk.com/ups-eyes-blockchain-in-bid-to-track-global-ship ping-data/, accessed November 1, 2018.

264. Staff, UPS blockchain patent to route packages through international supply chains via multiple carriers. 2018. Available from: www.supplychain247.com/article/ ups_blockchain_patent_to_route_packages_through_international_supply_chains, accessed November 1, 2018.

265. Pilkington, M., Blockchain technology: Principles and applications, in *Research Handbook on Digital Transformations*, ed. F. Xavier Olleros and Majlinda Zhegu. 2016, Edward Elgar.

266. Melone, M., Basics and history of PKI. 2012. Available from: https://blogs.tech net.microsoft.com/option_explicit/2012/03/10/basics-and-history-of-pki/, accessed May 2, 2017.

267. Ting, K.K., S.C.L. Yuen, K.H. Lee, and P.H.W. Leong, An FPGA based SHA-256 processor, in *International Conference on Field Programmable Logic and Applications*. 2002, Montpellier: Springer.

268. Plassaras, N.A., Regulating digital currencies: Bringing Bitcoin within the reach of IMF. *Chicago Journal of International Law*, 2013. 14: 377.

269. Johansen, B.E., Dating the Iroquois confederacy. *Akwesasne Notes*, 1995. 1(4): 62–63.

270. Olfati-Saber, R., J.A. Fax, and R.M. Murray, Consensus and cooperation in networked multi-agent systems. *Proceedings of the IEEE*, 2007. 95(1): 215–233.

271. Seibold, S. and G. Samman, *Consensus*. 2016, Delaware: KPMG.

272. Lamport, L., R. Shostak, and M. Pease, The Byzantine generals problem. *ACM Transactions on Programming Languages and Systems (TOPLAS)*, 1982. 4(3): 382–401.

273. Castro, M. and B. Liskov, Practical Byzantine fault tolerance, in *Third Symposium on Operating Systems Design and Implementation*. 1999, New Orleans.

274. Pîrjan, A., et al., Research issues regarding the Bitcoin and Alternative Coins digital currencies. *Journal of Information Systems & Operations Management*, 2015. 9(1): 1–14.

275. Christidis, K. and M. Devetsikiotis, Blockchains and smart contracts for the Internet of Things. *IEEE Access*, 2016. 4: 2292–2303.

276. Anwar, H., Consensus algorithms: The root of the blockchain technology 1. 2018. Available from: https://101blockchains.com/consensus-algorithms-blockchain/, accessed September 5, 2018.

277. Condos, J., W.H. Sorrell, and S.L. Donegan, Blockchain technology: Opportunities and risks. *Vermont*, 2016.

278. Zhang, Y. and J. Wen, The IoT electric business model: Using blockchain technology for the Internet of Things. *Peer-to-Peer Networking and Applications*, 2016. 10(4): 983–994.

279. O'Dwyer, R., The Revolution will (not) be decentralised: Blockchains. *Commons Transition*, 2015. 11.

280. Polemitis, A., Bitcoin series 24: The mega-master blockchain list. 2014. Available from: http://ledracapital.com/blog/2014/3/11/bitcoin-series-24-the-mega-master-blockchain-list, accessed February 11, 2017.

281. Pash, C., The Commonwealth Bank just used blockchain in a "world first" global transaction. 2016, October 24. Available from: www.businessinsider.com.au/the-comm

onwealth-bank-just-used-blockchain-in-a-world-first-global-transaction-2016-10, accessed February 11, 2017.

282. Hoffman, A. and R. Munsterman, Dreyfus teams with banks for first agriculture blockchain trade. 2018, January 22. Available from: www.bloomberg.com/news/articles/2018-01-22/dreyfus-teams-with-banks-for-first-agriculture-blockchain-trade, accessed February 2, 2018.

283. Bank, T.W., World Bank prices first global blockchain bond, raising A$110 million. 2018. Available from: www.worldbank.org/en/news/press-release/2018/08/23/world-bank-prices-first-global-blockchain-bond-raising-a110-million, accessed September 5, 2018.

284. Szabo, N., Smart contracts. 1994. Available from: www.fon.hum.uva.nl/rob/Courses/InformationInSpeech/CDROM/Literature/LOTwinterschool2006/szabo.best.vwh.net/smart.contracts.html, accessed July 5, 2017.

285. Crosby, M., P. Pattanayak, S. Verma, and V. Kalyanaraman, BlockChain technology: Beyond bitcoin. *Applied Innovation*, 2016. 2(6–10): 71.

286. Luu, L., D.-H. Chu, H. Olickel, P. Saxena, and A. Hobor, Making smart contracts smarter. 2016, Cryptology ePrint Archive, Report.

287. Finley, K., Someone just stole $50 million from the biggest crowdfunded project ever (humans can't be trusted). 2016. Available from: www.wired.com/2016/06/50-million-hack-just-showed-dao-human/, accessed February 11, 2017.

288. Alam, I., What are Ricardian contracts? A complete guide. 2018. Available from: http://101blockchains.com/ricardian-contracts/, accessed November 22, 2018.

289. Buterin, V., DAOs are not scary, part 1: Self-enforcing contracts and factum law. Ethereum Blog. 2014, February 24. Available from: https://blog.ethereum.org/2014/02/24/daos-are-not-scary-part-1-self-enforcing-contracts-and-factum-law/, accessed February 11, 2017.

290. Wright, A. and P. De Filippi, Decentralized blockchain technology and the rise of lex cryptographia. Available at SSRN: https://ssrn.com/abstract=2580664, 2015.

291. Norta, A., A.B. Othman, and K. Taveter, Conflict-resolution lifecycles for governed decentralized autonomous organization collaboration, in *Proceedings of the 2015 2nd International Conference on Electronic Governance and Open Society: Challenges in Eurasia*. 2015, St. Petersburg: ACM.

292. Norta, A., Establishing distributed governance infrastructures for enacting cross-organization collaborations, in *International Conference on Service-Oriented Computing*. 2015, Goa: Springer.

293. Kosten, D., Bitcoin mission statement: Or what does it mean sharing economy and distributed trust? MPRA Paper, 2015.

294. Rajesh, M., Inside Japan's first robot-staffed hotel. 2015, August 14. Available from: www.theguardian.com/travel/2015/aug/14/japan-henn-na-hotel-staffed-by-robots, accessed February 11, 2017.

295. Malmo, C., Bitcoin is unsustainable. 2017. Available from: https://motherboard.vice.com/en_us/article/ae3p7e/bitcoin-is-unsustainable, accessed September 20, 2017.

296. de Vries, A., Bitcoin's growing energy problem. *Joule*, 2018. 2(5): 801–805.

297. *The Economist*, Why bitcoin uses so much energy. 2018. Available from: www.economist.com/the-economist-explains/2018/07/09/why-bitcoin-uses-so-much-energy, accessed September 7, 2018.

298. CERN, Powering CERN. 2017. Available from: http://home.cern/about/engineering/powering-cern, accessed September 20, 2017.

299. Digiconomist, Bitcoin energy consumption index. 2017. Available from: https://digiconomist.net/bitcoin-energy-consumption, accessed September 20, 2017.
300. VISA, *Annual Report VISA 2016*. 2016.
301. Zyskind, G. and O. Nathan, Decentralizing privacy: Using blockchain to protect personal data, in *2015 IEEE CS Security and Privacy Workshops*. 2015, San Jose: IEEE.
302. Ruefli, T.W., Behavioral externalities in decentralized organizations. *Management Science*, 1971. 17(10): B-649-B-657.
303. Dewar, R.D. and J.E. Dutton, The adoption of radical and incremental innovations: An empirical analysis. *Management Science*, 1986. 32(11): 1422–1433.
304. Mintzberg, H., The structuring of organizations, in *Readings in Strategic Management*. 1989, London: Palgrave, pp. 322–352.
305. Pacanowsky, M., Communication in the empowering organization. *Annals of the International Communication Association*, 1988. 11(1): 356–379.
306. Strikwerda, J., An entrepreneurial model of corporate governance: Devolving powers to subsidiary boards. *Corporate Governance: The International Journal of Business in Society*, 2003. 3(2): 38–57.
307. Sedgwick, K., 46% of last year's ICOs have failed already. 2018. Available from: https://news.bitcoin.com/46-last-years-icos-failed-already/, accessed September 5, 2018.
308. Mougayar, W., Tokenomics: A business guide to token usage, utility and value. 2017. Available from: https://medium.com/@wmougayar/tokenomics-a-business-guide-to-token-usage-utility-and-value-b19242053416, accessed September 5, 2018.
309. Bonpay, Security tokens vs. utility tokens. 2017. Available from: https://medium.com/@bonpay/security-tokens-vs-utility-tokens-1aa7531aabe8, accessed September 5, 2018.
310. Commission, U.S.S.a.E., *Two ICO Issuers Settle SEC Registration Charges, Agree to Register Tokens as Securities*. 2018, SEC.
311. SEC, *SEC Issues Investigative Report Concluding DAO Tokens, a Digital Asset, Were Securities*. 2017, SEC: www.sec.gov.
312. BitTrust, Passing the Howey test: How to regulate blockchain tokens. 2017. Available from: https://medium.com/bittrust/passing-the-howey-test-how-to-regulate-blockchain-tokens-d218da93a8b6, accessed September 5, 2018.
313. Schor, L., 8 important things to know about security tokens / token regulation. 2017. Available from: https://medium.com/@argongroup/8-important-things-to-know-about-security-tokens-token-regulation-3d548a1a6367, accessed September 5, 2018.
314. Brenn, ICOs & token types for dummies: A buyers guide to crypto-tokens. 2017. Available from: https://hackernoon.com/icos-token-types-for-dummies-an-buyers-guide-to-crypto-tokens-b6edea16776e?gi=a26daee71903, accessed September 5, 2018.
315. Krueger, F., How to think about Tokenomics. 2017. Available from: https://medium.com/workcoin/how-to-think-about-tokenomics-b3da509444e5, accessed September 5, 2018.
316. Rosic, A., 99% of ICO's will fail and I will tell you why. 2017. Available from: www.linkedin.com/pulse/99-icos-fail-i-tell-you-why-ameer-rosic/, accessed September 5, 2018.

317. The Economist, Just spend. 2016. Available from: www.economist.com/finance-a
nd-economics/2016/11/17/just-spend, accessed September 7, 2018.
318. Kapron, Z., Measuring credit: How Baidu, Alibaba and Tencent may succeed
where Facebook failed. 2017. Available from: www.forbes.com/sites/zennonkapron/
2016/03/17/measuring-credit-how-baidu-alibaba-and-tencent-may-succeed-where-fac
ebook-failed/, accessed September 4, 2017.
319. Borak, M., China's social credit system: AI-driven panopticon or fragmented
foundation for a sincerity culture? *TechNode*, 2017, August 23. Available from:
http://technode.com/2017/08/23/chinas-social-credit-system-ai-driven-panopticon-or-
fragmented-foundation-for-a-sincerity-culture/, accessed September 4, 2017.
320. Ming, C., FICO with Chinese characteristics: Nice rewards, but punishing
penalties. 2017, March 16. Available from: www.cnbc.com/2017/03/16/china-socia
l-credit-system-ant-financials-sesame-credit-and-others-give-scores-that-go-beyond-fi
co.html, accessed September 4, 2017.
321. Nguyen, C., China might create a Black Mirror-like score for each citizen based
on how trustworthy they are. 2016, October 27. Available from: www.busi
nessinsider.com.au/china-social-credit-score-like-black-mirror-2016-10, accessed
September 4, 2017.
322. Hatton, C., China "social credit": Beijing sets up huge system. BBC News. 2015.
Available from: www.bbc.com/news/world-asia-china-34592186, accessed September
4, 2017.
323. O'Kane, S., China wants to track citizens' cars with mandatory RFID chips.
2018. Available from: www.theverge.com/2018/6/13/17458432/china-surveillance-ca
r-tracking-mandatory-rfid-chips, accessed September 7, 2018.
324. Russell, J., China's CCTV surveillance network took just 7 minutes to capture
BBC reporter. 2017. Available from: https://techcrunch.com/2017/12/13/china
-cctv-bbc-reporter/, accessed September 7, 2018.
325. Long, Q., China aims for near-total surveillance, including in people's homes.
2018. Available from: www.rfa.org/english/news/china/surveillance-03302018111415.
html, accessed September 7, 2018.
326. BBC, Chinese man caught by facial recognition at pop concert. 2018. Available
from: www.bbc.com/news/world-asia-china-43751276, accessed September 7, 2018.
327. Dement, D., China's new "social credit" system: Big data, mass surveillance and
judgment. 2017. Available from: http://thehigherlearning.com/2017/02/22/china
s-new-social-credit-system-big-data-mass-surveillance-and-judgment/, accessed
September 4, 2017.
328. Mendling, J., I. Weber, W. Van Der Aalst, J. Vom Brocke, C. Cabanillas, F.
Daniel, and S. Debois, Blockchains for business process management-challenges
and opportunities. *ACM Transactions on Management Information Systems
(TMIS)*, 2018. 9(1): 4.
329. Tapscott, A. and D. Tapscott, How blockchain is changing finance. *Harvard
Business Review*, 2017. 1.
330. Michelman, P., Seeing beyond the blockchain hype. *MIT Sloan Management
Review*, 2017. 58(4): 17.
331. Scuffham, M., Bank of Canada, TMX say blockchain feasible for securities settlement. 2018. Available from: www.reuters.com/article/us-canada-tech-blockchain/
bank-of-canada-tmx-say-blockchain-feasible-for-securities-settlement-idUSKBN1IC
18G, accessed September 7, 2018.

332. Hackett, R., Why big business is racing to build blockchains. 2017. Available from: https://fortune.com/2017/08/22/bitcoin-ethereum-blockchain-cryptocurrency/, accessed September 7, 2018.

333. Hackett, R., Walmart and 9 food giants team up on IBM blockchain plans. 2017. Available from: http://fortune.com/2017/08/22/walmart-blockchain-ibm-food-nestle-unilever-tyson-dole/, accessed September 7, 2018.

334. Akexandre, A., Walmart is ready to use blockchain for its live food business. 2018. Available from: https://cointelegraph.com/news/walmart-is-ready-to-use-blockchain-for-its-live-food-business, accessed September 7, 2018.

335. Bindi, T., Alibaba and AusPost team up to tackle food fraud with blockchain. 2017. Available from: https://www.zdnet.com/article/alibaba-and-auspost-team-up-to-tackle-food-fraud-with-blockchain/, accessed September 7, 2018.

336. Nott, G., Blackmores and Fonterra trial Alibaba food provenance blockchain. 2018. Available from: www.computerworld.com.au/article/640572/blackmores-fonterra-trial-alibaba-food-provenance-blockchain/, accessed September 7, 2017.

337. van den Dam, R., Blockchain in telecom: From concept to reality. 2018. Available from: www.ibm.com/blogs/insights-on-business/telecom-media-entertainment/blockchain-telecom-concept-reality/, accessed September 7, 2018.

338. Sallaba, M.G. and Mirko René, Blockchain @ Telco: How blockchain can impact the telecommunications industry and its relevance to the C-Suite. 2016. p. 22. Available from: www2.deloitte.com/content/dam/Deloitte/za/Documents/technology-media-telecommunications/za_TMT_Blockchain_TelCo.pdf, accessed April 29, 2019.

339. Kochhar, R., Blockchain in telecom: Hype or reality?2018. Available from: www.netmanias.com/en/post/blog/13145/blockchain/blockchain-in-telecom-hype-or-reality, accessed September 7, 2018.

340. Dickson, B., How blockchain can change the future of IoT. 2016, November 20. Available from: https://venturebeat.com/2016/11/20/how-blockchain-can-change-the-future-of-iot/, accessed September 7, 2017.

341. Reichert, C., Telstra launches Smart Home devices and pricing. ZDNet. 2016. Available from: www.zdnet.com/article/telstra-launches-smart-home-devices-and-pricing/, accessed September 7, 2017.

342. Reichert, C., Telstra explores blockchain, biometrics to secure smart home IoT devices. ZDNet. 2016. Available from: www.zdnet.com/article/telstra-explores-blockchain-biometrics-to-secure-smart-home-iot-devices/, accessed September 7, 2017.

343. Das, R., Does blockchain have a place in healthcare?2017. Available from: www.forbes.com/sites/reenitadas/2017/05/08/does-blockchain-have-a-place-in-healthcare/, accessed September 7, 2017.

344. del Castillo, M., T-Mobile's blockchain work is quietly coming together. 2018. Available from: www.coindesk.com/t-mobiles-stealth-blockchain-work-quietly-coming-together/, accessed September 7, 2018.

345. Russo, C. and Y. Gao, Huawei is in talks to build a blockchain-ready smartphone. 2018. Available from: www.bloomberg.com/news/articles/2018-03-21/huawei-said-to-be-in-talks-to-build-blockchain-ready-smartphone, accessed September 7, 2018.

346. McLaughlin, B., This week in China tech: Huawei's blockchain move, bike sharing goes bust, and more. 2018. Available from: www.forbes.com/sites/baymcla

ughlin/2018/03/27/this-week-in-china-tech-huaweis-blockchain-move-bike-sharing-go es-bust-and-more/#7d5a7976baf0, accessed September 7, 2018.

347. Deprez, E. and C. Chen, Medical journals have a fake news problem. 2017. Available from: www.bloomberg.com/news/features/2017-08-29/medical-journals-ha ve-a-fake-news-problem, accessed September 7, 2018.

348. Gottfried, J.S. and E. Shearer, News use across social media platforms 2016. 2016. Available from: www.journalism.org/2016/05/26/news-use-across-social-media -platforms-2016/, accessed September 7, 2018.

349. Kiloran, M., Senate hears Facebook pays news publishers average of $100 a day to use content. 2017. Available from: www.news.com.au/finance/business/media/sena te-hears-facebook-pays-news-publishers-average-of-100-a-day-to-use-content/news-s tory/4a98eaf6fd4a94e8210cdc67a429b4b4, accessed September 7, 2018.

350. Magee, C., The age of imagination, in *2nd International Symposium: National Security & National Competitiveness: Open Source Solutions*. 1993, Proceedings.

351. The Supreme People's Court of the People's Republic of China, 2018. Available from: www.court.gov.cn/zixun-xiangqing-116981.html, accessed April 29, 2019.

352. Cisco, *Cisco Visual Networking Index 2017*. 2017, Cisco.

353. Cisco, *Cisco Visual Networking Index 2012–2017*. 2013, Cisco.

354. Davis, J., Big data, analytics sales will reach $187 billion by 2019. *Information Week*, 2016. Available from: www.informationweek.com/big-data/big-data-analytics/ big-data-analytics-sales-will-reach-$187-billion-by-2019/d/d-id/1325631, accessed August 25, 2017.

355. Katal, A., M. Wazid, and R. Goudar, Big data: issues, challenges, tools and good practices, in *Contemporary Computing (IC3), 2013 Sixth International Conference on*. 2013, IEEE.

356. Lim, P., Equifax's massive data breach has cost the company $4 billion so far. 2017. Available from: https://time.com/money/4936732/equifaxs-massive-data-brea ch-has-cost-the-company-4-billion-so-far/, accessed September 7, 2018.

357. Surane, J.M. and A. Melin, Equifax CEO Richard Smith resigns after uproar over massive hack. 2017. Available from: www.bloomberg.com/news/articles/ 2017-09-26/equifax-ceo-smith-resigns-barros-named-interim-chief-after-hack, accessed September 7, 2018.

358. Melin, A., Three Equifax managers sold stock before cyber hack revealed. 2017. Available from: www.bloomberg.com/news/articles/2017-09-07/three-equifax-execu tives-sold-stock-before-revealing-cyber-hack, accessed September 7, 2018.

359. Cowley, S., Equifax faces mounting costs and investigations from breach. 2017. Available from: www.nytimes.com/2017/11/09/business/equifax-data-breach.html? _r=0, accessed September 7, 2018.

360. Cobb, S., 10 things to know about the October 21 IoT DDoS attacks. 2016, October 24. Available from: www.welivesecurity.com/2016/10/24/10-things-kno w-october-21-iot-ddos-attacks/, accessed July 4, 2017.

361. Hypponen, M. and L. Nyman, The Internet of (Vulnerable) Things: On Hyppo-nen's law, security engineering, and IoT legislation. *Technology Innovation Management Review*, 2017. 7(4): 5–11.

362. Poornachandran, P., R. Sreeram, M.R. Krishnan, S. Pal, A.U.P. Sankar, and A. Ashok, Internet of Vulnerable Things (IoVT): Detecting vulnerable SOHO routers, in *Information Technology (ICIT), 2015 International Conference on*. 2015, IEEE.

363. Tsesis, A., The right to erasure: Privacy, data brokers, and the indefinite retention of data. *Wake Forest Law Review*, 2014. 49: 433.

364. Fienberg, S.E., M.E. Martin, and M.L. Straf, *Sharing Research Data*. 1985, National Academy Press.

365. Joe, R., Coming in 2018: Comcast hopes to spur data sharing with blockchain technology. AdExchanger, 2017, June 20. Available from: https://adexchanger.com/data-exchanges/coming-2018-comcast-hopes-spur-data-sharing-blockchain-technology/, accessed August 31, 2017.

366. Fujitsu, Fujitsu develops blockchain-based software for a secure data exchange network. 2017. Available from: www.fujitsu.com/, accessed October 23, 2018.

367. Terbine, Terbine launches blockchain-enabled Internet of Things data exchange to accelerate commercial and public agency information sharing and monetization. 2018.

368. Alhassan, I., D. Sammon, and M. Daly, Data governance activities: An analysis of the literature. *Journal of Decision Systems*, 2016. 25(1): 64–75.

369. Malik, P., Governing big data: Principles and practices. *IBM Journal of Research and Development*, 2013. 57(3/4): 1.

370. Panian, Z., Some practical experiences in data governance. *World Academy of Science, Engineering and Technology Management*, 2010. 62: 939–946.

371. Tallon, P.P., Corporate governance of big data: Perspectives on value, risk, and cost. *Computer*, 2013. 46(6): 32–38.

372. Wende, K., A model for data governance: Organising accountabilities for data quality management. *ACIS 2007 Proceedings*, 2007: 80.

373. Cleven, A. and F. Wortmann, Uncovering four strategies to approach master data management, in *System Sciences (HICSS), 2010 43rd Hawaii International Conference on*. 2010. IEEE.

374. Umeh, J., Blockchain double bubble or double trouble? *ITNOW*, 2016. 58(1): 58–61.

375. Khatri, V. and C.V. Brown, Designing data governance. *Communications of the ACM*, 2010. 53(1): 148–152.

376. Rosenbaum, S., Data governance and stewardship: Designing data stewardship entities and advancing data access. *Health Services Research*, 2010. 45(5p2): 1442–1455.

377. Hern, A., Google's DeepMind plans bitcoin-style health record tracking for hospitals. 2017, March 9. Available from: www.theguardian.com/technology/2017/mar/09/google-deepmind-health-records-tracking-blockchain-nhs-hospitals, accessed May 4, 2017.

378. Metz, C., Google's untrendy play to make the blockchain actually useful. 2017. Available from: www.wired.com/2017/03/google-deepminds-untrendy-blockchain-play-make-actually-useful/, accessed May 4, 2017.

379. Piscini, E., D. Dalton, and L. Kehoe, *Blockchain & Cyber Security. Let's Discuss.* 2017, Deloitte.

380. Kissel, R., Glossary of key information security terms. *National Institute of Standards and Technology*.

381. McLaughlin, K., Google and Facebook fall for $100 MILLION phishing scam. 2017, April 28. Available from: www.dailymail.co.uk/~/article-4455652/index.html, accessed April 29, 2017.

382. Buldas, A., A. Kroonmaa, and R. Laanoja, Keyless signatures' infrastructure: How to build global distributed hash-trees, in *Nordic Conference on Secure IT Systems*. 2013. Springer.

383. Gault, M., Implementing data governance at internet scale. 2014. Available from: https://guardtime.com/blog/implementing-data-governance-at-internet-scale, accessed October 17, 2017.

384. Barzilay, O., 3 ways blockchain is revolutionizing cybersecurity. 2017. Available from: www.forbes.com/sites/omribarzilay/2017/08/21/3-ways-blockchain-is-revolutio nizing-cybersecurity/, accessed October 18, 2017.

385. Richmond, J., Advancing cybersecurity with blockchain technology. 2017. Available from: www.nasdaq.com/article/advancing-cybersecurity-with-blockchain-tech nology-cm780007, accessed September 7, 2018.

386. Treat, D., J. Velissarios, S. Francis, L. Freeman, and C. Hyland, *Blockchain Security Made Simple*. 2017. Available from: www.accenture.com/ t00010101T000000Z__w__/au-en/_acnmedia/PDF-43/Accenture-Blockchain-POV.pdf, accessed April 29, 2019.

387. David Birch, interview. April 24, 2017.

388. Rainie, L., The state of privacy in post-Snowden America. 2016, September 21. Available from: www.pewresearch.org/fact-tank/2016/09/21/the-state-of-priva cy-in-america/, accessed October 19, 2017.

389. Singer, N., Sharing data, but not happily. 2015. Available from: www.nytimes. com/2015/06/05/technology/consumers-conflicted-over-data-mining-policies-report-fi nds.html, accessed October 19, 2017.

390. Morey, T., T. Forbath, and A. Schoop, Customer data: Designing for transparency and trust. 2015. Available from: https://hbr.org/2015/05/customer-data -designing-for-transparency-and-trust, accessed September 14, 2018.

391. Mundie, C., Privacy pragmatism: Focus on data use, not data collection. 2014. Available from: www.foreignaffairs.com/articles/2014-02-12/privacy-pragmatism, accessed October 17, 2017.

392. Pentland, A., *Social Physics: How Good Ideas Spread – the Lessons from a New Science*. 2014, London: Penguin.

393. Turing, A.M., Computing machinery and intelligence. *Mind*, 1950. 59(236): 433–460.

394. Good, I.J., Speculations concerning the first ultraintelligent machine. *Advances in Computers*, 1966. 6: 31–88.

395. Barrett, A.M. and S.D. Baum, A model of pathways to artificial superintelligence catastrophe for risk and decision analysis. *Journal of Experimental & Theoretical Artificial Intelligence*, 2017. 29(2): 397–414.

396. Fleischmann, K.R., Sociotechnical interaction and cyborg–cyborg interaction: Transforming the scale and convergence of HCI. *The Information Society*, 2009. 25 (4): 227–235.

397. Goertzel, B. and C. Pennachin, *Artificial General Intelligence*. Vol. 2. 2007, Springer.

398. Shulman, C. and N. Bostrom, How hard is artificial intelligence? Evolutionary arguments and selection effects. *Journal of Consciousness Studies*, 2012. 19(7–8): 103–130.

399. Moravec, H., *The Role of Raw Power in Intelligence*. Unpublished manuscript, May 12, 1976: 124–135.

400. Anderson, M., S.L. Anderson, and C. Armen, Towards machine ethics, in *The AAAI-04 Workshop on Agent Organizations: Theory and Practice.* 2004, San Jose.
401. Bostrom, N. and E. Yudkowsky, The ethics of artificial intelligence. *The Cambridge Handbook of Artificial Intelligence*, 2014: 316–334.
402. Soares, N. and B. Fallenstein, Toward idealized decision theory. arXiv preprint arXiv:1507.01986, 2015.
403. Huang, J.C., S. Newell, and S.L. Pan, The process of global knowledge integration: A case study of a multinational investment bank's Y2K program. *European Journal of Information Systems*, 2001. 10(3): 161–174.
404. Russell, S. and P. Norvig, *Artificial Intelligence: A Modern Approach.* 1995, Malaysia: Pearson.
405. Bostrom, N., Existential risks. *Journal of Evolution and Technology*, 2002. 9(1): 1–31.
406. Carey, S., Rolls-Royce uses Microsoft IoT tools to cut down on engine faults and fuel costs, and wants to sell the insights back to airlines. 2016. Available from: www.computerworlduk.com/iot/rolls-royce-uses-microsoft-iot-tools-cut-down-on-engine-faults-3648777/, accessed September 20, 2018.
407. Fujitsu, Fujitsu estimates workers' heat stress levels with new AI-based algorithm. 2017. Available from: www.fujitsu.com/global/about/resources/news/press-releases/2017/0712-02.html, accessed April 29, 2019.
408. Hammon, K., Please don't hire a chief artificial intelligence officer. 2017. Available from: https://hbr.org/2017/03/please-dont-hire-a-chief-artificial-intelligence-officer, accessed September 21, 2018.
409. Accenture, *At Your Service: Embracing the Disruptive Power of Chatbots.* 2017. Available from: www.accenture.com/t20170503T135801Z__w__/us-en/_acnmedia/PDF-47/Accenture-At-Your-Service-Embracing-Chatbots.pdf, accessed April 29, 2019.
410. Hern, A., Microsoft scrambles to limit PR damage over abusive AI bot Tay. 2016, March 24. Available from: www.theguardian.com/technology/2016/mar/24/microsoft-scrambles-limit-pr-damage-over-abusive-ai-bot-tay, accessed June 19, 2017.
411. Vincent, J., Twitter taught Microsoft's friendly AI chatbot to be a racist asshole in less than a day. 2016. Available from: www.theverge.com/2016/3/24/11297050/tay-microsoft-chatbot-racist, accessed June 19, 2017.
412. Murgia, M., Microsoft's racist bot shows we must teach AI to play nice and police themselves. 2016. Available from: www.telegraph.co.uk/technology/2016/03/25/we-must-teach-ai-machines-to-play-nice-and-police-themselves/, accessed June 19, 2017.
413. Garcia, M., Racist in the machine: The disturbing implications of algorithmic bias. *World Policy Journal*, 2016. 33(4): 111–117.
414. Peyton, A., HSBC launching voice recognition and touch security services in UK. 2016. Available from: www.bankingtech.com/2016/02/hsbc-launching-voice-recognition-and-touch-security-services-in-uk/, accessed September 25, 2018.
415. Eyers, J., Peer inside ING's future of voice-activated, open banking. 2017. Available from: www.afr.com/technology/peer-inside-ings-future-of-voiceactivated-open-banking-20170818-gxzfxa, accessed September 25, 2018.
416. Taylor, H., Bank of America launches AI chatbot Erica: Here's what it does. 2016. Available from: www.cnbc.com/2016/10/24/bank-of-america-launches-ai-chatbot-erica–heres-what-it-does.html, accessed September 25, 2018.

417. Milnes, H., Fashion brands embrace bots as modern concierges. 2016. Available from: https://digiday.com/marketing/luxury-brands-facebook-messengers-chatbot-can-solve-digital-customer-service/, accessed September 25, 2018.

418. Steele, B., Learn a new language with Duolingo's chatbots. 2016. Available from: www.engadget.com/2016/10/06/duolingo-language-learning-chatbots/, accessed September 25, 2018.

419. Campbell, G., The impact of chatbots on the hotel industry. 2017. Available from: www.hotelspeak.com/2017/06/impact-of-chatbots-hotel-industry/, accessed September 25, 2018.

420. Acosta, E., Marriott International's AI-powered chatbots on Facebook Messenger and Slack, and Aloft's ChatBotlr, simplify travel for guests throughout their journey. 2017, Marriott. Available from: http://news.marriott.com/2017/09/marriott-internationals-ai-powered-chatbots-facebook-messenger-slack-alofts-chatbotlr-simplify-travel-guests-throughout-journey/, accessed April 29, 2019.

421. Andrew, S., Is Elon Musk scared of ai? Spacex founder urges tech company to develop "symbiosis" between man and machine. 2018. Available from: www.newsweek.com/elon-musk-urges-symbiosis-between-man-and-machine-1058900, accessed September 25, 2018.

422. Thompson, C., Elon Musk warns that creation of "god-like" AI could doom mankind to an eternity of robot dictatorship. 2018. Available from: www.businessinsider.nl/elon-musk-says-ai-could-lead-to-robot-dictator-2018-4/, accessed September 25, 2018.

423. Anderson, J., The Doomsday invention. *The New Yorker*, 2015, November 15.

424. Armstrong, S., N. Bostrom, and C. Shulman, Racing to the precipice: A model of artificial intelligence development. *AI & SOCIETY*, 2016. 31(2): 201–206.

425. Soares, N., *The Value Learning Problem*. 2015, Berkeley: Machine Intelligence Research Institute.

426. Core, M.G., H.C. Lane, M. Van Lent, D. Gomboc, S. Solomon, and M. Rosenberg, Building explainable artificial intelligence systems. *AAAI*, 2006: 1766–1773.

427. Taylor, G., K. Knudsen, and L.S. Holt, Explaining agent behavior. In *Proceedings of the 15th Conference on Behavior Representation in Modeling and Simulation (BRIMS06)*. 2006.

428. Gill, K.S., Artificial super intelligence: beyond rhetoric. *AI & SOCIETY*, 2016. 31(2): 137–143.

429. Lomas, M., et al., Explaining robot actions, in *Proceedings of the Seventh Annual ACM/IEEE International Conference on Human-Robot Interaction*. 2012, New York: ACM.

430. Sotala, K., Concept learning for safe autonomous AI, in *1st International Workshop on AI and Ethics, held within the 29th AAAI Conference on Artificial Intelligence (AAAI-2015)*. 2015, Austin.

431. Kaczmarek, S., The next big disruptive trend in business … explainable AI. 2017. Available from: https://disruptionhub.com/next-big-disruptive-trend-business-explainable-ai/, accessed September 25, 2018.

432. Hurtado, M., The ethics of super intelligence. *International Journal of Swarm Intelligence and Evol Comput*, 2016. 5(137): 2.

433. Anderson, M. and S.L. Anderson, *Machine Ethics*. 2011, Cambridge: Cambridge University Press.

434. de Spinoza, B., *The Collected Works of Spinoza, Volume II*. Vol. 2. 2016, Princeton, NJ: Princeton University Press.

435. Hume, D., *A Treatise of Human Nature*. 2003, Courier Corporation.
436. Brooks, D., The end of philosophy. *New York Times*, April 6, 2009.
437. Moor, J.H., Why we need better ethics for emerging technologies. *Ethics and Information Technology*, 2005. 7(3): 111–119.
438. Suwajanakorn, S.S., Steven, M., and Kemelmacher-Shlizerman, Ira, *Synthesizing Obama: Learning Lip Sync from Audio*. 2017.
439. Haberman, M.M. and J. Martin, Trump once said the "Access Hollywood" tape was real. Now he's not sure. *New York Times*, November 28, 2017.
440. Hillman, A.J. and T. Dalziel, Boards of directors and firm performance: Integrating agency and resource dependence perspectives. *Academy of Management Review*, 2003. 28(3): 383–396.
441. Soares, N. and B. Fallenstein, Aligning superintelligence with human interests: A technical research agenda. *Machine Intelligence Research Institute (MIRI) Technical Report 8*, 2014.
442. Fallenstein, B. and N. Soares, Vingean reflection: Reliable reasoning for self-improving agents. Technical Report 2015-2, Machine Intelligence Research Institute, 2015.
443. Baysinger, B. and R.E. Hoskisson, The composition of boards of directors and strategic control: Effects on corporate strategy. *Academy of Management Review*, 1990. 15(1): 72–87.
444. Hoskisson, R.E., M.A. Hitt, and C.W. Hill, Managerial incentives and investment in R&D in large multiproduct firms. *Organization Science*, 1993. 4(2): 325–341.
445. Ravenscraft, D.J., Ownership and control: Rethinking corporate governance for the twenty-first century. *Journal of Economic Literature*, 1996. 34(4): 1971.
446. Gupta, A.K., SBU strategies, corporate-SBU relations, and SBU effectiveness in strategy implementation. *Academy of Management Journal*, 1987. 30(3): 477–500.
447. Rindova, V.P., What corporate boards have to do with strategy: A cognitive perspective. *Journal of Management Studies*, 1999. 36(7): 953–975.
448. Pitcher, P., S. Chreim, and V. Kisfalvi, CEO succession research: Methodological bridges over troubled waters. *Strategic Management Journal*, 2000. 21(6): 625–648.
449. Conyon, M.J. and S.I. Peck, Board control, remuneration committees, and top management compensation. *Academy of Management Journal*, 1998. 41(2): 146–157.
450. Boyd, B.K., Board control and CEO compensation. *Strategic Management Journal*, 1994. 15(5): 335–344.
451. Strebel, P., The case for contingent governance. *MIT Sloan Management Review*, 2004. 45(2): 59.
452. Christen, M., G. Iyer, and D. Soberman, Job satisfaction, job performance, and effort: A reexamination using agency theory. *Journal of Marketing*, 2006. 70(1): 137–150.
453. Hilb, M., *New Corporate Governance*. 2008, Springer.
454. Baesens, B., R. Bapna, J.R. Marsden, J. Vanthienen, and J.L. Zhao, Transformational issues of big data and analytics in networked business. *MIS Quarterly*, 2014. 38(2): 629–631.
455. Hastie, T., R. Tibshirani, and J. Friedman, Unsupervised learning, in *The Elements of Statistical Learning*. 2009, Springer, pp. 485–585.
456. Leopold, T., V. Ratcheva, and S. Zahidi, *The Future of Jobs Report*. 2018.
457. Bourne, J., Mark van Rijmenam: On the "gestalt shift" of big data, blockchain and AI convergence. 2018. Available from: www.cloudcomputing-news.net/news/

2018/sep/27/mark-van-rijmenam-gestalt-shift-big-data-blockchain-and-ai-convergen
ce/, accessed November 25, 2018.

458. Lund, S., J. Manyika, and J. Bughin, Globalization is becoming more about data
and less about stuff. 2016. Available from: https://hbr.org/2016/03/globalizatio
n-is-becoming-more-about-data-and-less-about-stuff, accessed October 4, 2018.

459. Manyika, J., S. Lund, J. Bughin, J. Woetzel, K. Stamenov, and D. Dhingra,
Digital Globalization: The New Era of Global Flows. 2016. p. 156. Available from:
www.mckinsey.com/business-functions/digital-mckinsey/our-insights/digital-globaliz
ation-the-new-era-of-global-flows, accessed April 29, 2019.

Index

Page numbers in italics refer to figures. Page numbers in bold refer to tables.